ROTH FAMILY FOUNDATION

*Imprint in Music*

Michael P. Roth
and Sukey Garcetti
have endowed this
imprint to honor the
memory of their parents,
Julia and Harry Roth,
whose deep love of music
they wish to share
with others.

*The publisher and the University of California Press Foundation gratefully acknowledge the generous support of the Roth Family Foundation Imprint in Music, established by a major gift from Sukey and Gil Garcetti and Michael P. Roth.*

The La Traviata *Affair*

MUSIC OF THE AFRICAN DIASPORA

*Shana Redmond, Editor*

*Guthrie P. Ramsey, Jr., Editor*

1. *California Soul: Music of African Americans in the West*, edited by Jacqueline Cogdell DjeDje and Eddie S. Meadows
2. *William Grant Still: A Study in Contradictions*, by Catherine Parsons Smith
3. *Jazz on the Road: Don Albert's Musical Life*, by Christopher Wilkinson
4. *Harlem in Montmartre: A Paris Jazz Story between the Great Wars*, by William A. Shack
5. *Dead Man Blues: Jelly Roll Morton Way Out West*, by Phil Pastras
6. *What Is This Thing Called Jazz?: African American Musicians as Artists, Critics, and Activists*, by Eric Porter
7. *Race Music: Black Cultures from Bebop to Hip-Hop*, by Guthrie P. Ramsey, Jr.
8. *Lining Out the Word: Dr. Watts Hymn Singing in the Music of Black Americans*, by William T. Dargan
9. *Music and Revolution: Cultural Change in Socialist Cuba*, by Robin D. Moore
10. *From Afro-Cuban Rhythms to Latin Jazz*, by Raul A. Fernandez
11. *"Mek Some Noise": Gospel Music and the Ethics of Style in Trinidad*, by Timothy Rommen
12. *The Memoirs of Alton Augustus Adams, Sr.: First Black Bandmaster of the United States Navy*, edited with an introduction by Mark Clague, with a foreword by Samuel Floyd, Jr.
13. *Digging: The Afro-American Soul of American Classical Music*, by Amiri Baraka
14. *Different Drummers: Rhythm and Race in the New World*, by Martin Munro
15. *Funky Nassau: Roots, Routes, and Representation in Bahamian Popular Music*, by Timothy Rommen
16. *Blowin' the Blues Away: Performance and Meaning on the New York Jazz Scene*, by Travis A. Jackson

17. *The Amazing Bud Powell: Black Genius, Jazz History, and the Challenge of Bebop*, by Guthrie P. Ramsey, Jr.
18. *Jazz Diasporas: Race, Music, and Migration in Post-World War II Paris*, by Rashida K. Braggs
19. *Holy Hip Hop in the City of Angels*, by Christina Zanfagna
20. *The* La Traviata *Affair: Opera in the Age of Apartheid*, by Hilde Roos

*The publisher gratefully acknowledges the generous support of the AMS 75 PAYS Endowment of the American Musicological Society, funded in part by the National Endowment for the Humanities and the Andrew W. Mellon Foundation.*

# *The* La Traviata *Affair*

OPERA IN THE AGE OF APARTHEID

*Hilde Roos*

UNIVERSITY OF CALIFORNIA PRESS

University of California Press, one of the most distinguished university presses in the United States, enriches lives around the world by advancing scholarship in the humanities, social sciences, and natural sciences. Its activities are supported by the UC Press Foundation and by philanthropic contributions from individuals and institutions. For more information, visit www.ucpress.edu.

University of California Press
Oakland, California

© 2018 by The Regents of the University of California

Library of Congress Cataloging-in-Publication Data

Names: Roos, Hilde.
Title: The La Traviata affair : opera in the age of apartheid / Hilde Roos.
Description: Oakland, California : University of California Press,
    [2018] | Series: Music of the African diaspora; v.20 | Includes
    bibliographical references and index. |
Identifiers: LCCN 2018016617 (print) | LCCN 2018020844 (ebook) |
    ISBN 9780520971516 (ebook) | ISBN 9780520299887 (cloth : alk. paper) |
    ISBN 9780520299894 (pbk. : alk. paper)
Subjects: LCSH: Opera—South Africa—20th century. | Eoan Group. |
    Apartheid—South Africa.
Classification: LCC ML1751.S715 (ebook) | LCC ML1751.S715 R66 2018 (print) |
    DDC 792.50968—dc23
LC record available at https://lccn.loc.gov/2018016617

26  26  25  24  23  22  21  20  19  18
10  9  8  7  6  5  4  3  2  1

CONTENTS

List of Illustrations  ix
Acknowledgments  xi
Note on Terminology  xiii

Introduction  1

1 · We Live to Serve: A Demimonde before Art  18

2 · The *La Traviata* Affair: From Courtesan to Lover  45

3 · Eoan's Best Opera Success: An Amorous Fantasy  58

4 · Scala Is Scala and Eoan Is Eoan: The Struggle to Breathe  98

5 · Slow Death: On Twilight and Loss  140

Postscript  182

Appendix 1: Eoan's Music Productions  187
Appendix 2: The Eoan Group Constitution  211
Notes  219
Selected Bibliography  261
Index  267

ILLUSTRATIONS

1.1. Helen Southern-Holt. *21*
1.2. Joseph Manca. *25*
1.3. The Eoan Group Choir in 1946. *28*
1.4. Cartoon published in the *Torch* on November 24, 1947. *34*
1.5. Eoan Group poster outlining the group's values. *36*
2.1. The First Arts Festival Programme booklet. *51*
2.2. May Abrahamse performing the "Drinking Song" in Eoan's 1956 production of *La Traviata*. *52*
2.3. The "Dying Scene" from Eoan's 1956 production of *La Traviata*, with May Abrahamse as Violetta. *53*
3.1. Lionel Fourie in the role of Rigoletto. *67*
3.2. Eoan's principals in front of the Port Elizabeth City Hall in 1960. *76*
3.3. Eoan's principal mezzo-soprano, Sophia Andrews. *79*
3.4. Joseph Manca and Eoan's soprano soloists May Abrahamse, Patricia van Graan, Abeeda Parker, Ruth Goodwin, and Vera Gow. *88*
3.5. Manca conducting in City Hall during a rehearsal. *95*
4.1. Wardrobe Mistress Carmen Sydow in action. *106*
4.2. Alessandro Rota, Gordon Jephtas, and Joseph Manca discussing a production. *112*
4.3. Ismail Sydow. *115*
4.4. Example of a permit issued to Eoan for performing to mixed audiences. *128*
4.5. Soprano Vera Gow as Violetta. *131*
4.6. The Joseph Stone Auditorium, 1969. *136*

5.1. Joseph Gabriels as Canio in the 1972 Metropolitan Opera House production of Leoncavallo's *I Pagliacci*. *143*

5.2. Repetiteur Gordon Jephtas in conversation with Ismail Sydow in London. *153*

5.3. Seating plan of the Green & Sea Point Civic Centre, showing designated seating for whites and coloureds. *157*

5.4. Manca conducting the Eoan Group Choir. *169*

5.5. May Abrahamse and Gordon Jephtas during their recital in the Nico Malan Theatre on 3 March 1979. *175*

ACKNOWLEDGMENTS

The idea of writing this book started with the Eoan Group Archive. For almost forty years this archive was stowed away underneath the orchestra pit in the Joseph Stone Auditorium in Athlone, untouched and unexplored. In 2008 a ninety-nine-year loan agreement was negotiated between the Eoan Group and Stellenbosch University that enabled the transfer of the Eoan Group Archive to the Documentation Centre for Music in the Music Library. My thanks therefore go first to Shafiek Rajap, the managing director of the Eoan Group School of Performing Arts, as well as to the Eoan Group Board, who facilitated the transfer. Shafiek has over the past decade unfailingly supported research on the archive by granting permission to publications of all sorts, to exhibitions, and to films that came forth from the archive. Circling out from the archive is the Eoan Group community, which includes all who took part in the group's activities and those who supported the group in some manner or other. Many of them where interviewed by myself or other researchers for a number of Eoan Group History projects, and many have contributed additional materials to the archive. I am grateful to have been able to listen to them. I am even more grateful that we were able to capture the memories of those who have passed away since then, among them Ruth Fourie, Tillie Ulster, Patricia van Graan, John van der Ross, Ronald Theys, John Ulster, Gerald Arendse, Benjamin Arendse, Sophia Andrews, and Dirk Alexander.

The research environment and people that enabled my research include many to whom thanks is owed. First of all is my former supervisor and now my colleague, Stephanus Muller. His far-sightedness put this project on its path, his in-depth understanding of research and writing has been invaluable, and his generous collegial support is treasured. Thank-you to Santie de Jongh, the DOMUS archivist who has sorted the archive and made materials available whenever I needed them. My proofreaders, Aryan Kaganof and Neil Sonnekus, have both contributed to the shaping of my ideas and my use of language. Thank-you to my colleagues at Africa Open Institute, with whom I could share this journey. Finally, thank-you to my husband, Henk Dekker, who walked all the way with me, who cooked supper, did the laundry, and fed the dogs whenever my focus on this project banished domestic concerns to oblivion.

NOTE ON TERMINOLOGY

Throughout this text, the term *coloured* is spelled in South African English because it refers to a specific South African experience that is different to how the term *colored* is understood in US society. *Coloured* in South Africa includes mixed race but goes beyond this notion and refers to a conglomerate of diverse peoples and identities that were artificially grouped together during apartheid because they did not fit into easily identifiable racial categories such as "white" and "black." People who are referred to as coloured therefore share some political experiences, but to this day, *coloured* is marked by a heterogeneity of ethnicities, histories, and identities.

In South African discourse, debates exist regarding the capitalization of the word. During apartheid, capitalization (*Coloured*) was the norm, and all references to archival documentation in which it has been capitalized appear in that manner. Proponents of capitalization in postapartheid South Africa argue that the identity has emancipated itself from the past and from other identities. However, the term has an adjectival function similar to *white* and *black* and is used as such.

In some activist and postapartheid circles, preference is given to the phrase "so-called coloured," highlighting the term as an apartheid construct. Yet many South Africans who self-identify as coloureds take offence at being referred to as "so-called." Members of the Eoan Group also never referred to themselves as "so-called coloureds," and the phrase is therefore not used in this text.

# *Introduction*

Oh, no! Never! No, never!
You cannot know the kind of passion that burns in my heart!
—Violetta, act 2, *La Traviata* by Giuseppe Verdi

## LA TRAVIATA

The Eoan Group first opera production took place on 10 March 1956 in the Cape Town City Hall with a performance of Giuseppe Verdi's three-act opera *La Traviata*. Produced by Italian émigré Alessandro Rota with Eoan's artistic director, Joseph Manca, conducting the all-white Cape Town Municipal Orchestra, this production was part of the group's First Arts Festival.[1] All tickets for this performance (approximately one thousand seats) were sold out within the first day of booking open to the public.[2] Eight more performances followed before the end of the opening month of March 1956, including a special performance held for government dignitaries on 20 March 1956.[3] The cast included, among others, May Abrahamse and Ruth Goodwin sharing the role of Violetta, Lionel Fourie as Germont, and Ron Thebus as Alfredo; the group's choir and ballet corps sang and danced as Violetta and Alfredo's guests.[4]

Publicity for Eoan's performance of *La Traviata* happened through reviews and other informative articles in most local newspapers and magazines, including the *Cape Times*, the *Cape Argus*, *Die Landstem*, *Die Burger*, the *Sun*, and *Drum* magazine. The reviews were overwhelmingly positive, and Eoan seemed to have made a huge impact on Cape Town's classical music circles. Well-known Afrikaans critic Charlie Weich of *Die Burger* wrote that had he not seen with his own eyes what a coloured opera company had achieved on the night of 10 March in the City Hall, he would not have believed it. He singled out the voices of May Abrahamse and Lionel Fourie, and the decor and costumes, as outstanding.[5] The critic for the *Cape Argus* was of the opinion that "there must have been real astonishment at the sound and the spectacle of a non-European amateur cast performing Italian opera at a level that would put more than one professional company to shame."[6] The critic added that the "astonishment is to some extent an admission of failure to realize how far, with guidance, these underprivileged men and women from factories, shops and domestic jobs can travel in the realms of art."[7] The *Cape Times* described the performance as "an unqualified triumph."[8]

These reviews were, of course, written by whites for a predominantly white readership; given the state of local politics in the 1950s, it comes as no surprise that these white readers were astonished by this first "all-coloured" rendition of a Western cultural form such as opera. Yet reviews in newspapers that catered to the non-European community, namely the *Sun* and the *Drum*, were similarly positive. The *Sun* reported that "history was most certainly made last Saturday when the Eoan Group staged its most ambitious effort to date with *La Traviata* at the Cape Town City Hall."[9] The *Drum*'s headline read: "Cape Town's Eoan Group hits the sky with *La Traviata*."[10]

The group's artistic director, Joseph Manca, a South African of Italian descent, was more than delighted by the reception of the production, and on 2 April 1956 he wrote to Harold Rosenthal, then editor of the British opera magazine *Opera*:

> This Coloured Premiere of *La Traviata* was the greatest musical success Cape Town has ever witnessed and caused a furore among the local musical circles. Ever since the first night, the whole city has been talking and a special evening was given which was attended by the leading authorities of South Africa—The Governor-General, Members of the Cabinet, Full Diplomatic Corps, Members of Parliament, Senators, etc. etc. History was created in more than one sense. Not only was this the first Coloured performance in the world of a complete Italian Opera, but also all booking records were broken. All performances were "sold out" before the rise of the curtain on opening night. Altogether, nine performances were given, all playing to packed houses, and thousands of people were unable to gain admission. The results have surpassed all expectations.[11]

The event had far-reaching consequences for the functioning of the group. A mind shift took place within the group that changed its character from a humanitarian organization to one oriented toward Western arts production; this in the absence of an alternative nonracial institution in which the coloured population could explore and present its talents. Some years later, Manca gave his impression of what he thought the performance meant to group members:

> The presentation of the Italian Opera *La Traviata*, was the *dawn* of a new era for the Coloured People in their striving for the higher things of life. This introduction into the magical world of opera was the Coloured People's first intimate contact with one of the highest forms of musical art—an unforgettable baptism at whose front new horizons appeared on the educational landscape of the Coloured People's activities while new vistas of beauty were painted on the artistic canvas of their cultural progress.[12]

Today it is impossible not to read this interpretation of events as patronizing, politically compromised, and naive. It endorses apartheid themes of Western cultural superiority, cultural homogeneity, and the "civilizing" purposes of apartheid's separate (read *racial*) cultural development. If Manca is read at face value, opera in South Africa had a civilizing role to play that depended on its status as a European and uncompromisingly unindigenized art (as illustrated by Eoan's emphasis on performances in "traditional Italian style").[13] Indeed, not everyone in the coloured community was enthusiastic about Eoan's success. Two scathing attacks on Eoan's activities were launched immediately after the performances, illustrating the profound complexities of the politically charged environment in which the group operated. The first was a letter from the South African Coloured People's Organisation (SACPO), and the second was an anonymous circular distributed on the streets. Both letters expressed dismay to government officials about the Eoan Group's special performance of *La Traviata*, although a sense of admiration for the group's achievements was not entirely absent.[14] Alex La Guma, chairman of the SACPO, wrote to Eoan as follows:

> Allow us to congratulate you on your magnificent performance of "La Traviata." You have shown that, given the opportunities, Coloured people can excel in the realms of culture on par with all other peoples.
>
> It has come to our notice, however, that your group arranged a special performance of the opera for "Europeans Only" on Tuesday night 20th [of March]. Among those invited were the Cabinet Ministers and Members of Parliament whose attitude towards the Non-Europeans are well known.
>
> It [has been] rumoured for sometime that your group was financially supported by the government through the Coloured Affairs Department. People

can also conclude, therefore, that the Eoan Group supports Apartheid. In fact, the whole idea reminds one of the slave period when the farmers hired Coloureds to perform for them, their masters. Today in the 20th Century we do not recognise the white man as our master. This is the land of our birth and we demand government support for ALL cultural movements. BUT WITHOUT APARTHEID STRINGS.[15]

Manca's politically stilted version of events is also put into perspective by a critical pamphlet that was distributed on the streets:

### *THE LA TRAVIATA AFFAIR*

We do not share the amazement the columns of the daily press oozed over the recent production of Italian opera by a so-called "all coloured cast." We are not surprised that human beings can sing, dance and act.

However, the undoubted enthusiasm of both the performance and the majority of the audiences for "La Traviata" is an index of the cultural starvation and hunger of the majority of the people, cut off as they are by apartheid and poverty from the best in arts and culture. It is precisely this cultural starvation of the mass of the people that has tricked them into accepting Eoan's "La Traviata" as a step towards their cultural aspirations. In the same way a man driven by a burning thirst will drink at a sewer for the sake of life itself.

The Eoan Group is befouled by an apartheid atmosphere. But the most smarting humiliation to date, was the special performance of "La Traviata" for South African prominent racialists. People who publicly spit in the faces of the artists, who are horrified at the very thought of sitting next to them in the same bus, or even standing in the same que[ue] to buy a stamp, to these the Eoan Group was "thrilled" to give a special place of honour during the performance of La Traviata. To our shame, not one of the artists walked off the stage in protest against this outrageous insult. This sort of thing can only happen when people are so starved of artistic and cultural expression that the opportunity to express themselves artistically becomes all important.[16]

These documents show unequivocally that political resistance to Eoan's operatic activities occurred from the very beginning and, more important, that this resistance was publicized and known to Manca and group members. Notwithstanding the congratulatory letters, positive reviews, and enthusiastic reception by opera-loving Capetonians, these protest letters cut to the heart of issues that in the long run resulted in the group's demise. As illustrated in the pages of this book, throughout the group's existence (starting in 1933) its members subscribed to the ideals and agendas of white domination in one form or another. These included engaging with European cultural formats such as opera, ballet, and drama; endorsing European culture's "uplifting qualities"; functioning under white management; accepting funds from the apartheid state; assenting to performing for racially segregated audiences; suffering the stifling isolation resulting from apartheid laws; and steadfastly refusing to acknowledge that politics had anything to do with the group's work. These implicit and explicit endorsements of white domination are, in a nutshell, what caused the group's downfall and the branding of its members among their own community as stooges of the apartheid state.[17] And despite Eoan's many opera productions, group members continued to suffer "cultural starvation and hunger" as the system of apartheid undermined the group at every turn. These letters also bring home the seemingly untenable spaces that those who performed with whites had to negotiate in a time when governing structures insisted on racial difference.

The artistic success of the group's 1956 "Traviata," as former members fondly refer to the opera to this day, set it on a twenty-year course during which this opera became the group's flagship production. Catapulted into the sphere of Cape Town's semiprofessional opera world, the group continued to perform this opera during almost every season it presented. In 1975 "Traviata" was part of the last opera season the group ever staged. The work was also performed on other occasions, such as the group's countrywide tours in 1960 and 1965, its tour to the United Kingdom in 1975, its special appearances in rural towns such as Stellenbosch (in 1962) and Paarl (1971), and its appearance at the South African Republic Festival celebrations of 1966.[18] In 2004, a year after the group's seventieth birthday, Cape Town Opera produced *La Traviata* in Eoan's home, the Joseph Stone Auditorium in Athlone, in commemoration of the contribution the group made to opera production in Cape Town. For this occasion May Abrahamse, who had sung the role of Violetta for Eoan many times and was then seventy-four years old, was cast in the role of Annina.[19]

Although the reasons for the prominence of this opera in Eoan's performance repertoire probably rest on the availability of capable singers within the group and the familiarity that the group and Joseph Manca had with the opera itself, there are poetically tempting similarities between the fate of the leading character, Violetta, and that of the opera section of Eoan during the apartheid era.[20] Being socially and politically of "dubious" standing and living on the fringes of "respectable" (and in the case of Eoan, *white*) society, both the character Violetta and Eoan itself were enchanted by a utopian world for which they sacrificed all they had, were forced by figures of authority to give up that world, were publicly scorned and humiliated, and had their demise hastened as a result of their choices. Verdi's initial title for this work was *Amore e Morte*: "Love and Death." In 1980, when the group's opera endeavors were finally over, its reputation in its own community was in tatters, so much so that the antiapartheid organization South African Council on Sport (SACOS) declared Eoan a banned organization, a label it endured for decades to come. On the other side of the political divide, members of the group had been treated as second-class citizens by the apartheid state for decades, systematically eroding their personal and artistic aspirations; many in white professional opera circles regarded the capabilities of Eoan's established singers as below par.[21] By 1980 only a few younger singers (among them tenors Ronnie Theys and Keith Timms and soprano Virginia Davids) were given opportunities to perform with the then all-white Cape Performing Arts Board (CAPAB), where they were cast in minor roles or in the chorus.[22] This state of affairs came about gradually as the result of a history of political controversy and compromise, the denial of which was even more damaging.

Eoan's upwardly mobile social aspirations, resulting from its operatic performances, uncannily resemble the "Violetta predicament" of these endeavors. In *La Traviata*, Violetta is regarded as a reprobate whose questionable societal position threatens the purity of the Germont clan. Her marriage to Alfredo is therefore out of the question. Apartheid ideology, likewise, was built on the idea of racial purity, and the threat of contamination was projected by white patriarchy onto the coloured population. White descriptions of coloured identity in apartheid thinking focused on the "impurity of their race," viewing coloureds as a product of miscegenation—for which whites were largely responsible in the first place—that threatened the purity of the white family. Coloureds were also perceived as socially backward and in need of the civilizing qualities of Western culture.[23] During and before apartheid, coloureds were kept in place not only through myriad social conventions, but also by formal legislation, including the Group Areas Act, the Immorality Act, and the Separate Amenities Act.

Inherent to apartheid ideology was a degree of fascination with and an equal loathing for the racial other. *La Traviata* dramatizes this tension in the fascination and aversion with which its characters regard Violetta, expressed by both Alfredo and his father, Giorgio, from the first moment of sexual attraction between the protagonists and continuing in the private and public scorning of Violetta and the remorse both Alfredo and his father express upon her death. In *Mind Your Colour*, Vernon February explores racial stereotyping of the coloured population in Afrikaans literature and illustrates how "one is confronted with a picture ranging from ambiguity and almost near-kinship to total rejection and hatred."[24]

The simultaneous presence of affinity and rejection that existed between Eoan group members and Manca (and other white custodians of the group) is illustrated in the course of this book. It finds its most obvious manifestation in the story of white patriarchal control over the coloured voice. Manca, throughout his thirty-four years with the group, referred to Eoan members as "my musical children," minors who were never allowed to grow into equals. The archive clearly illustrates his autocratic management style, in which nothing happened without his consent and no one else was allowed to conduct performances. Former members often spoke of his possessiveness regarding the group and its endeavors, and Manca's marketing of the group's performers invariably described them as illiterates who could sing Italian opera. This fascination can also be read in the white operagoing public's continued support through concert attendance and in the newspaper reviews, which were seldom critical.

Despite this Manca's paternalistic, autocratic management of the group, many former members gave interviews in which they unapologetically testified to a sense of fulfillment and belonging that participation in Eoan's productions gave them.[25] Although interviews conducted forty years after an industrious performance career undoubtedly contain a degree of romanticizing of the past, documentation from the Eoan Group Archive also reflects the tremendous commitment and sacrifices that members and management made for the sake of opera, ballet, or anything with which the group engaged. Evidence of the group's conscious subjugation to authorities and its turning of a blind eye to the implications of that subjugation is similarly present in both the interviews and the archival documentation. Most members felt that their backs were against the wall: if there were no money, there would be no opera. As tenor Gerald Samaai conceded, "We had to take the [government] grant; otherwise we couldn't have performed anything. [We] knew that should [we] not take it, it's a slow death."[26] Yet never during my engagement with any of Eoan's former members were excuses offered for their desire to sing opera (or dance or act), to develop their talents, or to engage with Western classical formats such as opera. Instead, a sense of pride, albeit injured, accompanied their recollections of these endeavors.

## COLOURED IDENTITY

Terminology with regard to racial categorization and the notion of "coloured identity" is foundational to the narrative of this book and requires some illumination. The categorizing and labeling of human beings along color lines and ethnicity have had a long and painful history, and the extent to which such labeling was utilized as a mechanism of power and control in apartheid South Africa is still particularly alive in the collective memory of people across the world. It is therefore with a sense of trepidation that I, as a white South African who grew up during apartheid, discuss the term *coloured* and pen my take on the history of the Eoan Group. For the sake of historical authenticity, this book uses apartheid terminology, which perpetuates racial categorization up to today. Apart from this terminology, the residue of my privileged background, my predisposition toward the values of Western art and music, and my position of power as a white academic are all ever-present in this book. I realize that quite a different story would be rendered had this account of the Eoan Group been written from an alternative position, such as from a critical interrogation of white power or from a black/nonblack perspective. Furthermore, I cannot but acknowledge that inherent in the use of language lies the writer's control of the subject of this (hi)story.

The term *coloured* has been in use in South Africa since the nineteenth century to refer to a person of darker skin color who was not European, yet also did not belong to one of the black African tribes of Southern Africa. The term was characterized by a fluidity of meaning, but it became more or less fixed under apartheid law, which used it to group together all South Africans who did not fit into the clear racial categories of white, black, or Indian. In practice, *coloured* came to include a variety of ethnicities and nationalities from diverse social strata, incorporating people of mixed racial descent; indigenous groups such as the San, the Khoi, and the Griqua; descendants of former slaves; and immigrants from China, Malaysia, Indonesia, and St. Helena.[27]

To this day, the social and political identity of this conglomerate remains contested, as individuals either defend or reject the idea of "coloured identity" as a blanket concept. During the height of the apartheid era, activists rejected the use of the term because they regarded it as "an artificial identity imposed by the white supremacist establishment on weak and vulnerable people as part of a divide-and-rule strategy" and referred to themselves as *black* rather than *coloured*.[28] This view renounced apartheid's generalization that "colouredness" was chiefly "an in-bred quality that is the automatic product of miscegenation."[29]

Since the official abolishment of apartheid in 1994, coloured identity in South Africa has been the topic of much research, illustrating how identity formation goes far beyond skin color and is shaped by social, cultural, and political factors. Academics have provided historical, political, and social contexts to coloured identity formation in South Africa; documented the history of the coloured population; and debated the situatedness of the use of racial terminology. These authors include, among others, Mohamed Adhikari, Vivian Bickford-Smith, Sylvia Bruinders, Denis-Constant Martin, Roy du Pré, Zimitri Erasmus, Ian Goldin, Wendy Isaac-Martin, Wilmot James, Marie Jorritsma, Gavin Lewis, Carol Muller, Theodore Petrus, Birgit Pickel, Richard van der Ross, and Zoë Wicomb.[30] My aim here is not to repeat that extensive literature, but rather to provide a basic orientation toward the use of terminology as applied in this particular narrative and to highlight some aspects of coloured identity that Eoan's opera performances bring into critical focus.

According to the historian Mohamed Adhikari, the shaping of coloured identity during the twentieth century was determined by four main issues: the marginalized position of the community in terms of numbers, the intermediate status of coloureds that made them more privileged than Africans but below whites during apartheid, the derogatory connotations that often accompanied the essentialist view of miscegenation as their racial origin, and the aspiration to assimilate into powerful structures.[31] Among other points, he expounds on what he describes as "sensitive issues," and I highlight some of those here because they are of particular relevance when telling Eoan's story.[32] Among these are, for instance, the presence of cultural affinities for the West, the desire for assimilation into European culture (read *opera*, *ballet*, and *drama*), European culture's scope for upward social mobilization, hostility toward Africans, and a consciousness shaped by ambiguities and contradictions.

In the rest of this introduction I show how the Eoan Group exemplified certain features that Adhikari identifies as relating to coloured identity and how these features enlighten the context within which Eoan's history unfolded. The identification of these features is based on the theory of social constructionism, and it should be kept in mind that they are used here to explore the Eoan Group as the bearer of the culture of a section of the coloured community. The coloured population is by no means homogenous, and the ideas presented here should not be read as a blanket representation of the coloured community as a whole.

The first feature and, according to Adhikari, the most important element of the identity that dominated coloureds' day-to-day activities, is the state of marginality. Throughout the twentieth century coloureds never exceeded more than 9 percent of South Africa's population. Combined with a heritage of slavery, dispossession, and racial oppression, they chronically lacked the power to negotiate political or economic change for themselves, resulting in a degree of fatalism about their own capability to do so. As their political rights were increasingly eroded from 1948 onward, the only viable option for them was to "bow to white power and work towards incremental improvement in their conditions."[33]

When one explores the story of the Eoan Group through this lens, the group's attitude of cooperation with, and submission to, white management becomes strikingly evident. Although former Eoan members fondly referred to Joseph Manca as a father figure who called them "my musical children," they also reported on the dictatorial way in which he handled the affairs of the group, not taking kindly to resistance from members. Nothing happened without his permission. However, because the group aimed at the "upliftment" of the coloured community, members (consciously or unconsciously) accepted this style of management and believed that through the practice of opera, drama, and ballet, their lives would be improved. Their acceptance and belief accurately illustrate Adhikari's point about the disempowering effects of the condition of marginality over many generations, though this is not to say that the lives of the coloured community did not improve.

Adhikari describes the second characteristic of coloured identity as "a desire to assimilate into the dominant society." He elaborates on this by saying that "this assimilationism was less an impulse for acculturation than a striving on the part of the coloured people for acknowledgment of their worth as individuals and citizens and acceptance as equals or partners by whites."[34] Striking here is Adhikari's qualification that the desire for assimilation on the part of the coloured people was not an impulse toward the adoption or assimilation of white culture (in the case of Eoan, read *opera* and *ballet*), but rather a striving toward acknowledgment or acceptance as equals in white society. This distinction is important in the interpretation of Eoan's story, as the group's pursuit of excellence in performance should, in my view, be read primarily in the context of proving its members' worth as artists, and not as trying to buy into white favor by performing opera and/or ballet. It is also interesting to note that the performance of opera as such was not the reason the group was rejected by the coloured community; accepting funding from the apartheid state was the unpardonable error in this regard. There is no lack of evidence in the archive to see how thoroughly Eoan's undeniable aspirations toward acknowledgment by whites were thwarted. When the Performing Arts Councils were established in 1963, they provided professional career opportunities for whites only. After this date, many policy documents and much formal correspondence found in the Eoan Group Archive express a deep sense of frustration and bitterness that, despite Eoan's consistent opera production for many years, no provision was made by the government or within white opera circles to acknowledge Eoan Group members' status as professionals.

For Adhikari, the extreme example of the assimilationist desire manifested itself in the reclassification of some coloured people as whites.[35] Here the case of David Poole springs to mind. Poole received his training as a dancer in District Six, went on to study ballet in England, and enjoyed a career with the Royal Ballet. Being fair skinned, he had himself reclassified in England as white; after he came back to South Africa in 1959, he occupied top positions at the University of Cape Town Ballet School and later at the CAPAB ballet section, until his death in 1991. What is even more striking is that none of the fifty or so former Eoan members who were interviewed for an oral history book project in 2009 expressed any feelings of animosity or anger about this fact. By contrast, the lack of official acknowledgment of the contribution that Eoan made toward the cultivation of opera in the country was a prevalent theme in these interviews.

A third characteristic of coloured identity, which was also a direct result of apartheid policy, was the "intermediate status" of coloured people in the South African racial hierarchy: neither privileged white nor disadvantaged black, but an in-between position of relative privilege.[36] Despite being severely disenfranchised by apartheid, coloureds still enjoyed relative privilege compared to the black African population; they were supported with better schooling, tertiary education, and housing than black South Africans. Coloureds were also exempt from pass laws. Disassociation from the black majority has therefore been a contributory factor to racism in the coloured community. Adhikari states that colouredness is, among other things, marked by "a strong association with Western culture and values in opposition to African equivalents."[37] For the Eoan Group, relative privilege was afforded on various levels. The group received much media attention, and its performances had a popular following among coloureds and whites. Goodwill and support came from the white population in the form of donations, scholarships, educational support, and other assistance. Funding to help the Eoan Group meet production costs was provided by both the Cape Town municipality and the government's Department of Coloured Affairs (DCA; informally known as the Coloured Affairs Department). Although these contributions were a pittance compared to what, for instance, the state-funded, whites-only opera section of CAPAB received, the amount of these contributions was still more than what black artists received. In 1949 the group was able to purchase a building in District Six with the financial support of the white public as well as the government. In 1969 the pattern repeated itself when Joseph Stone, a white man who supported the group, and the government contributed funds toward the building of the Joseph Stone Auditorium in Athlone.

The fourth and last characteristic that Adhikari mentions is that coloured identity became "the bearer of a range of negative and derogatory connotations," which, he argues, were internalized by coloured people over the course of time.[38] A few examples of how these connotations influenced the group will suffice. Eoan was marketed in the media as a group of musically illiterate and professionally unskilled workers from poor backgrounds who were able to perform Italian opera on a high artistic level. Group members themselves were generally sensitive to these perceptions and felt they were being portrayed in a derogatory manner. Although some group members may have been unskilled and illiterate, many could read notation, and a number had studied at tertiary institutions and become teachers or social workers. During the height of the apartheid era, the Eoan Group was often paraded by government as an example of "how good coloureds can be" in its bid to legitimize the apartheid policy of "separate development."[39] In the end, this condescending praise struck a crippling blow to the Eoan Group, for whom personal excellence came at the price of political compromise.

### THE EOAN GROUP ARCHIVE

The documents that constitute the Eoan Group Archive are characterized by a diversity of voices and registers that have had an impact on the narrative of this book. During the process of writing I became aware of the dominance of some voices, whereas others had to be read between the lines. The characteristics of the various materials—whether letters, minutes, programs, rehearsal schedules, newspaper reviews found in the archive or sourced at the South African National Library, or interviews with former members conducted from 2008 onward—resulted in shifts in register. Some parts rely more heavily on personal letters, others on newspaper reports, and still others on memories. Throughout this book the archive remains a key informant to this narrative.

The contents of archives are often determined by happenstance, especially in circumstances where archiving as an industry is not highly regarded or where an infrastructure for archiving is largely absent. The Eoan Group Archive is no exception. The paper trail that arrived at the Documentation Centre for Music (DOMUS) at Stellenbosch University in February 2008 covered the period 1955–1989 in varying degrees of detail. Documentation included newspaper articles, a few photographs, minutes of meetings, some programs, annual financial statements, rehearsal schedules, notes, letters, telegrams, and the odd costume—but no recordings. Preliminary sorting filled 105 storage boxes that covered roughly 30 meters of storage space. Despite this large amount of documentation in the archive, the historical chronology is inconsistently represented, with a plethora of information on some periods and significant gaps on others, leaving the researcher the task of searching elsewhere for "missing information" and—when that search proves unsuccessful—to guess, project, or simply acknowledge that there are certain things we just don't know.

Except for a scrapbook containing newspaper cuttings of the group's activities from 1944 to 1949 (donated to DOMUS in December 2009), the archive contains no information on the years preceding the group's first opera production in 1956. The narrative of the first chapter of this book, which deals with that period, was therefore knitted together from newspaper articles, the odd reference to the "past" in later documentation, and interviews with members who were remembering events that took place more than sixty years earlier. Documentation on the period 1956 to 1980 has survived more comprehensively; documents concerning certain important events—for example, the 1956 and 1962 festivals, as well as the 1960 and 1965 countrywide tours—, have been meticulously preserved in files that were transferred to DOMUS in pristine condition. These files provided me with exceptionally rich information as they contained, among other things, almost every letter written or received in connection with these particular events. Because of the availability of personal letters, I had firsthand information on how the group's activities affected the lives of people on a very personal level.

Much of the Eoan Group Archive bears testimony to the methodical approach of Joseph Manca. Although he became involved with the group in 1943, the earliest documentation from his hand dates from 1955, when Manca started organizing the 1956 Arts Festival. Manca was an accountant by trade, with exceptional organizational skills and a penchant for detail, and was seemingly obsessed with the preservation of documentation, especially during the 1950s and 1960s. Paging through the files that contain the documentation on the arts festivals and the tours, one cannot but sense his conviction that history was being made and that its memory should be preserved for posterity. During the late 1950s he archived many letters and telegrams that were received from group members as well as the public, even if they were critical of the group or of him. Alex la Guma's scathing attack on the group during the 1956 Arts Festival is a highly significant document, and Manca's archiving of it is testimony to an inclusive approach. The contents of the archive in later years, however, portray Manca's increasingly autocratic management style, his diminishing tolerance of criticism, and the concomitant censuring of voices other than his own. The last evidence of a letter from the public that takes a critical stance toward apartheid dates from 1965.[40] From 1966 onward the few documents that do refer to the precarious political and social environment the group functioned in were written by either Manca or Ismail Sydow and illustrate a denial of the gravity of Eoan's day-to-day political environment. The documentation from the 1970s bears no trace of any of the political unrest in which Eoan members lived, worked, and performed. Instead, documents from this time pertain to Manca's never-ending plans and ambitions for the group, discussed in his customary superlatives. Introspection with regard to Eoan's artistic endeavors is similarly hard to find, and the only critical document preserved in the archive is a four-page summary of the problems pertaining to Eoan's 1965 production of Bizet's *Carmen*.[41] Due to Manca's gatekeeping of the archive and the fact that opera was his main interest, documentation of the group's many other activities is less visible.

In November 2008 DOMUS embarked on an oral history book project concerning the Eoan Group that preceded the academic study that makes up this book. The book *Eoan—Our Story* resulted from that project and became available to the public in January 2013. For that project, approximately fifty interviews were conducted during 2009 by former group members in collaboration with academics from the Music Department at Stellenbosch University. These interviews (also on film) documented former group members' recollections of opera production during the apartheid years. Although several decades had elapsed between the actual events and the interviews, for many group members these interviews were their first formal opportunity to reflect on a past filled with a passion for the arts yet plagued by complicity, political compromise, and disappointment. These interviews are fertile in displaying the diversity of experience and often contrasting opinions that group members held about the same events, issues, or role players. The interviews have also become a source of material for this book, as they often reflect wisdom gained from hindsight or recall events that have not been recorded elsewhere.

The oral history project also led to many additions to the Eoan Group Archive. Not only did the interviews and the filming of them become part of the archive, but also many interviewees donated personal collections of recordings, photographs, programs, and newspaper articles to the archive.

## THIS BOOK

The main objective of this book is to narrate an intimate institutional history of Eoan, a story fraught with complicity, political compromise, and disappointment, thus illuminating the predicament of "coloured opera" in the apartheid era. The text is interspersed with reflective detours on political, cultural, and social contexts in which the group operated; biographical details of dominant figures in the group; the repertoire the group performed; and discussions of the way opera became the undoing of the group in the apartheid setting. Although the group offered many other activities—such as ballet, drama, ballroom dancing, elocution, literacy classes, and after-school care centers for children—these are referred to only where relevant to the main theme of opera production. Accounts of the group's contribution to, for instance, ballet and drama productions, and the historical role the group played in these industries in the larger Cape Town area, remain in the background and are yet to be documented.

Chapter 1 deals with the twenty-five years that preceded Eoan's first opera performance, a period during which the group consolidated its existence as a cultural and welfare organization in District Six and other coloured residential areas in the Cape Peninsula. This period saw the drafting of the group's constitution, which set the tone for how management, operational policy, and the group's stance on politics were to influence opera production and human resources within the group in later years. Special attention is given to the trajectory along which the Eoan Group choir developed into an amateur opera company. Chapters 2 and 3 deal with the group's opera productions between 1956 and 1963, which in hindsight proved to be artistically their best years. At the time, the idea of a coloured opera group that produced Verdi operas continued to mesmerize Cape Town's white audiences and situated the group in the center of Cape Town's Western art music activities. Eoan was indeed the first "non-European" group in South Africa to formally and consistently produce opera on a semiprofessional level. A sense of excitement and wonder is palpable throughout this time, not only in documentation on the reception of the group, but also in the many artifacts in the Eoan Group Archive that document the internal operations of the group.

Chapter 4 covers the latter half of the 1960s, a time during which the group consolidated its reputation as an opera company, not only in Cape Town but also elsewhere in the country. The chapter illustrates how operatic activities were pursued with immense energy and dedication as members sacrificed time, family relations, and job opportunities to be able to participate in opera production. During this time they remained hopeful that acknowledgment as professional artists on a par with their white counterparts would be forthcoming. This period, however, also saw the tightening grip of apartheid starting to take its toll as the system relentlessly continued to foil the group's aspirations.

Chapter 5 illustrates the gradual stifling of Eoan's opera productions in the 1970s. After being moved out to Athlone on the Cape Flats, the group was effectively exiled from the central position it used to occupy with regard to cultural activities such as opera and ballet in the city of Cape Town. At the same time, the detrimental effects of the group's political compromise on the support it had enjoyed within the coloured community took on serious proportions. The underlying theme of this chapter is the increasing isolation (artistic and otherwise) that the group experienced and the ebbing away of willpower and creative energy that resulted in the cessation of operatic activities. The Postscript brings the book to a close by briefly contemplating why Eoan has thus far not been celebrated in the public domain and what the legacy of the group may be. A list of Eoan's music productions and the 1973 version of the Eoan Group Constitution are included as appendixes.

In 2018 the Eoan Group turned eighty-five years old, becoming the oldest organization of its kind in the coloured community of Cape Town. Throughout this period the group has had a constitution that defines its role as a cultural and welfare organization for the coloured community. Although opera overshadowed its activities and public profile from the 1950s through the 1970s, the group has always offered a range of other activities, such as literacy classes, children's centers, ballet classes, choral activities, and drama classes, run by branches of the organization located all over the Cape Peninsula. Opera was just one of many activities that the group participated in; after that died down, the group continued with ballet and drama, as well as other humanitarian activities, albeit on a much smaller scale. However, as a consequence of accepting funds from the apartheid government for opera production, the group became politically suspect in a way that to this day has proven difficult to overcome, even long after Eoan ceased applying for government funds. Today the Eoan Group still functions as a dance company and ballet school.

There are many former members and supporters who remember the group's opera performances and have long hoped for a revival of the group's extraordinary past. This has never happened, however, and the reasons are not difficult to find. Eoan performed opera during the apartheid era because coloureds were barred from performing opera with whites. With the transition to a democratic South Africa, the need for a separate opera company based on racial grounds has (fortunately) become obsolete. It is ironic, however, that the most difficult of circumstances led to the most extraordinary of opera performances.

ONE

## *We Live to Serve: A Demimonde before Art*

1933–1954

> Singing and mirth till the new day dawns on us in paradise.
> —CHORUS, act 1, *La Traviata* by Giuseppe Verdi

### BEGINNINGS

An understanding of the social and political environment of the suburb of District Six in Cape Town in the early twentieth century provides some explanation as to why a white woman from Britain—Helen Southern-Holt—started a humanitarian organization in the area. In *The Struggle for District Six, Past and Present*, Vivian Bickford-Smith provides a vivid description of the conditions at the time.[1] By 1900 this district, a suburb on the eastern side of the city of Cape Town, housed close to 30,000 inhabitants who were a diverse mix of people, including descendants of former slaves, people with a darker pigmentation who originated from racially mixed unions, Malays, Africans who migrated from the east of the Cape Province, recent immigrants from Britain, Jews from tsarist Russia, as well as Indians, Chinese, and Australians.[2] District Six was a culturally vibrant and racially diverse place, and, according to Bickford-Smith, "one of the most cosmopolitan areas in Cape Town."[3] However, its inhabitants were considered "low-class" because most people were poor, and educated individuals were far and few between. The neighborhood was overpopulated and, as a result of the neglect of basic services such as water supply and sanitation by the Cape Town municipality over a long period of time, living conditions were appalling.[4] White bourgeois Capetonians considered the area a slum.[5]

Driven by an urge to improve the lives of the poor and convinced of the "civilizing qualities" of Western culture, Helen Southern-Holt founded the Eoan Group as a cultural and welfare organization in District Six in 1933.[6]

Southern-Holt had emigrated from Manchester in the United Kingdom in 1929 as a trade manager for the department store Garlick's and had been actively involved in helping needy people in the greater Cape Town area since her arrival.[7] Information on the circumstances of the launch of the organization and the people involved (other than herself) is sparse. The Eoan Group Archive contains only a few artifacts concerning the group's activities during the first twenty years of its existence. Traces of the early history of the group are generally found in newspaper reports about its activities written in later years, or from interviews with members who were involved with the group at the time.[8] From a newspaper article published in 1947, it emerged that the organization was launched at a meeting in District Six that was attended by six people.[9] There were similar organizations active in the area, mostly church organizations who provided schooling and social support, but few catered for cultural activities in the way the Eoan Group did. Among these organizations were the African Methodist Episcopal Church, the Dutch Reformed Church, and the Anglican Church. The latter did much social work under the leadership of Bishop Sidney Lavis, who became a close friend of Southern-Holt and served as chair of the Eoan Group during the 1940s.[10]

Initially, Southern-Holt taught elocution to young people. During a speech held at the National Council for Women in 1947, she explained that "my first desire in giving help to the Coloured community was to start classes for clear, articulate speech. Having had to engage Coloured workers as well as European, I knew from experience that the mass of Coloured boys and girls entering the labour market were ill-equipped, and had not the power of the spoken word to aid them."[11] Shortly afterward, Southern-Holt also started a physical education section that incorporated remedial exercises for groups, a ballet section and a drama group, "recognising the talents and desire for development in the Coloured community."[12] Southern-Holt explained how she decided on the name Eoan: "On my programme, as I sat planning, I wrote 'Eos' the beautiful Greek word meaning Dawn—Eos ... Eoan ... pertaining to the Dawn. And so I named the new group Eoan, in the consciousness that through its illumination the Coloured People could realise the dawning of a new cultural expansion in themselves, and a new understanding of well-being, physical and mental, for their race."[13]

She also focused on young children, setting up nursery facilities or after-school care, where children were looked after, fed, taught to speak "proper English," and given physical education.[14] Classes were offered free of charge, but parents were expected to join parent committees and be involved in their children's upbringing.[15] This initiative continued to be an important part of Eoan's activities for decades to come, even long after Southern-Holt had left the organization, and opera, ballet, and drama came to dominate the activities of the group.

It is clear from Southern-Holt's use of the term "coloured" that her understanding was that the people thus defined constituted a homogenous group of people; the subtext was one of poverty and backwardness, a usage of the term that fitted into the white bourgeois discourse of the early twentieth century and that fed into apartheid notions on the nature of "the coloured race." As Bickford-Smith has pointed out, those who were grouped together under this term were in actual fact all but homogenous, and resistance to the levelling out of such diversity continues to this day. In 1950 the "boxing in" of this community was consolidated by the Population Registration Act, which stipulated that every individual in the country had to be classified within a racial category as defined by the government, and the diversity of the community within which Eoan functioned was reduced to, and formally institutionalized in, the one word: *coloured*.

Biographical information on Southern-Holt (see figure 1.1) is difficult to come by. Those who worked with her as staff members in the group do not recall ever having celebrated her birthday; nobody had an idea of her age, and enquiring whether she was a widow or a divorcee was taboo.[16] However, they vividly remember how her strong character often clashed with those around her. Tillie Ulster recalled how she was sternly reprimanded every time she mistakenly addressed Southern-Holt as "Mrs. Holt," and group members suspected that she left behind a bad marriage in the United Kingdom. According to Ulster, Southern-Holt was very possessive of the group, did not tolerate interference from others on managerial matters, and staff members frequently left the group after arguing with her.[17] She had one daughter, Mary (known to group members as Maisy), who came to Cape Town in 1935 to join her mother, and it is clear from documents in the archive that the two remained close throughout their stay in South Africa. Southern-Holt apparently never visited England during the thirty years she lived in Cape Town.[18] In 1958 she immigrated to Canada with Maisy and her family and died there in 1972.[19]

From sources regarding the group during its early years, one does glean something of Southern-Holt's value system. Not only was she well-connected with Cape Town's high society but also she was a lady with Victorian values. Great emphasis was placed within the group on the social and moral respectability that came from hard work, good manners, cleanliness, physical fitness,

FIGURE 1.1. Helen Southern-Holt. Source: Eoan Group Archive.

serving others, education, and sexual purity—values that informed the Eoan constitution, which was drafted some years later and had a profound influence on the functioning of the group throughout its history. During the 1940s phrases such as "Eoan stands for Progress, Health and Happiness" were commonly used in newspaper reporting on the group.[20] A 1946 article provides a fitting description of how the group lived these values: "The Eoan Group has achieved wonders in its efforts to encourage reliability, tidiness, helpfulness, team-work and decency by wholesome recreation for those who would otherwise be obliged to spend their leisure in the streets, in overcrowded dwellings or in shebeens."[21] These values also slotted in well with the Temperance Movement, which was widely influential in coloured society in Cape Town in the early twentieth century.[22] Former members remember, for instance, how Southern-Holt insisted on an upright bodily posture and would reproach each and every one who would slump in her presence. Office space and ballet studios were kept tidy, and no one was allowed to let shoes, costumes, or papers lie around.[23] More importantly, she emphasized the importance of the group as a whole above the individual. Ulster explained that "when the Eoan Group came into being, Ms. Southern-[Holt], being what she was, she would never allow names of individuals to appear on [the] programme. You would perform as either "Eoan grouper" or "Eoan chorister," or no name."[24] Alethea Jansen recalled that the group's mantra was "not for the self, but for the whole."[25] This principle proved difficult to sustain when the group developed into an opera company, causing much friction and resentment among aspiring soloists for years to come.

## DRAMA AND BALLET

The idea of starting ballet classes originated in 1934 when Southern-Holt attended a charity concert held in aid of widows and orphans of a fishing disaster that happened earlier that year in the Cape Town suburb of Hout Bay. During this incident a number of breadwinners within the coloured community of the area perished at sea. The concert included dance items and, after recognizing their enthusiasm and (in her view) the lack of skill of those who participated, she was convinced to start ballet classes.[26] In 1935 Southern-Holt's daughter, Maisy, formally started teaching ballet at the group.[27] The classes turned out to be an immediate success, so much so that Maisy accompanied two talented Eoan dancers, Bertha October and Myrtle Martin, to London in 1938 to participate in examinations at the Royal Academy of Dance in London. This one-time initiative was arranged through Southern-Holt's sister, who lived in the United Kingdom.[28] Although Maisy studied medicine and later moved to Grahamstown in the Eastern Cape, she continued to be the "honorary director" of the physical education and dancing sections at the group until at least 1946.[29]

Eoan's activities expanded to literature classes, which were soon followed by drama productions. Within a year the group produced a drama production, the English play *The Rivals* by Richard Brinsley Sheridan.[30] Over the following twenty years the drama section flourished under the guidance of Billie Jones, a white woman who annually produced "two three-act and eight to 10 one-act plays" with the group.[31] During the first decade of its existence, the group's dance and drama activities grew to such an extent that the group started performing in public venues in Cape Town. In 1937 a "Coloured

Dance Display" was staged with the Cape Town Municipal Orchestra.[32] Events such as this led to the first reviews being published in local newspapers, after which the group's cultural achievements started gaining wider attention among the public. The *Cape Standard*, for instance, reported on 3 May 1937 that William Pickerill, conductor of the Cape Town Municipal Orchestra, "praised the high standard of the work and expressed surprise at the polish and finish, congratulating both the teachers and the group."[33] Later that year the same newspaper reported that "[Eoan's] talented young dancers drew prolonged rounds of applause from a capacity house, while at times the verve and grace with which some of the dances [...] were executed, left the audience spell-bound."[34] From this year onward, the ballet section performed annually with the Cape Town Municipal Orchestra.[35]

Southern-Holt also established branches of the group in other coloured residential areas of the greater Cape Town area, expanding its reach beyond the city center. By 1940 a thousand children from fifteen Eoan branches took part in an open air "Physical Education Display" that included group dancing and physical exercises. Branch leaders were usually parents or teachers, and access to children who participated in such displays (and there were many in years to come) was facilitated via the existing infrastructure of schools where branch leaders were teachers.[36]

## FUNDING

A number of community organizations were active in the coloured community in the early twentieth century, most of which were church initiatives that brought with them a system that facilitated some sort of financial support.[37] Southern-Holt launched Eoan as an organization independent of church affiliations, and financial support had to come from elsewhere. According to former group members, she was well-connected with affluent citizens among city and government officials, and during her twenty-five-year tenure as leader of the organization she raised funds from these sources. This pattern was carried on until the late 1970s as well-to-do (white) individuals and the government continued to support the group financially through the efforts of Joseph Manca.

Money was never easy to come by, and the struggle to obtain funding remained a dominant (and controversial) theme throughout the history of the group. The group seemed to have applied for government funding for the first time in 1940. A 1947 newspaper article mentioned that "for eight years the Eoan Group functioned and grew without the help of any Government grant until the Government, realizing the power for good which lay in it, offered a grant, which has now [1947] been in existence for eight years."[38] From later sources it is clear that Eoan received an annual financial grant from the Department of Education, Arts and Science until 1956, after which the group suspended its applications for state funding for a decade.[39]

### THE EOAN GROUP CHOIR

At the invitation of Southern-Holt, Manca joined the music section of Eoan as choral conductor in 1943.[40] The Eoan Group choir had been set up some years earlier by two brothers, Dan and John Ulster, who played an important role in the group's early musical development.[41] The Ulster family lived in District Six; John was a bass soloist for many of its productions and Dan functioned as repetiteur, conductor, and training assistant to Manca until 1956. Dan Ulster also became the first coloured person to obtain a degree in music from the College of Music at the University of Cape Town in 1949.[42]

Joseph Salvatore Manca (1908–1985)[43] (see figure 1.2) was born in Cape Town of Italian parents, Leonardo and Maria Sara Manca, who had emigrated from Trapani in Sicily around 1903. Joseph was the eldest sibling, followed by his brother Angelo, sister Margarita, and his youngest brother Salvatore.[44] In 1924, aged sixteen, he matriculated at St. Joseph's College in Cape Town and two years later entered employment at the Cape Town City Council. He started as a junior clerk and, after completing the Municipal Treasurer and Accountant's examination, moved to the position of accountant.[45] He remained employed at the City Council until his retirement in 1969 at the age of sixty-one. Manca became involved in choral activities in and around Cape Town from 1934 onward and, despite his lack of formal musical training, played an important role in choral circles and in other amateur music sectors in the Peninsula until his resignation from the Eoan Group in 1977. Although primarily known for his involvement with the Eoan Group, Manca conducted various other choirs in the 1940s and 1950s, one of which was the Cape Town Municipal Choir and the Citizens' Service Choir, which gave many performances of oratorios with the Cape Town Municipal Orchestra.[46] In 1943, when he took over the position of choral conductor for Eoan, he was also director of the Camps Bay and District Musical Society,

FIGURE 1.2. Joseph Manca. Source: Eoan Group Archive.

which produced light operas and later became the Cape Town Light Opera Company.

The gradual development of Eoan's music section from a small choir in 1943 to an opera company in 1956 started in 1944 with a choral concert in the Cathedral Hall in Queen Victoria Street in the city center with approximately thirty-five choristers.[47] Excellence and popularity were clearly priorities for Manca. Barely two years after taking over choir direction, the Eoan Group Choir consisted of 185 singers and was described as "one of the best choirs in the country."[48] As illustrated in the course of this chapter, Eoan's choral productions grew ever more ambitious in the years to follow, adding dramatic elements such as the use of soloists, costumes, and movement to each new production. At the time, the drama section was equally active and continuously presented new plays. The *Cape Argus* publicly congratulated the group for "their prolific production of plays these days," while the ballet section had expanded and consolidated itself to such an extent that sufficient numbers of coloured dancers were trained to be employed in teaching positions within the group.[49] From this time onward, Eoan's ballet teachers always came from within the coloured community, a practice that was never extended to the music section.

## JAZZ AND OTHER COMMUNITY MUSIC

Denis-Constant Martin's 2013 publication *Sounding the Cape—Music, Identity and Politics in South Africa*, provides a broad overview of the kinds of music practiced by the coloured community in the Cape during the course of the twentieth century, sketching an important context within which Eoan's musical activities should be understood.[50] He writes that "music remained an indispensable ingredient of social life," an observation that echoes Carol Muller's 2008 statement that "musical renditions could be heard on the radio and through live performance at home, singing in the church or at school, [t]here was always live music on the streets."[51] Other than the new genre of jazz (introduced to the Cape in the 1940s), vocal and/or instrumental traditions included, among others, Christmas Bands, Langarm Bands, the Cape Coon Festivals, Qasidah Bands, and Malay Choirs, whose repertoire centered on songs such as Moppies and Nederlandsliedjies (Dutch songs).[52] Popular music styles from abroad (especially from the United States), disseminated through film and radio, became very popular, and, as Paula Fourie illustrated in her work on Taliep Petersen, influenced much local music making throughout the twentieth century.[53]

Yet within the political context of music making in the coloured community, Eoan's cultural activities were positioned in alignment with the system rather than in resistance against it. Early signs of the political divide between those practicing classical music and those playing jazz or popular music within the coloured community were present in the media in the 1940s already. An article discussing Eoan's cultural contribution to the community published in *Trek* in 1945 described the "edifying" or "civilizing" properties of classical music as "find[ing] temporary happiness, forgetfulness and satisfaction through artistic activities and to convey this elevation to thousands of their own people."[54] The article continues to denounce the influence of American popular and jazz music on the Cape Coon Festivals in blatantly racist terms as a "pathetic American Negro art," which is subsequently contrasted with classical music as practiced by the Eoan Group: "But now the impossible has been performed: the people whom Europeans [...] watched while they crooned silly and slushy jazz songs on the Green Point Common, present us in the City Hall with choruses by Bach, Händel, Mendelssohn, Wagner and the like. And it must be emphasised, they sang better, much better, than any other choir in this town."[55] Cultural formats such as drama, ballet, and choral singing were introduced through, among others, the Eoan Group with the help of (white) government funding and were perceived by some as important tools in the striving for social progress and the improvement of lives.

As the history of apartheid unfolded, the two musical genres of classical and jazz became increasingly informed by a language that situated them on either side of the political divide. Although not all local jazz musicians were by definition politically active, jazz became a space that allowed for political protest through music. A number of musicians, such as Abdullah Ibrahim (or "Dollar Brand" at the time); his wife, Sathima Benjamin,; Miriam Makeba; Johnny Dyani; and Hugh Masekela, went into exile in later years and were able to use their performances in the international jazz arena as platforms for resistance against apartheid.[56] The history of Cape Town jazz, as presented by scholars such as Carol-Ann Muller, Valmont Layne, and Denis-Constant Martin is therefore informed by a discourse of "the struggle."[57] In contrast to this, the Eoan Group, the main avenue through which the coloured community had access to performing and listening to live classical music, was in later years branded a cultural organization that supported apartheid. As much as this notion is reductionist and has been shaped by an antiapartheid discourse over time, the story of the group that emerges from the pages of this book will illustrate that due to the stance taken on politics by Eoan's management over the years, resistance against apartheid policies by coloured practitioners of classical music in the group was suppressed and contributed to the group's isolation within the community in later years.

## LARGE-SCALE CHORAL WORKS

On 21 and 22 June 1946, the Eoan Group choir (see figure 1.3) performed its first large-scale choral work: the cantata *The Redeemer* by Martin Shaw, composed in 1944 for soloists, choir, and orchestra, which was broadcast on the

FIGURE 1.3. The Eoan Group Choir in 1946. Source: Eoan Group Archive.

BBC in 1945.[58] Manca's ready use of such newly composed works from England is indicative of his vision for the group to have them perform new works. The work is composed for five soloists, choir, and orchestra, and, for this production, the Eoan Group choir consisted of a hundred voices, while the orchestra was replaced by an organ. The soloists for this production were Joey Daniels (soprano), Kitty Paulse (alto), James Adams (tenor), Andrew Mackrill (baritone), and John Ulster (bass), with John Juritz at the organ. The program notes mention that Dan Ulster was repetiteur during rehearsals, and according to his wife Tillie, he also trained the soloists.[59] The concert was held in the Cape Town City Hall, a venue where a racially mixed audience was freely tolerated until legislation prohibited this from the 1960s onward.

Already at this early stage, the image of Eoan singers as illiterate domestic workers, cleaners, or gardeners who performed "high art" was cultivated in the media. An article in the *Cape Argus* that appeared a week before this production reports as follows: "Well you won't remember the coloured messenger boy who passed you on his bicycle in the busy street of the city the other day. Do you know what he was humming, the coloured messenger boy bent on his errand that sunny morning along the city's asphalted artery of the road? He was humming a passage from Dr. Martin Shaw's oratorio *The*

*Redeemer*. You did not know it but you had just heard the humming of a trained singer." The article continues to address bourgeois (presumably white) housewives: "Your Maria who scrubs and polishes and dusts so assiduously, on Tuesday nights she takes off her apron and is transformed like Cinderella, into somebody quite new. That night she is no kitchen girl, but an interpreter of the arts; that night she voices beautifully the music of great masters, of Handel and Mendelssohn and Bach."[60]

The power of music to bring about a "Cinderella-like transformation" to the lives of domestic workers, gardeners, janitors, truck drivers, and factory workers had particular relevance for the coloured community at the time. In her book on jazz singer Sathima Bea Benjamin, Carol-Ann Muller quotes jazz musician Vincent Kolbe saying that "women would work a whole week in a factory, and Saturdays go to a dance with this gown, golden shoes, and a cigarette holder as they had seen in the movies. Young women fantasised on the weekend about being a 'princess for the night'. Men dressed up too—,they would wear bow ties and black suits."[61]

In March 1946 the ballet section presented a concert with the City of Cape Town Municipal Orchestra. The evening consisted of a variety of items ranging from existing ballets, such as Glazunov's *Tatiana's Birthday*, to new dances choreographed by Eoan's own dance instructors to music by Mozart, Delius, Schumann, and Albert Coates.[62] In the same month Shakespeare's *The Tempest* was staged by an all-coloured cast that included some of Eoan's actors.[63] This production was attended by the then prime minister, General Jan Smuts, and was sponsored by the South African Association of Arts. The organizers were thanked for "making a pleasant gesture towards the furthering of the art of Theatre among non-Europeans."[64] This comment clearly indicates that there was no intention within institutional circles of the time to allow coloureds to share the stage with whites and that segregation in cultural activities had been a reality long before the National Party officially legislated the practice. In fact, the newspaper The *Torch* went one step further and discussed tendencies toward "self-imposed segregation" by coloureds within cultural circles. The report mentioned that a concert was held to "raise funds for the formation of a 'School of Music and Culture' for Non-Europeans" and condemned coloureds who supported such a venture, stating that "we have more than enough segregatory measures which have been imposed on us against our will to contend with, without creating any new ones ourselves. Segregation means only one thing: facilities of a much inferior standard to those accorded to Europeans. In the sphere of music it means inferior tuition by inadequately trained staff and the setting up of an entirely false standard of criticism."[65] Not only did the article accurately identify the practical implications of what was later called "separate development," which had in effect been in existence for many years already and was to intensify in decades to come, it also spelled out the dilemma coloured artists faced in their endeavor to be regarded on the same level as whites:

> It is well known that critics who are considered quite competent as judges of performances of any kind by Europeans invariably regard performances of any kind by Non-Europeans in the same light as they regard the Coon Carnival and African Handwork, namely, something to be patronised and which might have some value in attracting tourists to the country. This was proved quite recently as the following extract from a critique of the Eoan ballet in the *Cape Times* (18/3/46) will show: "These Eoan Group dance displays are reaching up to a standard where they will have to be appraised from an absolute artistic standpoint rather than praised for a remarkable achievement coming from a non-European group."[66]

Being judged on the basis of performance excellence without interference from the associations that come with racial prejudice was an issue for Eoan's artists throughout their performance history. The issue raises the conundrum of discussing or critiquing musical performance independently of its social context. Could and should one discuss an Eoan performance as if the performance could have happened, for instance, on the stage of the Metropolitan opera house in New York rather than on the stage of the Cape Town City Hall, where they played to an audience who were well aware of and, in many instances, sympathetic to the social, educational, and political difficulties in which the performers lived?

The group had by this time expanded its branches throughout the Peninsula and by 1947 boasted twenty-one branches.[67] A branch was also launched in Port Elizabeth, the only one that ever existed outside the Cape Peninsula. This branch probably came about because Southern-Holt's daughter, Maisy, had been living in Grahamstown for some years (her husband was an academic at Rhodes University) and Southern-Holt visited her daughter often. At the time, Port Elizabeth had a large coloured population whose proximity to Grahamstown, combined with Southern-Holt's frequent visits there, facilitated the branch's functioning.[68] Although little archival material is available on this branch's activities, it functioned as an important support base for the group during its countrywide tours of 1960 and 1965.

In 1947 Shaw's cantata *The Redeemer* was repeated in a concert augmented with items such as excerpts from Handel's oratorio *The Messiah*, featuring Elizabeth April as soprano soloist. At the time, Eoan even boasted a pipe band that played music by Bach, Gounod, and Handel as arranged by Manca during a concert on 1 April.[69] In October the cantata for children's voices, *Sherwood* by Christopher Edmunds, was performed by a massed junior choir of five hundred children accompanied by the Cape Town Municipal Orchestra, while the Eoan Group (senior) choir performed Andreas Romberg's cantata *Lay of the Bell* on the same occasion.[70] This concert was attended by high-society guests, among them the London conductor and composer Albert Coates, who had settled in Cape Town in 1946 with his South African wife, Vera de Villiers. The *Sun* reported that "the world famous musician and conductor, Albert Coates, was one of many distinguished persons present on Saturday evening when the Eoan Choir rendered the beautiful cantata *Lay of the Bell* at the City Hall Cape Town. He was so struck by the excellence of the choral rendering that he personally conveyed to Mr. Manca and the choir his appreciation and his felicitations."[71]

During the 1940s the classical arts industry was fairly well established in Cape Town, and Eoan was able to make use of some of its infrastructure for their activities. The Cape Town Municipal Orchestra had been functioning as a professional orchestra subsidized in full by the city council since 1914, and the orchestra participated in many Eoan productions from the 1930s through to the 1970s.[72] Training in classical music on a tertiary level was offered by both Stellenbosch University (since 1904) and the University of Cape Town (UCT) (since 1910), while the latter also had a Ballet Company and a Ballet School, both established by Dulcie Howes in 1932.[73] Although Eoan had no access to training at Stellenbosch University and limited possibilities at UCT, examinations in the British Royal Academy of Dancing Exams could be taken by local dancers since the 1920s, and Eoan participated in these from the inception of their ballet section.[74] Several short-lived opera companies had been producing opera since the 1930s, and a number of venues were available in Cape Town for productions, some of which Eoan was able to use. Shortly after World War II, two prominent classical music figures from the United Kingdom, Erik Chisholm and Albert Coates, settled in Cape Town and contributed significantly toward the steady growth of a classical arts industry as well as a culture of concertgoing among the public. Both Chisholm and Coates publicly demonstrated their appreciation for the Eoan Group's endeavors. Despite its racial constituency and a degree of legislated segregation that existed before 1948, it is clear that Eoan participated in and contributed to the classical arts industry quite freely during this time.

Eoan's drama and dance sections continued to be equally active. Not only were a number of plays and ballets staged throughout the year, but many dancers took part in the Royal Academy of Dancing Exams with good pass rates.[75] In May the ballet section presented its annual display with the Cape Town Municipal Orchestra, conducted by Walter Swanson.[76] The performance was repeated in October. In August the drama department presented James Montgomery's comedy *Nothing But the Truth* with Andrew Mackrill as star actor. Mackrill was a versatile artist who not only excelled as an actor but also had a superb voice. He performed as a soloist in Shaw's *The Redeemer*, and reviews praised his performance as "simply magnificent."[77]

In 1948 Dulcie Howes, director of the University of Cape Town Ballet Company, sponsored coloured dancer David Poole to study ballet in the United Kingdom.[78] This gave him access to first-class training at a young age and enabled him to enjoy a professional career in London as a ballet dancer. In later years Howes made sure that dancer Johaar Mosaval was also given this opportunity.[79] There has always been a marked difference between the career possibilities of talented coloured dancers compared to singers from the Eoan Group. Howes seemed to have been acutely aware of the limited scope for coloured dancers in the South Africa and did her utmost to send abroad dancers with potential, in order for them to have access to professional careers outside of South Africa. Eoan's singers, on the contrary, were discouraged from leaving the country, as Manca was loath to give up his principals, without whom Eoan's opera performances would not have been possible. Those singers who did leave the country went at a later stage in their careers after being molded by local training and circumstances to a greater degree. With the possible exception of Joseph Gabriels, no Eoan singer was able to establish a singing career abroad on the same level as dancers such as David Poole, Johaar Mosaval, or Vincent Hantam did.

## THE SOCIAL AND POLITICAL ENVIRONMENT

In spite of its growing cultural activities, Eoan's main focus during the 1940s continued to be on social work, such as classes to "remedy defective speech," physical education, and training for nursemaids and club leaders.[80] Eoan joined other organizations (including the coloured political party, the

African People's Organisation) in a campaign to increase literacy among the adult coloured population.[81] In his dissertation on the history of sport in the coloured community, Francois Cleophas has shown that through its physical education programs, the group played an important role in the early development of a culture of sports activities in the coloured community.[82] In those years the group also received funding from the National Advisory Council for Physical Education for these activities.[83] One of the artifacts in the Eoan Group Archive that documents the early years of the group is a scrapbook containing media reports pertaining to the group's activities from 1944–1949.[84] Although cultural activities do have a presence in this book, its main focus clearly remains social work. The impression of District Six as a slum is reinforced in articles that describe the living conditions in terms of "squalor, misery and degradation," calling it a "social sore in the heart of the city," where "disease, dirt and poverty [reign] in [a] crowded slum."[85]

Although the group aimed to actively make a difference within coloured society, its relationship with politics had been ambivalent since its inception, and it remained so throughout its history. Eoan was a welfare and cultural organization run by a single-minded European woman who believed that social progress could be achieved through the qualities of Western civilization. Although the group's constitution stated that the organization was nonpolitical, a large portion of the financial means needed to run the group was sourced from government as well as wealthy white patrons, a situation that in later years made the group politically vulnerable.[86] Since the 1930s, newspapers that catered for the coloured public, such as the *Cape Standard*, the *Torch*, and the *Sun*, regularly ran front-page stories expressing anger at the social inequality and disempowered status of coloured society, and often called for active resistance against such conditions.[87] Under these circumstances, the premises on which Eoan was functioning—white management and white money—were bound to land the group in trouble sooner or later.

On 22 November 1947, for example, the group presented a concert comprising dance and choral items in Stellenbosch, where whites and coloured in the audience were allocated separate seating. Stellenbosch was at the time the political, financial, and cultural seat of white Afrikanerdom in the Cape, and it is clear that this arrangement was made to comply with the segregationist preferences of (white) Stellenbosch society who were, incidentally, also financial patrons of the group. According to a report published in the *Torch*, this arrangement was intended to "accommodate local conditions," and Eoan's management had full knowledge of this before the concert[88] (see the cartoon

FIGURE 1.4. Cartoon published in the *Torch* on November 24, 1947. Source: Scrapbook, Eoan Group Archive.

in figure 1.4). The incident caused a stir in the coloured community and was followed by a barrage of newspaper articles criticizing the group for "supporting the colour bar."[89] Eoan responded in the *Sun* with a statement that was to mark its stance toward political controversy in the years to come: "The Group need not feel disturbed about the unwarranted and deplorable attack made on it by the Press. The group is too firmly established, too highly respected and too outstandingly successful as a cultural body to be affected by those punitive efforts of the *Cape Standard* and the *Torch*."[90]

A letter from a mother whose child was participating in the group's activities is a stark foreboding of the loss of support that the group would suffer in later years: "For many years I have been an admirer and staunch supporter of the Eoan Group. I, however, got a rude shock when I read in the *Torch* that the Eoan Group openly supported the Colour Bar by giving separate seats to the Europeans at their performance in Stellenbosch. As a parent I have no use for chameleon-like organisations or people. I will not support the Group any longer. Such organizations should be shunned by all Non-Europeans who honestly oppose segregation."[91]

In May 1948 the National Party won the national elections by a slight margin, ousting the United Party of Jan Smuts that had been in power since 1933. This ushered in a period of intensified and formalized racial segregation that, in time, intensified the oppression, impoverishment, and disempowerment of South Africans who were not white. Under United Party rule, Eoan's management had forged ties with government as the provider of funds to run the organization. Barring the period 1956–1965, these ties were maintained with the National Party until 1989, when Eoan finally chose to terminate its fund applications to the government. However, in 1948 the change of government seemed to have little impact on the membership of the group or community support for its activities. By September 1948, Eoan's membership had grown to 2,037, indicative of the acceptance that the group enjoyed within the community at the time.[92]

## MANAGEMENT

The activities of the group bear testimony to the fact that managerial and administrative structures of the group were fairly stable, albeit heavily dominated by the person of Southern-Holt. Although the group's constitution was drafted during this time, the earliest version that has survived in the Eoan Group Archive is an amended version of 1959, the year after Southern-Holt left the country. Two early versions of the official aims of the group did survive in printed form as preambles to concert programs or marketing material and give some insight into the functioning of the group during this time. In a 1939 marketing brochure, the principles of the group were formulated in rather simple terms that focus on equality, brotherhood, and the training of the body and the mind.[93] Ten years later, however, these aims had been considerably expanded and reformulated with specific focus on "service to the group" in contrast to the "self-glorification of the individual."[94] This section was adopted in the 1959 version of the constitution, and the phrase "we live to serve" became part of the logo of the group (see figure 1.5). Servitude was upheld as a mantra by the organization throughout its opera-producing years.

**(THE DAWN)**

"We Live to Serve."

**BROTHERHOOD.**

To live a life which will be free from all bias, and free from all prejudice of creed, race and colour.

**UNITY.**

To live and work always for the good of the whole Group, forgetting the personal self, knowing that Unity is born out of the unselfish life.

**PURITY.**

To keep the body pure and clean, knowing that it is a temple of the living spirit. To control the thoughts, to keep the actions pure at all times. Fully to understand EOAN "dedication".

**JOYOUS SERVICE.**

To give service to the Group joyously; such service seeks no special thanks or self glorification but serves for the pure joy of serving.

**THE GROUP.**

To believe in the symbol of service as defined by EOAN and to take EOAN teaching only, for the purpose of becoming efficient so as to be ready to give to others those cultural arts embodied in EOAN. In order to keep up and advance the standard of EOAN not to re-teach, show class work or perform publicly without the Group's permission.

"My Word is My Bond."

Typex

FIGURE 1.5.  Eoan Group poster outlining the group's values. Source: Eoan Group Archive.

On a structural level, it seems that the group was able to offer salaried positions that included a principal, an administrator, and a number of ballet teachers. These positions were occupied by individuals from within the coloured community. In 1945 Marie Adams was appointed as vice-principal of the group and in 1947 was promoted to principal, overseeing the educational sections of the organization, a task that was taken over by Alethea Jansen in the early 1950s.[95] Tillie Ulster was secretary of the group from the early 1940s through to about 1952, and coloured ballet teachers had been appointed at the group since 1945. A newspaper article of 1947 indicates that Southern-Holt's position was unsalaried, as were the positions of other Europeans involved with the group, including Manca as choral conductor and Billie Jones as director of the drama department. Reports for the first time also mention that Manca functioned as the treasurer of the group.[96] An accountant by trade, it seemed a natural role for him to play in the management of the group, and he remained in charge of Eoan's finances until his resignation in 1977.[97]

### *A SLAVE IN ARABY*: EOAN'S FIRST OPERETTA

In February 1948 the drama department presented its first Shakespeare play, *A Midsummer Night's Dream*, the largest drama undertaking the group had managed so far and an event that had been in preparation for months.[98] In November the children's musical *The Rose and the Laurel* by Herbert Walter Wareing, was performed "with singing and dancing by 500 participants," while another Eoan dancer, Sheila van Breda, was sponsored by the group to study ballet in the United Kingdom.[99]

The year 1949 was an industrious year for Eoan's music section, which made important strides in its development toward the production of musical drama and opera. In April Manca produced a dramatized version of Martin Shaw's *The Redeemer*.[100] The work was now performed by the group for the third year running, this time with costumes and movement that incorporated actors from the drama section. Manca described the production as "a form of passion play."[101] In July a children's operetta, *The Wonderful Inn* by May Sarson, preceded the choir's first attempt at representing opera choruses in concert, a production that included choruses from Giuseppe Verdi's *Il Trovatore* and *Nabucco*, Giacomo Puccini's *Madama Butterfly*, Wagner's *Tannhäuser*, and *The Flying Dutchman*, as well as Pietro Mascagni's *Cavalleria Rusticana*, featuring Elizabeth April as soprano soloist.[102]

A major breakthrough came a month later when Billie Jones produced the group's first complete operetta, *A Slave in Araby* by Alfred Silver and Stanley Guise, using 75 performers and starring soprano May Abrahamse in her first principal role.[103] Andrew Mackrill was once again singled out in reviews as a polished performer, and the critic predicted that Abrahamse would develop into a "fine singer."[104] This operetta included all the elements that were needed for the opera productions from 1956 onward: soloists, choir and dancers, and telling a story through song and movement under the guidance of a director and conductor. This production was also Eoan's first musical production using stage scenery and a producer, as well as a full orchestra. The work was staged with the Cape Town Municipal Orchestra in the City Hall in Cape Town.[105] Manca's ambition to produce opera with the group was described in a newspaper article as follows: "Mr. Manca makes no secret of the fact that his great ambition is to see the group [...] produce the best opera. This latest production brings Mr. Manca nearer to the accomplishment of his hopes."[106] The production received good reviews, and tickets to all performances were sold out. The *Cape Argus* described the production as a "Triumph for the Eoan Group," the *Cape Times* mentioned that the production was "most commendable," while the *Sun* stated that the repeat performance was a "show not to be missed."[107] In December the choir presented yet another choral concert, this time under the baton of Enrique Jorda, consisting of excerpts from choral works by Mozart, Brahms, Handel, and Borodin.[108] Staging four large musical productions in one year, of which three consisted of new material, was no small achievement and foreshadowed the energy and enthusiasm with which the group produced opera in later years.

Many of the cantatas, musicals, operettas, and choral or theatrical works that the group performed in the run-up to their first opera production have sunk into oblivion today, with little or no information available on the music or their composers. The bulk of these works were composed in the first half of the twentieth century in England and represented a repertoire that played into English middle-class musical tastes of the prewar era. These works functioned as important stepping stones for the group in its journey toward opera production. For Manca, who never received formal training as a musician, these works must have been equally important as a method of instruction. By 1949 he had already produced a substantial number of large-scale dramatic works with great success and was steadily working toward the production of

Italian opera, a challenge for any amateur musician. Manca's musical capabilities were the center of much debate over the years, not only among Eoan members but also among his peers in the (white) classical music industry.[109] On the one hand, claims were made that he could not read an orchestral score, was a poor conductor, and sidelined group members with better skills. On the other hand, Manca was a composer who wrote an operetta, *San Maratto*, in 1932 (when he was 24 years old) that was performed in that year with the Cape Town Municipal Orchestra under the direction of William Pickerill.[110] Later in his life he composed piano works as well as songs with piano accompaniment (mostly settings of Afrikaans poems), of which a number have been performed and recorded by Eoan artists. To this day appreciation of Manca as a musician ranges from adoration to vilification; for many in the coloured community, he made a life as an opera singer or chorister a reality; for others, he represented the low expectations of inferior education that was deemed good enough for South Africans who were not white. In order to stage Verdi operas as an untrained musician with an amateur opera company, music must have been part of his life since childhood, and learning the trade probably came through trial and error.

Apart from having some talent in music, the knowledge Manca had about the technical and musical aspects of choral and opera production was probably learnt from fellow Italian and professional singer Alessandro Rota, with whom he worked closely for more than four decades. Rota came to South Africa in 1930 as a dramatic tenor with the Gonzales Opera Company, decided to stay and started his own (short-lived) voice production school in 1932.[111] By 1934 Manca, who was twenty-six at the time, served as choir master and conductor for some of Rota's opera productions, and from 1956 onward Rota became closely involved with Eoan as voice trainer and opera producer until the late 1970s.[112] Apart from the debate around Manca's musical abilities, it is also clear that he was ambitious. The opportunity to produce large-scale opera within the professional and semiprofessional worlds of white opera production at the time—in which musicians such as Albert Coates, Erik Chisholm, Gregorio Fiasconaro, and later Angelo Gobbato were important figures—would not have materialized. As a white man at the helm of a talented group of artists who lived and worked on the fringes of mainstream arts production in the Cape, the Eoan Group was the perfect vehicle for this ambition.

## THE ISAAC OCHBERG HALL IN HANOVER STREET, DISTRICT SIX

In 1949 Eoan was finally able to acquire a building that would be the group's home for the next two decades and that grounded the group solidly into the narrative of District Six. During the first fifteen years of its existence the group had no permanent office, and the organization's administrative hub moved from one place to another. Eoan's activities took place in schools and church halls in the city and throughout the Peninsula where the group had branches, while choir rehearsals were held in the Banqueting Hall in the City Hall in Cape Town. Initially, Southern-Holt used the Hyman Liberman Institute in District Six as a base, but soon this location became unavailable.[113] Bishop Lavis offered offices to the group at the St. Paul's Primary School in Bryant Street in Cape Town, but this proved to be short-term as well.[114] By 1939 the group started petitioning the government and the public to raise funds for a permanent home, but it took ten years before it reached this goal.[115] In 1945 the group's offices were located in Room 50 in the Old Post Office in Adderley Street, and by 1946 its headquarters had moved to the Zonnenbloem College in Woodstock.[116] Southern-Holt lived in a house at 29 Glen Garith Road in the leafy suburb of Sea Point, and much of the administration was run from there.[117]

A new initiative was started in January 1945, when the support group "Friends of Eoan" was launched with the aim to "secure wider support among Europeans for the activities of the Eoan Group."[118] This group, consisting of well-to-do and politically influential whites, specifically focused on raising funds for a building for the group. From the start, government officials were invited to attend Eoan's concerts and other activities as "it was hoped the government would make a substantial contribution" toward funds for the building. In 1946 the Department of Social Welfare indeed pledged £8,300 toward the building fund.[119]

After extensive fundraising by the group and the "Friends of Eoan," £22,000 was collected, and the group was able to purchase an old church building belonging to the Dutch Reformed Church at 302 Hanover Street in District Six for £10,500. The remaining funds were used to renovate the building.[120] The hall was named after Isaac Ochberg, who had bequeathed £3,000 toward the fund.[121] The Isaac Ochberg Hall remained Eoan's artistic and administrative headquarters until 1969, when Eoan was evicted from the area and the group moved to the Joseph Stone Auditorium in Athlone, a designated coloured residential area on the Cape Flats. Although many of the group's activities took place at the Ochberg Hall during these years, church and school halls elsewhere in the city continued to be used for their extensive branch activities. In the early 1960s it also became clear that the Ochberg Hall could not accommodate everything the group was involved with, and from 1961 onward the music section rented premises on the third floor of a building in Bree Street in the city center, where rehearsals and the training of soloists took place.[122] This venue was used by the music section until the group moved to Athlone in November 1969.

### THE EARLY 1950S

Shortly after the National Party came into power in 1948, a number of laws were implemented that saw the steady passing and implementation of legislated racial segregation. In 1949 the Prohibition of Mixed Marriages Act was passed, followed a year later by an amendment of the 1927 Immorality Act that forbade sexual relations between whites and any other racial groups.[123] In 1950 the Group Areas Act was passed that assigned racial groups to different residential and business sections in urban areas.[124] In the same year the Population Registration Act made it obligatory for every South African to register as a member of a specific racial category. In 1951 the Separate Representation of Voters Act was passed whereby coloureds were removed from the voters' roll.[125] The Pass Law Act of 1952 made it compulsory for all black South Africans over the age of sixteen to carry a "pass book" at all times when they were in white areas. Coloureds, however, were exempt from this legislation. The year 1953 saw the promulgation of the Separate Amenities Act, which designated public spaces, such as beaches, parks, ablution facilities, entrances to buildings, and so forth, for the exclusive use of specific racial groups. The latter law was branded "petty apartheid" as it dominated the day-to-day practicalities for the ordinary citizen. For Eoan's activities this had far-reaching consequences because it influenced access to concert venues, public attendance of their performances, rehearsal facilities, teaching areas, as well as back-stage operations. On 2 November 1951, the *Sun* ran a front page article on the government's threat to withdraw subsidies to cultural organizations that "do not fall in line with the Government's apartheid policy," which precluded racially mixed audiences.[126] The article mentioned that the Camps Bay and District Musical Society, of which Manca was the chair at the time, refused the grant. Manca is reported to have said "Rather than sell its soul to the Government, the Society decided to refuse the money." However, the article remains silent on the issue of Eoan's acceptance of a government subsidy at the time.

Interviews with former members sixty years after these events took place have rendered limited information on how the newly instituted legislation affected the group. Over time the memory of these events seems to have disappeared into nostalgia, forgetfulness, or denial. Hints from newspaper articles and program overviews indicate that although Eoan continued to add to its impressive list of music productions, the group did not avoid political controversy. The year 1952, for instance, marked the three-hundredth anniversary of the Dutch settler Jan van Riebeeck's arrival at the Cape, an event the National Party chose to commemorate countrywide and through which it advanced the ideological agenda of white nationalism. According to a study on this festival, a large part of the coloured community boycotted the Tercentenary Festivities, including the "government-funded" Eoan Group.[127] Seen in the context of the group's explicit stance to refrain from becoming involved in politics, this decision was highly unusual and presented the essential elements of the dilemma the group faced throughout its history. The *Torch* reported on 9 October 1951 that the Eoan Executive indeed decided to boycott the celebrations and described the arguments for and against:

> There was a section which favoured participation "to show the world how good the Coloured people are," i.e. no longer monkeys. A similar section wanted to take part for fear of losing a £400 a year grant from the Government and £500 from the Council, their combined principles were not worth more than £900.
>
> Those against comprised an oddly assorted mixture of two groups. One group opposed participation correctly: because "we cannot celebrate 300 years of discrimination." The other "anti" group was anti-African. For them the Celebrations were an insult. They would do a Spanish dance in the City Hall for the (other) descendants of Van Riebeeck. But it was unthinkable that their little girls be asked to dance like Zulus and "Kaffirs."[128]

Not only was the group blackmailed by the fear of losing funds provided by the government, but also this incident illustrates various aspects of coloured identity referred to in the Introduction to this book and illustrated in writings by various scholars on the subject.[129] The derogatory description of a coloured person as a "monkey" is a typical example of the "negative signification" that coloureds had been subject to for generations. The *Torch* also suggests that coloureds referred to themselves as the "other" line of descendants of Jan van Riebeeck, designating their origin exclusively as the offspring of racial mixing that followed the Dutch settlement at the Cape in 1652. As the historian Mohamed Adhikari explained, seeking acceptance as "good" in the eyes of whites and therefore being treated as equals was something many coloureds desired and, in later years, resistance groups often smirked at Eoan's activities as "parading how good coloureds can be."[130] The boycott, however, also proved that individuals within the group were politically aware and were willing to take the risk that came with resistance against apartheid. Racial prejudices against black Africans prevalent in the coloured community are also clearly illustrated here, an issue that often caused tensions within the group.

By this time, the group had been functioning for twenty years and was one of a few organizations that provided opportunities for coloureds to take part in Western classical art forms such as choral and solo singing, ballet, dance, and drama. Similar opportunities were available with, for example, the Spes Bona Orchestral Society, which was started in 1917 at the Battswood College in the coloured residential area of Grassy Park.[131] This college offered training in classical instruments from the 1930s onward. Newspaper articles reveal that concerts, choir festivals, and *eisteddfods* (choir competitions) were held under the auspices of the Battswood College, as well as the (coloured) Teachers League of South Africa. Eoan member Dan Ulster, who headed the college for many years, also conducted the Spes Bona Orchestra from 1960 onward.[132] This orchestra consisted of amateur musicians who performed classical music concerts, often in conjunction with the Battswood College Choir.[133] There were also a number of coloured church choirs that performed cantatas and oratorios. In March 1951, for instance, May Abrahamse and Andrew Mackrill sang solo roles in a rendition of John Henry Maunder's cantata *Olivet to Calvary* with the St. Paul's Choir, which was located in the coloured residential area of the Bo-Kaap.[134] There was a dance studio in Ashley Street in District Six, and the Zonnebloem College not only presented occasional operettas and choral concerts, but also had an art school that held regular exhibitions.[135] These activities were all held within the confines of the coloured community in the Cape with little interaction across racial or spatial borders. But Eoan had greater ambitions. Not only did the group have whites in their management structure, from 1937 onward they performed with the (white) Cape Town Municipal Orchestra, and many whites attended their concerts. When their reputation as an opera company became nationally established in the course of the 1960s, the group's principal singers were often invited to sing in towns throughout the country, and some even recorded with the South African Broadcasting Corporation. The Eoan Group was a cultural organization that provided a space for coloured people to perform Western classical art forms within an environment that potentially transgressed racial boundaries and challenged perceptions of racial exclusivity in the genre of opera. This highly significant endeavor and the way it was thwarted at the hands of the apartheid regime is the story that unfolds in this book.

The five years preceding the group's historic production of *La Traviata* saw a continuous stream of production of new works as well as repeats of existing repertoire, preparing the group for opera performances and illustrating the enormous amounts of time and energy group members were willing to spend on the practice of Western art music. New works included the two-act operetta *Hong Kong* by Charles Jessop in 1950 and Harold Fraser-Simson's musical comedy *The Maid of the Mountains* in 1951.[136] In 1953 Eoan embarked on a full-scale production of Mendelssohn's *Elijah* with soloists, a choir of more than one hundred singers, and organ accompaniment, followed by a production of the operetta *The Gypsy Princess* by Hungarian composer Emmerich Kalman, which "played to packed houses" and of which "all repeat performances were sold out."[137] The group celebrated its twenty-first birthday in 1954 with George Posford and Bernard Grun's musical *Magyar Melody* that saw one hundred performers on stage accompanied by the Cape Town Municipal Orchestra.[138]

During this time the group's activities regularly reached the front page of the newspaper the *Sun*, a weekly publication aimed at a coloured readership.[139] As illustrated earlier in this chapter, their activities were also noted in newspapers such as the *Cape Times* and the *Cape Argus*, which had a wider readership. Reviews of Eoan's concerts were generally positive, praising the group for its high-quality musical entertainment and running many articles on the group's ballet and drama activities. The group enjoyed a good standing within the coloured community, and its achievements were also admired within the larger Cape community. With hindsight it is easy to see how early complicities paved the way for major political compromises, which in time caused the group (in Manca's own words) to "sell its soul to the government." At the time, however, its achievements, combined with Manca's ambitions toward opera production, heralded a future that was bright and exciting.

TWO

## *The* La Traviata *Affair: From Courtesan to Lover*

### 1955–1956

With you I would share my days of happiness;
Everything is folly in this world that does not give us pleasure.
Let us enjoy life, for the pleasures of love are swift and fleeting
As a flower that lives and dies and can be enjoyed no more.

—VIOLETTA'S "DRINKING SONG,"
act 1, *La Traviata* by Giuseppe Verdi

### PREPARATIONS

The year 1956 witnessed a landmark in the history of Eoan: its first performance of a full-length opera, Verdi's *La Traviata*. The production was part of an arts festival that consisted of five music and drama productions as well as a number of other cultural events. Joseph Manca had been preparing the group for opera production for several years, and as early as 1949 the *Cape Argus* reported on Manca's explicit ambition to produce opera with the group.[1] As illustrated in the previous chapter, the productions staged during the decade before 1956 functioned as a gradual buildup toward the performance of opera, and by 1955 Eoan's music section had gained considerable experience in musical theater and had performed numerous operettas, operatic concerts, large-scale choral works, and costumed versions of oratorios. However, not only was the performance of *La Traviata* the culmination of an ambition toward which Manca had been patiently striving, but the success of this production as well as the larger undertaking of the Arts Festival changed the standing of the group within Cape Town's cultural environment and, as illustrated in the course of this chapter, had significant implications for Eoan's future.

In the course of the decade preceding the group's first opera performance, the political landscape had changed considerably, and for the coloured community the developments were largely detrimental. Since the National Party had ascended to power in 1948, racial segregation had been continually reinforced through legislation. In the year of Eoan's First Arts Festival, legislation was adopted that introduced racial segregation on public buses. The township of Sophiatown near Johannesburg was declared a white residential area, after which thousands of people were forcibly removed from their homes.[2] In August that year twenty thousand women marched to the Union Buildings in Pretoria to protest the pass laws.

Eoan's relationship with politics had been problematic since its inception. Conflicting opinions regarding the group's official stance on apartheid legislation surfaced before and during the festival, forcing important managerial changes shortly afterward. Helen Southern-Holt appears to have been aware of the potentially disruptive influence of politics on the organization and deemed this important enough to formally separate politics from the functioning of the group. When the group's constitution was drawn up (presumably in the 1940s), the statement that "the Eoan Group shall be non-political" preceded even the declaration of the aims of the group.[3] The phrase "we live to serve" was one of several values included in this document and became the group's motto. The phrase was also formally incorporated into its emblem.[4] In the years to come, resistance from within the organization was more often than not quashed by repeated calls from management that this was an organization of service. Despite this approach, Eoan's artistic endeavors clearly cannot be interpreted independently from political contexts, since the program of the National Party and the group's response to it influenced the workings of the latter to the core. Not only was the group restricted and directed by all sorts of rules and regulations derived from apartheid legislation, but resistance to the political situation manifested itself in various ways and in the long run brought the organization to its knees.

Manca's position on the relationship between politics and music seemed somewhat different from Southern-Holt's. It appears that he was more dismissive, and he is alleged to have always said to Eoan members that "politics is a dirty word."[5] As this chapter illustrates, this attitude is apparent in his response to the critical voices directed at the group from outside as well as from within. For Manca, it seems, the practice of opera by the Eoan Group was only sustainable within a system in which the ruling party's policy was the accepted norm. In situations where that normativity was challenged, his reaction was to either dismiss the claims or refuse to take the issues seriously. It is ironic that despite this attitude, or perhaps as a result of it, politics became the group's downfall.

Early in 1955, Manca proposed to the Eoan Group that it should present an arts festival administered and organized by the group itself. He felt that "the time had now arrived for the Group to undertake a more ambitious venture and that, as in the past, the Group would be the pioneer in the presentation of the first all Coloured Arts Festival."[6] The program for the festival was to include four music productions: a performance of *La Traviata*, a children's version of Gilbert and Sullivan's *The Mikado*, the South African premiere of George Posford's musical comedy *Zip Goes a Million*, and a performance of Felix Mendelssohn's oratorio *Elijah*. The drama section was to present the 1940 play *Johnny Belinda* by Elmer Harris, and other cultural activities such as classical ballet shows, massed physical education displays, flower exhibitions, and a floral-arrangement competition were also planned. The Arts Festival was the most ambitious initiative the group had ever undertaken.

Preparations were characterized by a frenzy of administrative tasks (mostly taken care of by Manca), the training of singers and dancers, arrangement of venues, agitated correspondence with the Cape Town Municipal Orchestra's management regarding the availability of the orchestra, an extensive marketing campaign, and internal resistance. Already at this early stage in the group's history some members had left the organization because of Eoan's perceived ties with the government, the most tangible evidence of which was the funding provided by the Department of Coloured Affairs (DCA) since approximately 1940.[7] A letter to a former Eoan member, Andrew Mackrill, in which Manca offered him the principal part in the musical *Zip Goes a Million*, provides some insight into Manca's personal motivation for working with Eoan and the difficulties experienced in doing so:

> My one great regret is and has always been that you decided to disassociate yourself from active participation in the Group's activities. What hurts me is now that I would have thought that I would enjoy the support of all those who value art and who would rise above their personal feelings. Let us set aside "personal questions" and let us serve the people. In spite of the importance of this event I have met and found some sort of passive resistance. This grieves me immensely, as I feel that both the Group and myself do not deserve this sort of treatment. Tell me, Andrew, what is behind all this?[8]

This letter is one of the very few documents preserved by Manca in which he acknowledged the presence of some form of resistance among members to the political status quo. Exactly how this "passive resistance" manifested itself is difficult to gauge, but already here Manca resentfully relegated politics to the realm of "personal feelings" and disengaged the practice of art from day-to-day life. Mackrill's reply to Manca, dated 13 July 1955, made it clear that politics rather than personal animosity was responsible for the resistance among some coloured people to Eoan's activities:

> It may help you to understand the new spirit motivating non-Europeans and why there is this "passive resistance" to your fine efforts in the work you are doing in the Group. Up to ten years ago, Non-Europeans counted it an honour and privilege, as well as a pleasure, to be associated with Europeans. There was so much you could teach us, so much we could learn from the European. And the European enjoyed working with us. Then came the advent into power of the Nationalist Party as the government of the day. They brought with them the seeds and virulent poison of race-hatred as between White and Non-White. They destroyed over night the happy relations and mutual regard existing between Coloureds and Europeans and Africans, and they did it all in the name of God and the Holy Bible. And then they formed a Coloured Affairs Department. That was the final nail in the coffin containing the once peaceful and happy relationships that existed between White and Black.
>
> Non-Europeans hate and loathe that particular Government Department with an intense and savage bitter loathing and hatred. It stands for the Government of the Nationalist Party, the Party at whose feet history will lay the blame for all the bitterness and animosity now existing between Black and White in this country. People are suspicious of the ties existing between this Department and Eoan.
>
> No, Mr Manca, it's not "jealousy" or "a desire by some individuals to be at the head of affairs." The reasons are as I set them out briefly above. During the time I was in Eoan, I was the most politically conscious member in the Group. I was also its stormy petrel, and most outspoken critic. But that's because I love the Group so. Eoan made me, in the world of Art, the man I am today. All my success I've had, on stage in theatre as a singer in big musical works, and now lately as a producer of plays, I owe it all to Eoan. My grateful thanks to them always for all this.[9]

Mackrill's letter poignantly reflects the dilemma artists (who were not white) faced when practicing their art within the existing structures. Yet he also named one of the main causes for the growing rejection of the group by their community: the DCA. The idea for the creation of such a department was already mooted in 1942 by the United Party under the leadership of Jan Smuts, and the eventual establishment thereof was a decade in the making.[10] It was discussed extensively in parliament at the time, but only implemented by the National Party after it came to power. Throughout the 1940s, several bodies in the coloured community, among them the Teachers League and the Anti-

CAD Movement, were outspoken in their resistance to such a department, as it signified an increase in segregation and the further erosion of the small amount of political power that the coloured population had at the time. Jan Smuts's resistance to the creation of such a structure however also points toward the kinship that had existed between the coloured and white populations up to this point: "[They] want to be treated the same way as, and together with the European," he said.[11] It is in this spirit that one can understand the acceptance of and support for Eoan's activities during the early years of its existence. The creation of the CAD by the apartheid government to "look after coloured affairs" was indeed a mechanism that entrenched racial separateness and subjugated the coloured community to white control. Accepting money from the CAD to fund opera activities not only required submission to apartheid legislation but also forced the group to perform before racially separate audiences. Mackrill's tone and choice of words pointed ahead to a time twenty years later when Eoan would be branded an apartheid organization.

Manca's dismissive approach to politics was evident when he replied to Mackrill on 27 July, "thanks for your very interesting letter and the information contained therein," and proceeded to discuss other organizational matters without a single word of engagement with or comprehension of the issues that Mackrill had raised.[12] It is clear from the archive, however, that Manca's determination and ambition to succeed with and for the group were as strong as ever. His response in this letter perhaps most clearly reveals his character: ambitious, but unwilling (or perhaps unable) to engage with the issues that could threaten his goal.

Manca launched an extensive marketing campaign, writing to dozens of newspapers and arts magazines in South Africa as well as the United Kingdom and Italy, requesting publicity for the upcoming festival.[13] He even invited Ricordi in Italy, the copyright holder of Verdi's music, to send a representative to attend the performance, stating that this would be the world premiere of a Verdi opera by "an entirely Non-European cast and company."[14] Manca used the racial dimension of the production as the criterion for the uniqueness of the occasion, and without exception, the "colouredness" of the cast was used to distinguish this performance from any other performance of the opera. Within the historical context of South Africa in the 1950s, this approach may seem self-evident, but from the vantage point of opera production per se, it needs to be said that foregrounding "race" had become an opportunistic strategy for Manca. It implied that the ability of coloureds to perform opera was "impressive" or "unusual," a perception that, despite its condescension, was used as a marketing ploy for years to come. Manca described the forthcoming production: "The performance of *La Traviata* is an epoch-making event and will create music history in that it will be the first time in the history of world music that a complete Italian opera is performed in the traditional Italian style and sung in the Italian language by an entirely Coloured Cast."[15] Elsewhere he added that it "represents the boldest and most thought-provoking experiment in the musical life of both the City of Cape Town and of South Africa as a whole."[16] He continued his marketing campaign by stating that this feat was to be performed "by people who have never seen opera and who are not professional singers but are drawn from the rank and file of the Coloured Community, i.e. from maidservants and qualified teachers."[17] The festival was certainly noticed within the greater Cape Town area. Although it is doubtful whether it attracted much attention elsewhere in the country or abroad, evidence in the archive suggests that the British magazine *Opera* published an article on this historic production.[18]

## THE ARTS FESTIVAL

The Arts Festival opened on 10 March 1956 with Eoan's first production of Verdi's *La Traviata* (see the programme booklet, figure 2.1). The production resulted in many excellent reviews, creating hopeful expectations of sustained operatic endeavors, yet the event did not take place without critical questioning by resistance movements within the coloured community.

Verdi's position as one of the foremost opera composers rested on his ability to write parts that showcased vocal brilliance, and it is the rendition of such parts by skillful singers that enthralls audiences to this day. The forces required to perform this opera include singers who can perform some of the most difficult and revered roles in the operatic repertoire; given the circumstances of educational (also music educational) deprivation of the coloured population in South Africa, it *is* astonishing that Eoan had singers with the vocal and artistic capacity to do just that. Although local opera production in the larger Cape Town area was consolidated with the establishment of the Opera School at the College of Music in Cape Town in 1954 (the first formal opera school in the country), Eoan's singers had limited access to quality training and generally came from backgrounds in which opera was unlikely to be entrenched in education or environment. Yet Manca had access to exceptional singers who impressed critics and audiences.

# EOAN GROUP

# ARTS FESTIVAL

### March to August 1956

City Hall, Cape Town

*Souvenir Programme* 1/3

FIGURE 2.1. The First Arts Festival Programme booklet. Source: Eoan Group Archive.

FIGURE 2.2. May Abrahamse performing the "Drinking Song" in Eoan's 1956 production of *La Traviata*. Source: Eoan Group Archive.

None of the participants in Eoan's production were professionally paid artists, and most had other daytime jobs. In fact, with a few exceptions, this was the rule for all the productions of this Arts Festival and continued to be the case for all opera productions throughout the group's existence. At the time of the production May Abrahamse (see her performing the "Drinking Song," figure 2.2), for instance, was working in the "Cheque Room" at the *Cape Times*. The April edition of *Talk of the Times*, the magazine supplement of the *Cape Times*, reported: "From factory bench to stardom is usually a transition reserved for dreams and fiction. It is a reality, however, for Miss May Abrahamse, the Coloured opera star who created such a tremendous impression with her distinguished acting and singing in the Eoan Group's presentation of the Verdi opera *La Traviata*, in the City Hall last month. Her job is in our Cheque Department at Parow. It is there that she earns a living but it is in Eoan Group productions that she is earning stage fame."[19]

FIGURE 2.3. The "Dying Scene" from Eoan's 1956 production of *La Traviata*, with May Abrahamse as Violetta. Source: Eoan Group Archive.

Abrahamse (born 6 May 1930) went on to become one of Eoan's most prominent and celebrated soloists, singing principal roles with the group for twenty years.[20] She initially received vocal tuition from producer Billie Jones, followed by further training with Beatrice Gibson and in later years training with Olga Magnoni.[21] But it was during her time with Jones that she learned the role of Violetta, a role she sang with Eoan throughout her career (see figure 2.3), including the last time the group performed this opera, in 1975.

The soprano Ruth Goodwin studied bookkeeping and shorthand at a commercial school and worked as a secretary at a trade union during this time, but she had already been taking private singing lessons at the College of Music for some time. The baritone Lionel Fourie was teaching at a primary school in District Six. The exception to those who worked at other jobs was the accompanist and repetiteur Dan Ulster, the first coloured person to obtain a degree in music at the College of Music and one of the few Eoan members who was able to earn a living in the music world as an educator and conductor.[22] Ulster also served as conductor for the productions of *The Mikado* and *Zip Goes a Million* during the festival.

Although *La Traviata* was more than a century old by the time of Eoan's production, evidence of homegrown productions before 1956 is difficult to find. Désirée Talbot writes in *For the Love of Singing: 50 Years of Opera at UCT* that her first experience of the work was a production by the Carl Rosa Company that toured the country in 1934; on her list of UCT's opera productions, *La Traviata* is entirely absent.[23] Alessandro Rota, who settled in Cape Town in 1930, produced a number of operas with local singers, but the traces of these productions are lost or buried, and one can only speculate on how often *La Traviata* was performed in Cape Town before and by whom. On the other hand, the idea that Eoan's was the first local production of this opera seems unconvincing. By 1956 Rota had lived in South Africa for more than twenty-five years, and he must have had experience with the work to be able to produce Eoan's staging of it. Furthermore, although Manca claimed that this would be the first production by "an all-coloured cast," the extensive marketing campaign nowhere mentions that this would be the first local production of the work. However, we can safely assume that local audiences up to that time had not often heard this work performed in Cape Town.

The archive contains numerous letters from friends and admirers congratulating Manca and Rota on a sterling performance and praising them for what they had achieved with the group. The following letter indicates the general tone of these comments:

> May I add my mite of praise to the torrent which must be pouring in on you both for your production of La Traviata. It was indeed a "miracle" and you must feel like men with a mine of untapped wealth at your feet! I only hope you will continue to provide us with opera in the future, but I hope too, that your ambitions include an Eoan Theatre. The stage was woefully small for the magnificent chorus, and not the least part of the evening's enjoyment was the happy atmosphere in the auditorium itself. My heartiest congratulations to every member of the cast, and my thanks to you both for a wonderful evening.[24]

An extensive collection of correspondence between Manca and Eoan group members regarding all sorts of organizational matters is also found in the archive, and it is in reading these that one gets a sense of the personal impact that Eoan's musical activities, and in many instances Manca as a person, had on the lives of individuals. These letters tell stories of how group members struggled with day-to-day activities such as their daytime jobs, finding the time to practice or attend rehearsals, trouble with transport to and from the City Hall, not feeling confident enough to sing a specific role, complaints about jealousy among choir members, and parents who were worried that their children spent too much time with the group and neglected their homework. Witnessing the sincere relationships between Manca and group members through these often highly personal letters provides an angle on the festival that is rather different from the story that unfolds via newspaper reviews.

One would assume that the choice of *La Traviata* as the group's first opera production was not an arbitrary one, but it raises the questions of why *this* opera and why it played such a significant role in the history of the group. Verdi composed this work shortly after *Rigoletto* (in 1850) and *Il Trovatore* (in 1852). It confirmed the composer's stature as one of the foremost opera composers during his lifetime and one of the most popular of all time. In the decade following Eoan's production of *La Traviata*, *Rigoletto* and *Il Trovatore* were added to its performance repertoire, which by 1970 comprised eleven operas, nine of which were Italian and the other two popular German and French works.[25] However, the most obvious reason for the predominantly popular Italian opera repertoire probably lies with Manca; being of Italian descent, he preferred the Italian repertoire, and not being a trained musician, it is possible more technically challenging works were beyond his abilities.

### THE AFTERMATH

The bad press the group received for the performance given for government dignitaries also resulted in an unhappy ending for the founder of the group, Helen Southern-Holt. Documentation in the archive shows that she was involved with organizing this specific performance, as she supplied lists of dignitaries who were to be invited.[26] Alethea Jansen, principal of the group at the time, defended Southern-Holt's approach to the government as pragmatism: "She always used to say, 'Oh don't worry Mrs. Jansen, we work with the government of the day. Today that one, tomorrow next one, next week we find another one.'"[27] Opposition to the special performance was expressed during a meeting of the group's executive shortly after the festival. Jansen explained that various Eoan members were unhappy about the perception the incident created: "I don't think she was ever forgiven for it. You know what they said? 'She's making apartheid.' That's how it was interpreted by the people, she's making apartheid."[28] After the incident, Southern-Holt further withdrew from the organization, and in January 1958, after being with the group she had founded for twenty-five years, she left Cape Town permanently, immigrating to Canada.[29]

Sidestepping politics was impossible, and in 1957 the group decided to stop applying for annual funding from the government, as the condition connected to the acceptance of state funding was that Eoan had to perform to segregated audiences and had to apply for a permit to perform in so-called white venues.[30] The threat of withdrawal of state funds should organizations not endorse apartheid policy had already been raised in 1951, and despite Eoan's artistic success, it eventually did have an impact on the group.[31] In 1951 Manca went on record to say that he would not sell his soul to the government for money. In 1957, after a hugely successful artistic season (the profit netted from the festival amounted to £994), Eoan had the financial luxury to take such a stance.[32] Except for the continuation of the annual £500 grant from the Cape Town municipality, the group remained financially independent until 1966.

The resounding artistic success of the festival was Manca's defense to those who voiced political objections and, for some years afterward the group's success seems to have silenced criticism from political corners, even if only superficially. The 1956 Arts Festival functioned as a springboard for annual opera productions for the following twenty years. In these years Eoan contributed significantly to the establishment of local opera production within the larger Cape Town area, a relatively new development for the time. Although no professional opera company existed in South Africa at the time, Cape Town audiences had access to various opera productions in these years; Erik Chisholm's University of Cape Town Opera Company staged many student performances of operas from the standard repertory in the Little Theatre.[33] The year 1956 was also the bicentenary of Mozart's birth and, after Eoan's successful season in March, the (white) operagoing public in Cape Town could attend performances of Mozart's *Don Giovanni* in May and *Le Nozze di Figaro* in June, both produced by Chisholm and staged in the

Little Theatre on the University of Cape Town campus.[34] Reviews mention that the soloists in these productions were Désirée Talbot and Gregorio Fiasconaro, both teachers at the Opera School (and teachers of some of Eoan's principals), while singers from the same generation of Eoan's principals, such as Emma Renzi, Nellie du Toit, and Dorreen Berry, sang the minor roles in these productions.

THREE

## *Eoan's Best Opera Success: An Amorous Fantasy*

1957–1963

> I want to live, faithful to you alone!
> I have forgotten the world and lived like one in heaven.
> —ALFREDO, act 2, *La Traviata* by Giuseppe Verdi

### SINGING ON

Applause for the group's first opera production had scarcely died down when Joseph Manca started planning the next Eoan opera season. On 27 April 1956, while the Arts Festival was still in full swing, an advertisement was placed in the *Sun*, announcing auditions for the "forthcoming Eoan Opera Season."[1] No date was mentioned, but the advertisement listed a number of operas that would be considered for the second opera season. These included *Rigoletto*, *Il Barbiere di Siviglia*, *Cavalleria Rusticana*, *La Bohème*, *Madama Butterfly*, *Carmen*, and *La Traviata*.[2] Two years later, in March 1958, the group held its second opera and ballet season, performing Pietro Mascagni's *Cavalleria Rusticana*, Giuseppe Verdi's *La Traviata*, and Leo Delibes's ballet *Spring Song*; in the course of the following decade, all the operas considered for performance in the abovementioned advertisement were indeed added to Eoan's performance record.[3]

The timing and content of this advertisement not only confirm that Manca had great ambitions, they also make clear that the success of the first opera production did not come entirely as a surprise. Manca's plans to perform many more operas with the group had been in the making for some years, and Eoan's successful debut on the local opera scene provided the confirmation he needed to continue. Having access to people with singing talent, a degree of operatic skill, and heaps of goodwill and enthusiasm, Manca went on to present to the city, in a fairly consistent manner, a repertoire that opera lovers had no regular access to.

The years 1957 to 1963 were a period in the group's history during which it was astonishingly productive as a theater, dance, and opera company. Although other organizations existed in Cape Town and the rest of the country that also produced these art forms (and some of them, such as the University of Cape Town Opera Company, had a higher turnover with regard to number of productions), none combined the various arts in one company as Eoan did.[4] In 1957 the chairman of the Eoan Group, William Richardson, quite rightly stated that the group was "an outlet in the fields of music, song, dancing, ballet, drama and physical education."[5] Combining the performance of various art formats in one organization was only later followed by other bodies, when the South African government instituted the Performing Arts Councils (PACS) in 1963. During 1957–1963 the group held four more opera and ballet seasons (in 1958, 1959, 1960, and 1962), adding five operas, three musical comedies, and eight ballets to its performance repertoire. In 1960 Eoan embarked on an exceptionally successful three-month tour of the country. It also held its second Arts Festival in 1962, during which the group premiered a new South African ballet, *The Square*, composed for it by Stanley Glasser. And in 1963 Eoan's drama section premiered Flora Stohr's play *Behind the Yellow Door* in the Little Theatre in Cape Town, which dealt with the life of a coloured family in Athlone and expressed strong antiapartheid sentiments.[6] The productivity and many successes of this period culminated in June 1963, when Manca was awarded an honorary doctorate by the University of Cape Town in acknowledgment of his work with the group and his contribution to opera production in the country.[7] For a trained accountant with no formal musical education, this was no small achievement.

The extraordinary productivity of this period can be attributed to a number of factors. First, it is clear that apartheid legislation did not yet impact the group's activities as profoundly as it did later, from the mid-1960s onward, and during this time neither political resistance nor the limitations of apartheid disrupted the functioning of the group in a significant way.[8] The group also seemed to be on a "motivational high" during this time; the thrill of excitement among group members, production staff, and the operagoing public is palpable in much of the archival material and newspaper reporting on Eoan. Added to this, the group remained fairly independent financially during this time; the budgetary constraints that plagued the group from 1964 onward seem not to have hampered its production output noticeably. In hindsight, this period was a time in its history when the atmosphere in the group was particularly positive and the members were able to practice their art in a relatively unfettered manner. However, these conditions were conducive to a mode of thinking in which the practice of opera and the social and political environment of its participants could be treated as parallel worlds that had nothing to do with each other. In such thinking, the means required to practice opera or the circumstances of its presentation did not have to answer to the everyday lives of the people who practiced it. Manca's insistence that "politics is a dirty word" that should not interfere with Eoan's opera production could more easily be upheld at that time than in later years. This separation of music and the everyday lives of musicians (and its audiences) has of course had a long history in Western art music, in which art has existed for art's sake, and Manca certainly came from a tradition in which this was the default position. It is safe to say that opera production in South Africa and the public engagement with Western art music upheld this position for most of the twentieth century.

The political situation for the community within which Eoan functioned worsened significantly during this time as self-governance was replaced by white custodianship. Having removed coloureds from the voters' rolls in 1956, the apartheid government proposed that they might elect a number of whites to represent them in the House of Assembly. This caused much debate in local newspapers, with many voices for and against such a move.[9] In April 1958 the proposal was pushed through, and four white representatives were elected to act on behalf of the coloured community in parliament.[10] This move was significant in the construction of the relationship between the white and coloured racial groups as engineered during the apartheid era. It is in this context that one can understand the nature of the hierarchical relationship that existed between Manca and Eoan's members. Coloured rights had been deliberately reduced to dependency on whites, and this political move illustrates the (white) assumption that coloureds could not govern themselves and should be looked after by whites. At Eoan the corollary was that Manca took care of all major decisions, and even the smallest of organizational arrangements had to carry his approval.

However, dependency on white representation in governance structures was still better than the situation for black South Africans, who had no representation. The benefit of white representation for Eoan was that white funding made opera possible, which was still better than not being able to produce opera at all. This situation is an apt illustration of Mohamed Adhikari's notion of the in-between status of "relative privilege" that the coloured community found itself in and one of the aspects that affected the formation of its identity.

White custodianship also had an impact on Eoan's long-term sustainability. Throughout the group's history, management by whites was a contentious issue, and rebellion against white custodianship of coloured interests can be regarded as one of the contributing impulses toward the ousting of Manca from the organization in 1977. The meltdown of organizational structures after 1977 can also be attributed to the lack of professional empowerment. However, the management styles of Southern-Holt and Manca during the early years do not present a simplified picture in which white management opposed coloured self-determination. Although the documentation in the archive and many interviews with former members indicate that both individuals were domineering personalities, Southern-Holt insisted on the development of coloured management throughout her time as leader of the group.[11] This is illustrated by the appointment of Alethea Jansen (in 1950) and later Mabel Canterbury (in 1957) as principals. Up to the mid-1960s, Manca's management style also did not demonstrably oppose coloured leadership in the group, and his right-hand man remained Ismail Sydow throughout his career with Eoan. However, as described in the ensuing chapters of this book, Manca's management style did change over time, and by the 1970s his authoritarian manner of engagement with group members became evident. Yet anyone familiar with the production of opera will attest to the necessity for a strong leader who can oversee and manage its many aspects.

For the group an important change occurred when Southern-Holt immigrated to Canada in 1958. With her departure, the period during which the humanitarian concept of "social change through the arts" was the dominant sentiment within the group came to an end. Although "social upliftment" remained part of the group's official policy for many years, arts production now became an end in itself, providing opportunities for people of color to participate in opera, drama, and ballet on a semiprofessional, yet unsalaried, level. Although the image of Eoan's principal singers as so-called unskilled workers who could perform high art continued to be cultivated in the media, many were in fact trained in a variety of fields (as teachers, nurses, and social workers, among others), and "social upliftment" was scarcely the reason they chose to sing opera or devote their lives to theater or ballet. Alethea Jansen, the principal of the group from 1950 and Southern-Holt's assistant during these years, also left, and a new principal, Mrs. E. Canterbury, was instated from 1957 onward.[12] Except perhaps for "the old guard," who had worked closely with Southern-Holt during the group's early days and continued to expound the values upon which she had founded the organization, the change in focus that came with her departure did not seem to be a major loss to the group. It was only in later years, when the group started experiencing serious problems such as the loss of membership and community support as well as debilitating internal strife, that the organization's founding values were resuscitated, in (seemingly fruitless) attempts to solve its problems.

## THE 1958 AND 1959 SEASONS

The broader operatic scenario of Cape Town during this period provides an important backdrop against which Eoan's opera performances took place. Opera production in the white community of Cape Town in the 1950s and 1960s was mainly driven by Erik Chisholm, a prolific composer and an enterprising and experienced musician who immigrated to South Africa in 1946 to take up the post of dean of the College of Music at the University of Cape Town. In the 1930s local opera production was started by William Henry Bell (at the time dean of the college) as part of the college's musical activities, but it was Chisholm who established the University of Cape Town Opera Company in 1954, with Gregorio Fiasconaro as director. Cape Town audiences were treated to a variety of opera productions from the standard repertory as well as lesser-known works.[13] The UCT Opera Company also regularly toured South Africa, extending its tours to Northern and Southern Rhodesia (today Zambia and Zimbabwe) in 1956 and the United Kingdom in 1956–1957.[14] Notable premieres of locally composed operas included Chisholm's *The Pardoner's Tale* (1961) and John Joubert's *Silas Marner* (1961).[15]

The repertoire choices of Eoan and the UCT Opera Company, however, were significantly different, with surprisingly little overlap. Although both companies sang works from the canon, the UCT Opera Company was more experimental in staging a number of lesser-known works as well as twentieth-century operas, while Eoan clearly presented mainstream nineteenth-century Italian opera repertoire.[16] The UCT Opera Company did perform a number of operas from the standard canon, among them some by Mozart (*Zauberflöte, Le nozze di Figaro*, and *Don Giovanni*), Verdi (*Fallstaff* and *Othello*), and Puccini (*Tosca, Turandot*, and *La Bohème*). The only overlap with Eoan was the Opera Company's 1966 production of Rossini's *Il barbiere di Siviglia* (which Eoan performed in 1969 and 1974) and its 1969 production of Giacomo Puccini's *La Bohème* (which Eoan performed in 1960, 1962, and 1965). The years 1957–1963 may have been productive for Eoan, but they were equally productive for the Opera Company, which staged no fewer than twelve operas on twenty-seven occasions. Five of those were on tour within the country as well as abroad.[17] Although the Opera Company clearly had a larger artistic output, the roles the two companies played within the cultural arena in Cape Town were different. Eoan's repertoire choices were directed to a more popular audience, while Chisholm's artistic inventiveness and daring are unparalleled in the city even to this day. Significantly, the two companies seldom performed in the same venue: most of the Opera Company's productions where held in the Little Theatre situated on UCT's Hiddingh campus in Orange Street, with an audience capacity of 250.[18] Eoan's productions where held in the City Hall, a much larger venue with a seating capacity of 900, which the Opera Company never used. The only venue they shared for a few productions was the Alhambra Theatre in Riebeeck Street, to the north of the city center, a hall with an audience capacity of close to 2,000.[19] However, their diverging financial, artistic, and educational resources, not to mention the contrasting social and political circumstances within which the two companies operated, have to be taken into account when discussing their operatic endeavors; unsurprisingly, these aspects influenced the nature of their productions.

Cape Town also had an active Gilbert and Sullivan Society, established in 1947, that produced one or two operettas per year.[20] This group, of which Chisholm was vice president for a number of years, performed in the Labia Theatre, a small venue in Orange Street at the top end of the city center and close to the Little Theatre, where the UCT Opera Company performed. During the years under discussion here, the society produced *Ruddigore, Iolanthe, Yeomen of the Guard, Cox and Box, Pirates of Penzance, Mikado, Princes Ida, Patience,* and *Gondoliers*.[21] The venue was managed as a commercial enterprise and received state funding for its operations. In 1950 the Labia's management accepted the conditions imposed for receiving state funding, namely performing to racially segregated audiences, and introduced a policy of performing to whites and coloureds on separate evenings. This caused anger in the coloured community, after which many boycotted the venue.[22]

Collaboration between the white and coloured opera groups was minimal during these years; the UCT Opera Company and the Eoan Group shared Fiasconaro as producer, but never exchanged singers or dancers. Whites attended Eoan's opera performances, but coloureds were not allowed in most venues in town and therefore had little exposure to opera production by other companies.[23] In an interview with former Eoan member Tillie Ulster, it emerged that Chisholm made provision for coloureds to attend dress rehearsals of his opera productions in the Little Theatre, but these seem to have been for the select few.[24] Ulster's husband, Dan Ulster, was one of Chisholm's students at the time, and through their friendship the Ulsters had easier access to productions than other group members did.[25] In the long run, the lack of exposure to opera production by other companies and the resultant isolation of Eoan's artists had a detrimental effect on the quality of the group's artistic standards.

After 1956 Manca kept the momentum going with regard to musical productions, adding at least one new work to the group's repertoire for every new performance season. Although he worked toward the production of opera rather than operetta or musical comedy, the latter had been a standard item in Eoan's annual performances since 1949, and three more musical comedies were added to its repertoire in the late 1950s. In August 1957 Eoan performed Emmerich Kalman's *Maritza* with the Cape Town Municipal Orchestra; Rudolph Frimi and Herbert Stothart's *Rose Marie* was added a year later, and in August 1959 Harry Tierney's *Rio Rita* was performed.[26] As usual, these productions were held in the Cape Town City Hall. Eoan's principal soprano, May Abrahamse, had sung the lead roles in all the musicals and operettas Eoan had performed up to this time (there were six between 1949 and 1956, not counting the many children's productions). In *Maritza*, *Rose Marie*, and *Rio Rita*, the baritone Gerald Arendse sang the male counterpart.

But Manca's main aim was the production of opera, and Eoan's second opera and ballet season opened on 10 March 1958, during which productions were held every evening until 22 March. A number of matinees were also scheduled. On the program was the group's second production of Verdi's *La Traviata* and a new addition to its repertoire, Mascagni's *Cavalleria Rusticana*, both produced by Fiasconaro. The ballet presentation was *Spring Song* (the last act from Delibes's ballet *Coppelia*), choreographed by David Poole. The group's production of *Cavalleria Rusticana* on opening night did not disappoint, and on 11 March 1958 the *Cape Times* reported that "another milestone in the eventful career of the Eoan Group was passed with overwhelming success when it opened its opera and ballet season before the wildly enthusiastic audience which filled the City Hall last night. The production of Mascagni's *Cavalleria Rusticana* was a colossal feat for a cast of singers, many of whom had learnt the music and its Italian words note by note."[27] Although the group could not rely on the surprise element of its first opera appearance two years before, opera lovers in the city were yet again enthralled. On 22 March the *Cape Times* reported that "owing to the big public demand for seats, extra performances of 'Cavalliera Rusticana' and 'Spring Song' will be given next Saturday at 2.45pm and 8.10pm."[28] The (white) opera-loving public developed into a large and loyal support base that could be counted on in the decades to follow. Chisholm, one of Cape Town's most celebrated classical musicians, continued to be a loyal friend of the group until his early death in 1965. His praise of the group, printed in the program booklet for the 1958 season, stated that "the cultural work of the Eoan Group, in width of scope and in standard of achievement, is without parallel anywhere in the African continent; indeed there are few non-professional cultural organizations anywhere in the world with a record to equal this unique organization."[29]

In choosing Mascagni's *Cavalleria Rusticana* as the group's second opera, Manca selected an opera he knew would be popular. This work is Mascagni's best-known opera, and its immediate popularity made the composer a celebrity in Italy overnight.[30] Set in a Sicilian village (incidentally the region where Manca's parents originated from), the well-worn story of thwarted love, deception, and revenge that end in death is set to music based on "the values of tradition Italian opera, firmly focused on cantabile melody, and on arias and choruses in the simplest forms."[31]

As was the case with Eoan's production of *La Traviata*, it is impossible to know if this was the first local production of this tremendously popular work. Touring companies may have performed this work in Cape Town before, but since records of these performance are unknown, alternative claims to a first production do not exist. According to Talbot's list, the UCT Opera Company did not perform this opera, and although the records of various other short-lived local opera companies that were set up in Cape Town during the 1930s and 1940s are unaccounted for, the chances that this popular work had been produced locally cannot be ruled out.[32] A number of soloists made their debut with the group in this production. Among them were Sophia Andrews in the role of Lucia, Benjamin Arendse as Alfio, Shirley Smit as Lola, and the tenor Yusuf Williams as Turrido. Of these, the *Cape Times* reviewer reported that "Sophia Andrews, as Lucia, showed real histrionic talent as well as possessing a voice of rich quality. Benjamin Arendse was one of the best actors in the cast as Alfio, with a baritone that should take him far."[33] Andrews, who became the group's principal mezzo-soprano until 1970, recalled how she struggled with the role. She was in her third year of study with Fiasconaro and felt she did not want to sing a part composed for an alto. However, she explained that being offered a principal role at such a young age, she had "no right" to refuse the role and had to adjust her voice to produce the darker quality required for the role.[34]

The group's second production of *La Traviata* was met with equal praise. The cast remained the same as in the 1956 production, with May Abrahamse and Ruth Goodwin sharing the role of Violetta, Ron Thebus singing Alfredo, and Lionel Fourie as Germont, although the smaller role of Flora was this time shared by two new soloists, Matilda Theunissen (Tillie Ulster) and Shirley Smit. Charlie Weich of *Die Burger* reported on 12 March 1958 that the Eoan Group had repeated its "miracle performance" of two years before, heaping much praise on Ruth Goodwin for her rendition of the role of Violetta and describing the duet between Fourie and Goodwin in the second act as the high point of the production.[35] In a similar vein, the *Cape Times* reported that Goodwin "exhibited unexpected talent in portraying the character, while at the same time displaying a voice of much sweetness and warmth, particularly in the upper register" and felt that she had earned the "rousing reception and curtain call at the end."[36] The *Cape Times* review furthermore provided a lengthy description of David Poole's choreography in the ballet presentation, praising several individual dancers—Joan Boonzaaier, Khadija (Didi) Sydow, and Kathleen Enoch—and concluded by saying that "it is the reawakening of the spirit of the dance in the Eoan Group which I welcome, and I salute David Poole, for giving so many budding dancers the chance to blossom briefly in a ballet designed with tact and great ingenuity."[37]

Success continued a year later when Eoan presented its third opera and ballet season from 7 to 21 March 1959, as usual in the Cape Town City Hall. This time the program consisted of three operas: a repeat of *La Traviata* and *Cavalleria Rusticana* as well as a new addition to the repertoire, Verdi's *Rigoletto*. All three operas were produced by Fiasconaro. The dance production was *Pastorale*, a ballet choreographed to music by Verdi.[38] The season opened on 7 March with a performance of *Rigoletto*, and the production was extremely well received by the music critics of Cape Town's three major newspapers. The *Cape Argus* called it a "triumph," the *Cape Times* described it as "Eoan's best opera success," and *Die Burger* referred to it as a great achievement.[39] Although most of the soloists were reviewed positively, Lionel Fourie, who sang the title role in this opera (see figure 3.1), made a huge impression on critics and received the lion's share of praise for his "outstanding acting and singing" and his "remarkably sustained performance."[40] The group's third performance of *La Traviata* was again met with much appreciation by the

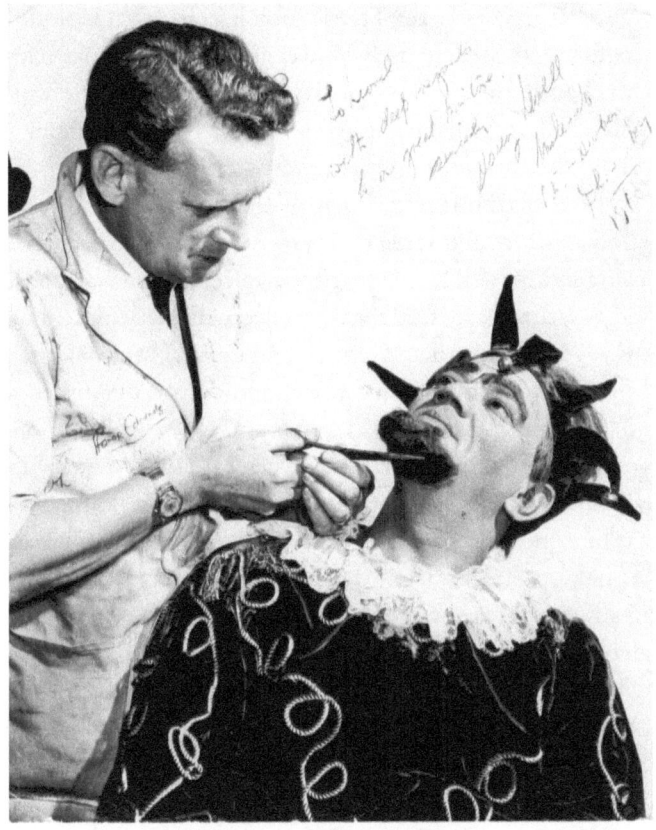

FIGURE 3.1. Lionel Fourie in the role of Rigoletto. Source: The *Evening Post*, published with permission from the Tiso Blackstar Group.

public and critics. The *Cape Argus* reviewer mentioned that "from the start bursts of applause (sometimes at awkward moments for the singers) made it clear that the big audience keenly appreciated the quality of the presentation" and went on to praise May Abrahamse's performance by stating that "in a finely sustained piece of acting, [she] made an even more convincing Violetta than she did in that first memorable production three years ago."[41]

Lionel Fourie, who sang the title role of this opera, played a dominant and larger-than-life role in the consciousness of the group. Born on 21 April 1926, Fourie grew up in the rural town of Ladismith in the Little Karoo, where he worked as a tailor for six years before moving to Worcester (another rural town) to qualify as a teacher.[42] His received some vocal training in Ladismith from a Dr. Blythe, for whom Fourie's mother cooked. While studying to become a teacher in Worcester, Fourie took lessons from Con de Villiers, a zoology professor at Stellenbosch University, who was a part-time singing connoisseur. Fourie moved to Cape Town in 1955, where he worked as an Afrikaans language teacher at the Ashley Street Primary School in District Six and joined the Eoan Group.[43] According to his widow, Ruth Fourie, he received no further training from any of the singing teachers at the UCT Opera School, with whom some of Eoan's other principals trained.[44] A tall and imposing figure with a large baritone voice, Fourie was politically outspoken and a natural leader. He was intellectually articulate, was fluent in several languages (among them German and Dutch), and was one of the few coloured people who published political and cultural commentary in the (predominantly white) Afrikaans newspaper *Die Burger*.[45] Although Fourie made his operatic debut in 1956 as Germont in *La Traviata*, it was in *Rigoletto* that he gained the reputation that long outlived his premature death in 1963. Not only is he remembered as one of Eoan's great baritones, but his life also traced the Shakespearean tragedy that marks the plot of *Rigoletto*. Fourie was a splendid singer with a superior intellect and political candor, but he was also an alcoholic and a diabetic, which severely disrupted his career and, according to his widow, led to his death at the age of thirty-eight.[46] Fourie was also responsible for one of Eoan's legendary stories, which relates directly to the character of Rigoletto. According to a number of singers, Fourie had vowed that no one in the group would sing the role after him; his exact words were "nobody will wear my cloak."[47] It is interesting that Eoan indeed struggled to perform *Rigoletto* after that. In 1968 the annual opera season that included this opera was canceled due to the illness of many singers and insufficient preparation of the group.[48] In 1969 Eoan's production of *Rigoletto* was canceled shortly before the beginning of the season when its principal baritone, Robert Trussell, who was to sing the role of Rigoletto, died unexpectedly. It was only in 1971 that the group managed to perform this opera again. However, principal singers allege that during this performance they saw a second Rigoletto in ghostly form roaming about onstage. After the performance they apparently burned the cloak that was originally made for Fourie in order to dispel the curse.[49]

It was also during the 1959 season that Eoan's best-known tenor, Joseph Gabriels, made his debut, in the role of the Duke of Mantua in *Rigoletto*. Gabriels was immediately popular with critics as well as the public and was subsequently regarded as Eoan's star tenor, a reputation he continued to hold even after he left the country in 1967. The *Cape Argus* wrote of this performance that "Gabriels, made an immediate impression. Here is a real tenor voice which, trained and husbanded with care, will be an invaluable asset to the group."[50] The *Cape Times* mentioned that "Joseph Gabriels, a newcomer to the Group, created something of a sensation with his tenor of strong and resonant timbre as the Duke of Mantua. With serious and intensive training, he should go far in the musical world."[51]

Gabriels's career as an opera singer is an important part of the group's legacy. He was the only Eoan singer who had a notable singing career abroad; he made his debut performance at the Metropolitan Opera House in New York in 1971 as the first South African singer ever to perform in that venue. This achievement is remembered today with much pride by former members as well as the opera fraternity, and it is indeed a significant happening in the history of the group and of South African opera production. However, his career as an opera singer, locally and abroad, was not easy or glamorous, and his achievements as an international singer turned out to be less spectacular than supporters at home remember. Born on 27 April 1937, Gabriels was the youngest in a family of nine.[52] His father was a fishmonger, and the family lived in Salt River, a poor suburb southeast of District Six. After school, Gabriels was employed at a clothing company and started singing in Malay Choirs, despite not being of the Muslim faith.[53] According to his widow, Mabel Kester-Gabriels, he also sang much popular music and jazz and toured the country with Morris Smith's Golden Dixies Show. It was while Gabriels was singing in a Malay Choir competition that Manca, who was adjudicating, discovered him and brought him to the Eoan Group.[54] It is difficult to know whether Gabriels had had any exposure to opera or any form of classical music up to this point in his life, but it is certain that his first training in (classical) music or voice production was with the group. From interviews with his widow and other former members, it is clear that Gabriels could not read staff notation throughout his performance career in South Africa and was taught all his roles by rote.[55]

His lack of experience was evident during his first opera performance. *Die Burger* noted that although Gabriels had a splendid voice, he was beating the time with his hand while performing onstage and seemed to have less understanding of the artistic essence of his role than his fellow artists did.[56] The *Cape Times* critic even suggested that Gabriels was not ready for the role: "[The] role is a heavy one for a partially untrained young voice, and care should be taken not to force it unduly."[57] Gabriels's singing improved significantly in the next few years, and he performed all of Eoan's principal tenor roles until 1965. During this time he also built up a national reputation among the opera-loving public.

An important musical event that challenged apartheid ideology took place in 1959. Although unconnected to Eoan and presenting a political and musical ethos far removed from the environment in which Eoan performed, it holds an important place in the bigger picture of local music production, in which Eoan's history should be understood. South Africa's first "jazz opera," *King Kong*, opened in Johannesburg in February 1959 and was performed countrywide to thousands of South Africans of all races.[58] This work is based on the life of champion boxer Ezekiel "King Kong" Dlamini (1925–1957), who became famous in the crowded townships of Johannesburg.[59] The production was an interracial team effort, with the text written by Harry Bloom, music composed by Todd Matshikiza, lyrics by Pat Williams, and stage direction by Stanley Glasser.[60] Bloom's description of the work as a "jazz opera" found its way into most marketing and newspaper reviews of the time, but it is somewhat misleading. The similarity it shares with opera is that of a story told through song, but today musicians and scholars refer to this historic work as a musical. David Coplan describes the musical fabric of the work as "big band," in which "African musical and dramatic stage traditions [were infused] into a narrative structure [that] presented a mixture of African and Western song and dance."[61] The production drew from members of Johannesburg's township bands, such as the Manhattan Brothers, the Jazz Dassler Orchestra, and the Harlem Swingsters, and launched the careers of a number of jazz musicians who in later years became household names internationally. Among them are Miriam Makeba, Kippie Moeketsi, Sol Klaaste, Mackay Davashe, Jonas Gwangwa, and Hugh Masekela.[62] Politically the work was neutral, and Coplan argues that "the play did not make a strong political statement, but it did show something of the hardships, violence and frustration of African township life."[63] *King Kong* toured to Cape Town, where it was performed in the Camps Bay Civic Theatre; went on to Durban; and eventually also toured to London in 1960. Although Eoan's members probably did not have the opportunity to see the production (they had no access to whites-only halls), the artistic environment created by *King Kong* affected the group a few years later. In 1962 *King Kong*'s producer, Stanley Glasser, took his collaboration with artists of color further by recording his musical, *Paljas*, with a cast that included Eoan singers and dancers, as well as a number of black musicians.[64] In the same year he composed a "jazz ballet," *The Square*, for the group, the only indigenous and new composition ever composed for the Eoan Group.

## THE FOURTH OPERA AND BALLET SEASON
## AND THE 1960 OPERA AND BALLET TOUR

South Africa experienced turmoil and unrest in 1960 that signaled the beginning of the mass public action that characterized the country's political life in later years. The African National Congress and the Pan Africanist Congress, political organizations that at the time represented the majority of the black African population in South Africa, were banned by the government under the Unlawful Organisations Act.[65] On 21 March 1960, a massacre took place during which scores of protesters were shot and killed by police responding to a march in the township of Sharpeville in the (then) Transvaal.[66] This ushered in a thirty-year period of resistance activities, which culminated in widespread repression of the antiapartheid movement, political killings, and a state of emergency by the 1980s.

Although the Sharpeville Massacre took place in a township approximately fifteen hundred kilometers northeast of the Western Cape, the rise of the resistance against apartheid also affected Eoan's immediate environment. Days after the shootings the (then) president of South Africa, Hendrik Verwoerd, declared a state of emergency and used the opportunity to crack down on antiapartheid activists, including those in the coloured community. One of Eoan's staunchest critics, Alex la Guma, who was born and raised in District Six, rose to prominence during this time. Resistance movements in the Cape, however, were divided because coloured and black African communities were not yet organized into a united front, as became the case in later years. Divisions existed within the coloured community, too, where a number of resistance movements operated that did not support each others' campaigns; among them were the Non-European Unity Movement (NEUM) and the South African Coloured People's Organisation (SACPO).[67] SACPO later morphed into a new a new organization called the Coloured People's Congress (CPC).[68] In the wake of the Sharpeville Massacre, residents of Langa township, just north of the city of Cape Town, took part in strike action, and thousands of people marched into the city of Cape Town via De Waal Drive (the main transport artery into the city) on 30 March 1960, bringing the city center to a standstill. These protest actions were supported largely by Cape Town's African workforce but took place on the doorstep of Eoan's home in District Six and in the middle of Eoan's 1960 opera season. Political resistance within the coloured community steadily escalated in the years thereafter, with ever-growing numbers joining boycotts and strikes. On the first anniversary of the Sharpeville Massacre, tens of thousands of coloured men and women stayed away from work. During this time coloured activists such as Alex la Guma, Reggie September, and Barney Desai were arrested for taking part in antiapartheid activities and charged with treason, resulting in a weakening of the organizational structures of the CPC.[69]

Despite this turmoil, support for Eoan seemed to be at an all-time high during this period, and the year was an unusually busy one for the group, which presented its largest and most ambitious program thus far. Not only did the group present its annual opera and ballet season in March and April in the Cape Town City Hall (comprising four operas and a ballet), it also undertook its first full company tour of the country from June to September, presenting programs in Port Elizabeth, Durban, and Johannesburg. Keeping in mind that the entire cast and most of the production team were amateurs who had other daytime jobs and received no remuneration for their performances, the sacrifices that they made of time, career, and family life are all the more remarkable.[70]

The fourth opera and ballet season was held from 10 March to 2 April 1960, again with Gregorio Fiasconaro as producer and Joseph Manca as conductor.[71] The program included repeat performances of the three operas produced in the past few years (Verdi's *Rigoletto* and *La Traviata* and Mascagni's *Cavalleria Rusticana*), but the season's opening night was dedicated to another new addition to the repertoire, Puccini's *La Bohème*. Eoan also continued to add more singers to its list of principals, and soloists who made their debut in this season were Winifred Domingo as Musetta in *La Bohème* and Vera Gow as Lola in *Cavalliera Rusticana*. The ballet performed for the Cape Town season was Glazunov's *The Seasons*, which was choreographed by Pamela Chrimes, a South African dancer who had been dancing with Sadler's Wells for some years and who joined the staff of the University of Cape Town Ballet School upon her return to the country.

Reviews were once again glowing, and Cape Town's critics and audiences seemed to be continuously impressed by the achievements of the group. "The Eoan Group passed another milestone in its career with flying colours when it presented 'La Boheme' before a crowded audience in the City Hall last night" wrote the reviewer for the *Cape Times*, while *Die Burger*'s critic described the production as a personal best for the group and wished its members the privilege of performing in a proper opera house in the near future.[72] The *Cape Argus* review focused on the "fund of talent this group possesses" and praised Joseph Gabriels's rendition of Rudolfo, stating that "he displayed a splendidly true tenor, sang with confidence and acted with animation."[73] Reviews of the other productions were equally upbeat, under headlines such as "Sensational Success of Rigoletto," "Confident and Polished Eoan Group Rigoletto," and "Eoan Group's Vitality Shines in *La Traviata*."[74] The group's production of *Cavalleria Rusticana* was described by the *Cape Times* as "the crown on the Eoan Group's fourth operatic production this year."[75]

The story of *La Bohème* is based on a sentimental novel by the French writer Henri Murger and concerns the romance of a poor poet, Rodolfo, with the equally poor Mimi, a seamstress who is dying of consumption. Set against the backdrop of the merriment of Paris cafés, Rodolfo and his bohemian (read *artistic*) friends spend their time socializing in cafés. The popular appeal of this work certainly fitted Eoan's repertoire in general, and at the time the work had been a favorite with several local opera groups, which had performed it in Cape Town before. In 1947 and 1948, for example, Johannesburg opera producer John Connell brought his opera troupe to Cape Town to perform *La Bohème* in the Alhambra Theatre, and in 1950 Alessandro Rota's short-lived Labia Grand Opera Company, of which Manca was chorus master, also performed the work.[76]

Examining the documentation in the Eoan Group Archive pertaining to 1960, it is clear that Manca's control over the group and its activities was strong and that he created the infrastructure for the group to perform opera. In the "Advance Publicity Information" for the 1960 opera season, his involvement is described as follows: "The whole opera season is under the direction of Joseph Manca, who in addition to conducting the operas has been responsible for its complete administration and organisation. Added to this has been his unstinted training of the principals in the learning of their music, language and translation of the various roles."[77] Perusing the archival documentation, one comes across hundreds of documents pertaining to the detailed planning of finance, festivals, rehearsals, interviews, permits, and many other organizational matters, bearing testimony to the huge task Manca assumed and his penchant for detail, but also to the control he exercised over the group and its movements. Evidence of this can be seen everywhere in the documentation for the tour that the group was to embark on shortly after the opera season. All travel arrangements were planned to the minute, and he even went as far as planning the sleeping arrangements for every member in each hotel the group stayed in during the tour. And when individuals decided to swop rooms, these details did not escape Manca's attention (they possibly had to be consented to by him) and were noted.[78]

Not only did the group receive favorable reviews in the newspapers, performances were generally sold out, and most of Eoan's seasons during this time were extended due to public demand. Understanding what "public support" meant in this particular context needs to be qualified. Coloured (as opposed to white) attendance at productions has been a contentious issue throughout the group's existence, one that cannot be discussed without reference to cultural heritage, racial identity, politics, and social strata. As mentioned in chapter 1, the infrastructure for the practice of classical art forms such as ballet and opera was minimal within the coloured community. The few avenues available for coloureds to take part in these activities and thereby build a culture of appreciation and practice of these formats were introduced through organizations such as churches, schools, and other bodies like the Eoan Group. By the 1960s these structures had been formally in place for no longer than a few decades, and most of them functioned on minimal financial resources. Although Adhikari argues that a common feature of coloured identity is "a strong association with Western culture in opposition to African equivalents," widespread attendance of, for example, classical music concerts among the coloured public was not the norm.[79] Apartheid policies, Eoan's increasingly compromised political standing, and the much lower income levels of the coloured community in general exacerbated the situation, and coloured attendance at Eoan's opera performances was always numerically small and in later years dwindled to almost nothing. Not everybody in the group found this situation acceptable, and in 1959 Lionel Fourie wrote an article for the Afrikaans newspaper *Die Burger* in which he lambasted the coloured community living in the city for its poor support of the group, stating that only 5 percent of those attending Eoan's concerts were coloured, the rest being white.[80] During this time the group operated without state funding and was not subject to legislation that forced it to perform to segregated audiences. Coloureds therefore had relatively unhindered access to City Hall; the allocation of separate seats for coloureds at Eoan's performances, which alienated the coloured public from the group and its activities, only came into effect after 1965, when the group reapplied for government funding due to its financial woes. As far as membership (for which fees were payable) was concerned, support for the group from within the coloured community reached its peak during the period under discussion here. The group had close to two thousand members who benefited from the variety of activities it offered.

After completing a successful opera season in Cape Town, Eoan undertook its first tour through South Africa. It visited Port Elizabeth, Durban, and Johannesburg, presenting the program performed during its March opera season in Cape Town (four operas and two short ballets).[81] Manca reported in his customary superlatives: "The tour lasted for three months from June to September where the Eoan Group played to absolute capacity houses, making a deep impression on the citizens of these cities. People queued night and day and houses were sold out long before the seasons opened thus proving that South Africa is an opera loving country."[82]

The tour was a financial and artistic success, and newspaper critics in the various cities provided as many positive reviews as Eoan held performances.[83] The Eoan Group Archive also holds many letters by individuals expressing sincere thanks, appreciation, and well wishes to Manca and the Eoan Group, many indicating that no consistent or quality opera production was available in their own cities. An overview of the tour's itinerary provides a good indication of the scale of this undertaking.

In Port Elizabeth, Eoan presented fourteen sold-out performances in the Feather Market Hall, which had a capacity of 1,496 seats.[84] (See the principals in front of Port Elizabeth City Hall in figure 3.2.) The season coincided with Port Elizabeth's centenary celebrations, and the visit was organized with the help of the Council of Coloured Women. A degree of resistance from antiapartheid organizations during this time came from the Port Elizabeth branch of the Coloured Teachers' Organization, which decided to boycott the town's Centenary Festival and requested that Eoan cancel its performances in protest against government policies, a call that Eoan (obviously) did not heed.[85] Documentation from the Eoan Group Archive suggests that at this stage a fair degree of freedom of movement for coloured people was still allowed, and there are no documents related to the obtaining of permits to perform in the Feather Market Hall or regarding their accommodation.[86]

In Durban, Eoan presented another fourteen performances at the Durban City Hall, where all performances were well attended, although a reviewer noted that the support from the coloured community was "somewhat disappointing."[87] It is clear from the archive that, already in 1960, Eoan's principal tenor, Joseph Gabriels, had a professional reputation stretching far beyond the Cape Province. The Natal Department of Music and Entertainment, for instance, was not easily convinced that Gabriels was still working as a shop

FIGURE 3.2. Eoan's principals in front of the Port Elizbeth City Hall in 1960. From left to right: Joseph Gabriels, Ruth Goodwin, Sophia Andrews, Robert Trussell, Winifred Domingo, Gerald Arendse, Lionel Fourie, May Abrahamse, and Benjamin Arendse. Source: Eoan Group Archive.

assistant and therefore to be regarded as an amateur and exempt from taxation.[88] In both Port Elizabeth and Durban, racially mixed audiences were freely admitted to the venues.

The reviews were generous, although not without criticism. *The Natal Mercury* reported on 30 July that the packed Durban City Hall experienced a brilliant *La Bohème* and that "every South African, regardless of colour, can be justifiably proud of this company."[89] Three days later, the same critic commented:

> Seldom has a Durban audience responded so enthusiastically and warmly to a performance as it did last night at the close of the Eoan Group's production of *Rigoletto*. Loud and prolonged, the applause seemed almost deafening at times when any of the principals took their curtain calls. After an unfortunately indifferent start in Act 1, the company soon rallied, but it was not until

the magnificent final act that it reached its peak. This act was brilliant from any point, but nothing touched such great heights as the singing. This was the Eoan Group at its best.[90]

Eoan's success during its season in Johannesburg proved to be unsurpassed. On arrival in mid-August, the group's seventeen performances were sold out; due to public demand, it was decided to extend the season by three weeks. This added another twenty-seven performances to the schedule, and the group performed every evening from Monday to Saturday, with three additional matinees per week.[91] The performances were held in the University of the Witwatersrand's Great Hall and the Alexander Theatre. Again, all racial groups were allowed to attend the performances in these whites-only venues, although for the Alexander Theatre this was an exception to the rule.[92] Again, keeping in mind that all participants on this tour took unpaid leave from their daytime jobs, were not paid for their performances, and only received compensation for lost wages, the achievement of presenting seventy-two performances in three months at an apparently high artistic level is remarkable.

### APPLAUSE FOR A CAUSE?

When writing about Eoan from contemporary scholarly perspectives, issues such as its approach to opera and the artistic qualities of its performances need to be critically examined. Scholarly inquiry in the twenty-first century into the performance of Western art music in colonial contexts often directs its focus toward tracing, for example, the indigenization of opera, ways in which Western music may or may not have been appropriated and changed in performance, and the relativism (or not) of Western artistic criteria in such practices. Historical studies of the practice of Western art music by musicians of color during apartheid South Africa is currently an underresearched area, but Christopher Cockburn's work on the performances of Handel's *Messiah* by African choirs in the 1950s and 1960s, for example, points toward a dilution of the authority of the composer and European performance traditions in these performances.[93] In the case of Eoan, searching for indigenization in the context of postcolonial studies or against the backdrop of the authenticity debate in Western art music challenges the expectation of an "African operatic practice," as the group subscribed to the idea of performing opera in "true Italian tradition" throughout its performance history. The Eoan Group

Archive, the numerous newspaper reviews, and the many interviews held as part of the Eoan History Project attest to the group's adherence to unapologetic Italianate ideals, its striving for performance excellence as understood in Western art music, and its regard for the authority of the composer. The question to explore here is rather who and what served as the group's musical benchmark and what this says about the social and political environment in which its members lived.

The artistic quality of an opera production in the West is to a large extent dependent on the vocal expertise of singers and the level of musical education of all artists involved, both of which were severely compromised by the circumstances in which Eoan operated. If Manca's claim of having "unskilled workers who can sing high opera" is to be taken seriously, anyone familiar with the skills required to sing nineteenth-century Italian opera would be forgiven for wondering if one can realistically expect a high-quality result within the social, political, and artistic context in which the group operated. Sophia Andrews, principal mezzo-soprano for the group from 1958 until 1970 (see figure 3.3), for instance, did indeed work in a textile factory throughout the time that she performed with the group.[94] She grew up in District Six in a family where there was no money for tertiary education, but through the group she was given a bursary for singing lessons with Fiasconaro at UCT's College of Music. During the five years she studied with him, however, she left school without completing her high school education and worked as a domestic worker with an employer who gave her leave on Tuesdays and Thursdays to practice and attend her lessons at the college.[95] Fiasconaro seems to have taught her by ear and gave her many records to listen to; during an interview with Andrews, it became clear that she never really mastered reading staff notation. When asked about her vocal range during an interview, she replied, "very wide, one of the biggest." When she was asked how low she could sing, she replied equally vaguely, possibly trying to evade a question that would expose her lack of technical knowledge: "as low as you throw me."[96] Her wide range is indeed illustrated by recordings of her voice dating from 1960 and later, but she did not seem to have an exact technical knowledge of the pitch she was singing.

Most of Eoan's principal singers received their vocal training in similar fashion. May Abrahamse, Ruth Goodwin, Arthur Ackerman, Lionel Fourie, Vera Gow, and many others took singing lessons with individual teachers at UCT or elsewhere, but not one of them had a music degree. Of Joseph Gabriels it is said that he had no voice training or music education whatsoever; it is certain that for the first decade of his singing career with Eoan,

FIGURE 3.3. Eoan's principal mezzo-soprano, Sophia Andrews. Source: Eoan Group Archive.

although having mastered principal roles in *Rigoletto* and *La Bohème*, he could not read staff notation. Ruth Goodwin remembered: "I was listening to [Joseph] on this recording, the way he sings that. Amazing! And he couldn't read a note of music. Lionel [Fourie] sat with him and taught him to take the top C."[97] Manca also took responsibility for much of the training. His daughter, Ruth Grevler, explained that "the whole of Sunday [the principals] would come and my father taught them at the piano in the lounge. He used to sit at the piano and play a bar of music and they used to have to sing it. And as they got better, they sang together. It took him one whole day to teach Joseph Gabriels eight bars of music."[98]

Criticism of the artistic standards of the group was seldom openly raised, and when it was, it is not clear how Manca or individual artists within the group reacted to it. The Eoan Group Archive contains a few such documents, the first dating from 1965, but they are the exceptions.[99] In contrast, the archive holds hundreds of congratulatory letters, telegrams, and reviews on the group's performances, and the occasion of Manca's being given an honorary doctorate in 1963 certainly must have boosted his (and the group's) self-image with regard to the quality of its performances. It can be reasonably argued that the reception of the group's opera performances by the broader public as well as opera connoisseurs was influenced by the knowledge of the difficult political and social circumstances, and the compromised educational background, of the group. Not only did music critics constantly refer to Eoan's opera productions as somehow "miraculous," but the entire marketing vocabulary of Eoan's seasons was based on the appeal of "unskilled workers who can sing opera." This in all likelihood contributed to a scenario of lower expectations, in which "unskilled workers" could more easily be forgiven for musical mishaps.

During 1957–1962 Fiasconaro produced all of Eoan's opera productions. In 1982 he published his autobiography, *I'd Do It Again*, which provides a rare instance of (surprisingly harsh) criticism of the group. The gist of the four-page description of the group, written in stinging invective, is that Eoan had soloists of great talent, but the group lacked education and discipline, and that Manca, despite working with "unbelievable patience," was completely unrealistic about his own and the group's musical abilities and artistic expertise.[100] Fiasconaro's description exposes some of the group's shortcomings. There is no doubt that there was much talent, but the effects of the lack of education and training cannot be ignored. Andrews's case was similar to most of Eoan's principals: talented singers who went for voice training on a part-time basis, without having access to a full-time course at the UCT Opera School, where they could immerse themselves in nothing but opera to gain a broader knowledge of operatic performance, classical music history, and theory. Fiasconaro's account also illustrates the practical problems for a producer when working with a large cast that had little training or exposure to the tradition of opera. "I had to try to teach people whose trades were, perhaps, street vendors or factory workers, how to wear tails, how to bow, how to kiss a lady's hand, how to curtsy and flirt with a fan—endless small things which were large hurdles."[101] A lack of discipline may be something that all opera directors complain of, irrespective of the social circumstances of the performers, but absenteeism remained chronic throughout the group's performance history, and traces of it can be found in a number of documents in the archive.[102]

Furthermore, Manca's limited musical training and insight have been commented on by various musicians and former Eoan members over the years, and his steadfast belief that their seasons were "on par with the finest opera houses in Europe," points to a painful lack of broader artistic awareness.[103]

Central to the issue of quality is the fact that the group was artistically extremely isolated, with almost no exposure to opera production by other companies and little encouragement for members to test themselves against others. It was fenced in by apartheid legislation, the effects of a history of slavery, substandard training, and successes that had few realistic links to the "La Scala" Manca liked to compare the group to. Fiasconaro remarked on the results of the continued praise by newspaper critics and the overwhelming support from the public: "Everything they did was superb; the press used every complimentary adjective in the dictionary and many people praised them to the skies, purely as a political ploy. This of course gave everyone in the Group a totally false idea of their own ability."[104] His dismissive language points out that the political environment stimulated such behavior. Throughout its history, Eoan was used for political gain by different stakeholders and for different reasons. White guilt may have contributed to the uncritical support for artists of color who were the victims of an unjust system, while the same situation was used by the apartheid government to showcase "how well the system of separate development worked for coloureds." On the other hand, it can also be argued that an uncritical, opera-loving public is no unusual occurrence anywhere in the world, and in the context of Cape Town's cultural environment at the time, this could well have played a role in the formation of the group's image.

There were artists in the group who were aware that the public's sympathy and enthusiasm could be indifferent to compromised musical standards. The most vocal of these was Eoan's repetiteur, Gordon Jephtas (born 8 March 1943). Jephtas joined the group in 1958 on invitation from Manca, who had heard him accompany a singer at a private concert, and went on to play an instrumental role in the group as vocal coach, repetiteur, and accompanist.[105] Limited biographical details are available on Jephtas's early life, but during interviews conducted with former Eoan members in 2009, it emerged that Jephtas had few family ties and lived with the Sydow family for a number of years.[106] Between 1961 and 1963 Eoan sponsored his studies for a teacher's licentiate at the College of Music at UCT and he left the country in October 1965 to pursue a career as repetiteur abroad. Apart from a number of Eoan dancers who had notable careers abroad, Jephtas's career in the field of opera can be regarded as the most successful, surpassing even that of Joseph Gabriels.

Until his death in 1992 he worked with several world-renowned opera singers and companies in Europe and America, including singers such as Renata Tebaldi, Franco Corelli, Marilyn Horne, Monserrat Caballè, Leontyne Price, and Luciano Pavarotti.[107] His lifelong friend and confidante, Eoan's principal soprano May Abrahamse, often sent him taped recordings of Eoan's operatic concerts, on which he commented in detail by return letter to her. On one such occasion Jephtas wrote, "I was overjoyed to hear some familiar voices even though some of it is pretty embarrassing."[108] About the enthusiastic audience applause he commented, "I find it difficult to analyze whether the applause is just complimentary because of the cause and the circumstances, or whether they really enjoyed what they had just heard."[109] During the latter part of the 1960s and 1970s Jephtas regularly returned to South Africa and worked with principal singers to prepare them for their performances. Oral testimonies by former Eoan singers reveal Jephtas as an extraordinary musician who had an uncanny capacity to bring voices and roles to life in the most difficult of circumstances.[110] Although he was deemed the successor of Manca, it seems that he never stayed long enough for his critical commentary and expanded frame of reference to lift the group out of its artistic isolation.

Returning to Fiasconaro's discussion of the group, his lack of empathy for the position of coloured artists and the stinging tone of his remarks call for comment. He describes Eoan's singers as insufficiently trained and undisciplined, but fails to acknowledge that they were denied decent vocal and musical education in a system from which he benefited and through which he had a professional career that earned him an excellent reputation.[111] He seems to have suffered from a limited willingness to educate coloured singers himself; although he writes flatteringly of Sophia Andrews that she "amply justified my expectations," in the five years during which she was his pupil, he failed to teach her to read staff notation.[112] She may have been a factory worker with no secondary schooling certificate, but mastering all the major mezzo roles of Eoan's repertoire and devoting all her free time to the group during the prime years of her singing career certainly does not demonstrate a lack of intelligence or discipline.

The need for education was not lost on Eoan's management, and in the early 1960s the group continued to provide funds for some for its dancers, singers, and musicians to study. For most of the members this came in the form of lessons with singing teachers at the College of Music at the University of Cape Town, but there were a few who enrolled as full-time students.[113] Dan Ulster was the first coloured person to obtain a degree in music at a

South African university. Gordon Jephtas studied at UCT from 1960 to 1963, and in later years Cecil Jacobs and Lydia Johnson both studied dance at UCT's Dance School. Eoan also sponsored the ballet dancer Didi Sydow to study with the Royal Ballet School in London from 1964 onward.[114] In later years, however, these educational initiatives diminished.

## THE SECOND ARTS FESTIVAL OF 1962

During 1961 Eoan's music section moved to premises on the third floor in Delta House at No. 7 Bree Street in the heart of Cape Town's business district.[115] Alternative rehearsal and office space was needed not only because the Ochberg Hall in District Six was by this time too small to house all of the group's activities, but also because the area was deemed unsafe.[116] In accordance with the Group Areas Act, Eoan, as a coloured organization, had to apply for a permit to use the Bree Street premises because it was situated in a white area. The permit was granted on 24 April 1961, and Eoan's music section used these premises until 1969, when the group finally moved out of District Six to the Joseph Stone Auditorium in Athlone.[117]

In preparation for the Second Arts Festival, planned for 1962, no public performances were held during 1961. Manca dreamed big (as usual), not only preparing for the festival, but already starting to plan a second tour of the country for 1963, this time to include visits to the then Rhodesia and South West Africa (today Zimbabwe and Namibia). He also planned an extended tour of Europe and England; he wanted Eoan to take part in the Commonwealth Arts Festival in Britain in 1964.[118] Appealing for financial assistance for the planned activities, Manca wrote:

> There are few cultural organizations which can, out of their own resources, finance such costly ventures. It is felt that South Africa could have no better "show window" than by presenting the Eoan Group in Europe and Great Britain, thus showing to what extent South Africa has culturally progressed. Its very appearance would silence the many critics of South Africa and have much more propaganda value than the publication of thousands of magazines and pamphlets. The South African government should not lose this opportunity of sponsoring the Eoan Group and making possible its overseas visit, and an appeal is made to the authority, to South African Commerce and Industry and to the Government itself to see that the Eoan Group's ambition to tour overseas is made a reality.[119]

From these comments it is clear Manca was convinced that a tour abroad would not be possible without substantial funding from the state. Whether he used a phrase like "propaganda value" as a ploy to please those in power into funding Eoan or really stood behind these ideas, we do not know. However, he did seem to be aware that the government's funding system was conducive to projects with propaganda value rather than for the sake of opera production or the upliftment of the coloured community.

Although Eoan was at this time not receiving funding from the DCA the debate on government funding for cultural activities and the political compromises it entailed must have been alive in the Eoan Group. In March 1961 issues such as segregated audiences, government funding, and the notion of "art above politics" were discussed in the newspapers, and Manca filed newspaper cuttings on these issues in Eoan's 1961 papers. Because performance for racially segregated audiences was seminal in the eventual demise of Eoan's opera activities in the late 1970s, it is worthwhile quoting portions of two such articles:

### *Actors and Apartheid*

The cruel dilemma in which opponents of segregation find themselves is whether to accept the benefits of segregated institutions or to reject them on stern principle. We can understand and sympathize with the cultural non-White whose aversion to apartheid is so strong that he cannot bring himself to attend segregated performances. But there is a broader view which compels even greater respect – the view that the liberating power of culture can exert itself even in a segregated audience, and that the sense of human brotherhood can be communicated even in a building which denies it.[120]

### *Conflict on Theatre Apartheid*

The whole question of segregated audiences is one of inconsistencies and contradictions. On the one hand Europeans apparently are determined in their opposition to mixed audiences at shows, and a benevolent Government is only too happy to legislate supporting this opposition. Yet one finds these same Europeans perfectly happy, attending very mixed performances of productions staged by such prominent non-White theatre groups as the Eoan Group. Let the European look round him in his daily life. There can never be apartheid. The lives of everybody in this land are so interwoven that in spite of the fanatical efforts of legislators, the scourge of apartheid must finally break down.[121]

Both articles appeared in the *Cape Times*, a newspaper known for its liberal views throughout the apartheid era, written by whites for a predominantly white readership. It illustrates how white liberal benevolence could state that apartheid "can never be" and believe in the power of art to transcend injustices done in the name of apartheid, yet partake of the best of what white society offered and never suffer the deprivations the system imposed on its victims. The articles highlight that some whites who attended Eoan's opera performances still preferred not to sit next to coloured people in the theater and supported the idea of segregated audiences. The discussion among politically aware individuals within the coloured community regarding such issues had been ongoing since the National Party came into power in 1948 and was reported on widely in newspapers such as the *Torch*. In a number of these articles the Eoan Group was accused of submitting to party politics, and it is clear that the organization was regarded with suspicion in politically activist circles. However, the threat of withdrawal of state funds from organizations that did not submit to apartheid legislation was real, as it endangered the very survival of the group's opera productions.

Racially mixed events were still possible, and Eoan's Second Arts Festival was an example thereof. The festival was held in cooperation with the Peninsula Round Table, which consisted predominantly of white patrons and whose members regarded themselves as nonpolitical and nondenominational. From the start of the preparations until all organizational matters had been dealt with, all correspondence was typed on a letterhead that stated "EOAN Group—Peninsula Round Table Arts Festival 1962" and included both organizations' logos and directors. Although the Round Table did not present or take part in any of the productions, it played a financial and organizational supporting role, and it was clear that this was a racially mixed initiative.[122] It was also the last such initiative the group ever participated in.

The festival productions were again spread over several months, starting with opera in March and ending with a ballet in September. The opera season opened on 17 March with yet another new addition to Eoan's repertoire, Puccini's *Madame Butterfly*, and repeat performances of its existing repertoire of *La Traviata* and *La Bohème*.[123] The group produced a drama in April and two children's operettas in July, Martin Shaw's *Travelling Musicians* and Harvey Paul's *Alice in Wonderland*. In August Eoan added two new works to its repertoire, performing Verdi's *Requiem* as well as Johann Strauss's operetta *Die Fledermaus*. In September Eoan premiered *The Square*, a new ballet composed for the group by Glasser. This meant having to master four new major productions for this season—an opera, an operetta, a choral work, and a new ballet—as well as two smaller works in the form of children's operettas.[124] Allusions to

Manca's famous comparison of Eoan to La Scala and his goal of presenting opera in "true Italian style" also appeared in the press. The *Cape Times* reported on 7 March that "[a]iming not only to maintain its already high standard of presentation but also to raise it to further heights, the Eoan Group is doing its best to give Cape Town audiences opera as it is done at La Scala in Milan. To this end Joseph Cappon has planned large-scale lavish settings, Mavis Taylor has designed costumes described as 'sumptuous' and to lend authentic special effects period furniture has been made."[125]

Reviews were again extraordinarily complimentary, and the headlines published in the *Cape Times* alone indicate that the season was deemed another major artistic success. "Eoan Group's 'Butterfly' Is Outstanding Success," published on 19 March, was followed by "New Laurels for Eoan Group in Bohème" on 20 March and "Applause for Debut of New Violetta in La Traviata" on 23 March. Eoan's first production of *Madame Butterfly* was described as an "instantaneous and unqualified success," and the reviewer mentioned that "May Abrahamse, for many years one of the group's shining stars surpassed herself in her portrayal of the ill-fated little heroine."[126] Other principal singers, such as Joseph Gabriels, Sophia Andrews, Benjamin Arendse, Robert Trussell, and Samuel Amos, were similarly praised for good singing and acting.[127]

The review of Eoan's second production of *La Bohème* was similarly positive, highlighting the progress made by principals such as Joseph Gabriels, whose aria at the end of the first act was acknowledged by a "storm of applause," and Robert Trussell, who was "rapidly coming to the fore as one of the outstanding members of the operatic group."[128] Vera Gow's "naturally full and ringing soprano" also received good reviews as she made her debut in the role of Musetta.[129] Gow was to play a major role as one of Eoan's principal sopranos in years to come. It was, however, the debut of Abeeda Parker as Violetta in Verdi's *La Traviata* that astonished not only the press and the public, but also Manca himself. The *Cape Times* wrote:

> At the City Hall last night, a new star in the Eoan Group made a sensational début. This was Abeeda Parker, a girl of 18 who, a year ago, had no musical tuition, but who sang and portrayed a role that in the ordinary way is only attempted by coloratura sopranos of wide experience with outstanding voices. For this slip of a girl, the task of memorizing the notes of a four-act score, the Italian words of it and the actions accompanying them, was alone arduous. What captivated the audience and drew continual rounds of applause was the bell-like purity of her voice and the ease with which she used it in her brilliant arias.[130]

The *Cape Argus* reported in a similar vein that "this young singer of undoubtedly outstanding talents took the audience by storm, not only her beautiful singing, but also by her assured bearing and acting. Here we have a potential star of international status, I am sure, if one is to judge by this one performance. In Abeeda Parker we have an exceptional operatic find, who should be given every facility and encouragement to continue in her operatic career."[131]

Parker (born 6 December 1943) made her debut with Eoan at age eighteen. Only one year after she had joined the group, her rendition of the role of Violetta astonished everyone. Manca was also clearly quite taken with her, as evidenced by his detailed notes in the archive on her background and his great plans for her future career as an opera singer. Parker came from a prestigious family in the Indian community of the Cape, where she grew up in the Muslim faith. She received good schooling, knew several languages (Arabic, among others), and was the second youngest in a family of eight girls. Manca's notes make no mention of her vocal training, but state that she sang at school, listened to recordings of opera, and was enrolled for a course at Battswood College, where members of the coloured community could be educated in Western art music. His notes also state that Eoan would arrange a bursary for Parker to study abroad and that she would "be one of South Africa's foremost opera singers in the future."[132] Although his plans for her did not materialize, it was unusual for Manca to plan training abroad for one of his principal singers. Interviews with other principals indicate that he was generally unwilling to let go of singers that he knew would draw crowds. (See the soprano soloists who participated in this Arts Festival, figure 3.4.) Although relatively little is known about Parker's training, it is safe to assume that she did have limited exposure to operatic techniques; according to Ruth Grevler, Manca's daughter, she was taught the role of Violetta in the Manca family's living room in a very short space of time.[133]

The archive also contains many letters and telegrams congratulating Manca and the group on their performances. One of these came from David Bloomberg, who at the time was a lawyer and theater director. Bloomberg later served on the Eoan Group Trust, produced one of the group's most successful musical programs in the late 1960s, and went on to become a public figure of note when he became the mayor of Cape Town in 1973. On 21 March 1962, he wrote a letter that is reflective of much of the admiration that opera enthusiasts had for Manca and the group: "My very heartiest congratulations to you on the wonderful ovation that you have received from the press and the

FIGURE 3.4. Joseph Manca and Eoan's soprano soloists May Abrahamse, Patricia van Graan, Abeeda Parker, Ruth Goodwin, and Vera Gow. Source: *Alpha Magazine*, published with permission from Government Printing Works, Republic of South Africa.

public for the current season of opera. I enjoyed the evening tremendously, and marveled at the degree of professionalism which you have attained for the Group. I think that you have achieved absolute wonders."[134]

It may be true that Eoan suffered from the dangers of too much uncritical praise (as both Fiasconaro and Jephtas pointed out), but Bloomberg was no artistic philistine either. He traveled abroad often and was well known in theater circles as a producer, and it is unlikely that he misjudged the situation entirely.

Paging through the documentation in the archive on the 1962 festival, it is evident that behind the scenes life was less glamorous than the reviews projected. Lack of funding started to make serious inroads into the group's bank account, and the absence of decent remuneration for artists cost the goodwill of participants. Minutes of the meetings of the finance committee of January to March 1962 show, for instance, that the tenor Joseph Gabriels was not willing to sing free of charge and was engaged in a paid singing position elsewhere in the country, so the committee agreed to pay him a fee of R26 per week to sing for Eoan during the festival. Baritone Robert Trussell was unemployed at the time of preparations for the festival and was paid R20 per week for his role. Lionel Fourie also had financial troubles, and the committee resolved to loan him R80, although the minutes state that the committee realized there was little chance that the money would be repaid.[135] Shortly afterward, Fourie became ill (according to his widow, Ruth, this was due to alcoholism and diabetes) and had to withdraw from the festival entirely. At short notice his role as Germont in *La Traviata* was taken over by Fiasconaro, who was also directing the operas of this season. This incident was probably the first and last time that a white singer joined the Eoan cast onstage. Fiasconaro, too, provided Manca with a fair share of headaches. He seemed to be chronically negative about the group, and on 14 February he wrote Manca a lengthy letter in which he withdrew from directing Strauss's *Die Fledermaus* later that year, complaining about the coloured singers' alleged bad attitudes and nonattendance at rehearsals and the lack of remuneration offered by the group. He attacked Manca's lofty cultural aspirations and his seemingly untouchable position, stating that "you might argue that nobody can offer them opportunities of singing in opera, but, dear Mr. Manca, you know as well as I do that gold is the most powerful force and 'cultural ideas' will never prevail."[136] Although the performances of the opera season went well, there was little profit from ticket sales, and by June the group had to apply for additional funds from private donors in order for the July, August, and September productions of the festival to continue.[137]

On 4 August, Eoan's production of Verdi's *Requiem* triumphed, with reviewers giving it yet again "full marks for all concerned," praising the "dramatic qualities" of May Abrahamse's voice and Sophia Andrews's "rich mezzo voice."[138] The tenor and bass solo parts were sung by Joseph Gabriels and Robert Trussell. For this performance, the Eoan Group Choir was augmented by the Cape Town Choral Society, illustrating that despite apartheid, interracial productions were still possible.

### DANCING *THE SQUARE*

Some weeks later the group presented a new ballet, *The Square*, a work composed for Eoan by Glasser and choreographed by David Poole.[139] The story was a depiction of gang life in the racially mixed yet poor District Six, and the principal role was created for and danced by Johaar Mosaval, who grew up in District Six and was a principal dancer with the Royal Ballet in England at the time.[140] The music was composed for the (in South Africa at least) unusual combination of symphony orchestra and jazz band. Created to respond to the social and musical environment of the group at the time, this work forms an important part of its legacy. New ballet compositions for local companies were unusual. The first one on record seems to be a ballet by William Henry Bell, *Le Jongleur de Notre Dame*, composed in 1936, and the second is John Joubert's 1952 ballet *Vlei Legend*, composed for the Jan van Riebeeck Tercentenary Festival. Both works were composed for and performed by the UCT Ballet School.[141]

Ballet had been a substantial part of the group's activities since 1935 and, as numerous newspaper reports over time reveal, a very successful one. Not only did the group put many coloured dancers through Royal Academy Dance exams on various levels, it also presented annual "dance displays" together with the Cape Town Municipal Orchestra and was in a position to employ dance teachers in paid positions. In the early history of the group, ballet was in fact a more prominent activity than choral or operatic singing. Although opera production overshadowed Eoan's ballet activities in later years, the existence of its ballet section has had a much longer and consistent history. Today, after eighty-five years, the Eoan Group still teaches ballet and presents productions to the public annually, whereas operatic singing was part of its history for less than half that time. Program notes of Eoan's productions show that David Poole of the University of Cape Town Ballet School was the choreographer for most of Eoan's ballet productions during the early years. In practice this meant he was responsible for teaching dancers their movements, and despite not being part of Eoan's staff, it is clear that he spent substantial amounts of time with the group.

Poole was born in 1925 into a coloured family and trained with Dulcie Howes at the UCT Ballet School, after which she arranged for him to go to England for further training.[142] There he danced with Sadler's Wells from 1947 until 1958, after which he returned to South Africa permanently.[143] Being fair skinned, he had himself reclassified by the South African authorities in England as a white person.[144] At the time of Poole's return to South Africa, professional dance opportunities were only available at the (white) UCT Ballet School, where he was offered a post. Poole remained committed to the development of ballet in the coloured community, despite (or maybe because of) the fact that his "change of colour" afforded him access to a professional career in South Africa that he otherwise would not have had. Documentation in the Eoan Group Archive includes many letters between

Poole and Manca regarding a host of ballet-related concerns, and even after Manca had left the organization in 1977, Poole continued to attend Eoan's annual general meetings and took part in discussions regarding the future of the group.[145]

Up until about 1962 the ballet section's artistic output was on a par with that of the music section. It presented its own productions during the course of each year, contributed to Eoan's annual City Hall performance seasons, and took part in operas and operettas in which dance scenes were required. The composition of *The Square* illustrates the prominent position Eoan's ballet section enjoyed within the broader spectrum of Cape Town's cultural life.

One of the characteristics of the Eoan Group Archive is that it focuses primarily on arrangements in and around the group's activities, while information on issues such as the choice of repertoire or artistic concerns with regard to a new commission such as this ballet is entirely (and unfortunately) absent. For example, the archive holds correspondence with Glasser about his fees for this commission and whether or not he was going to conduct the orchestra during the performance, but no information is available on how he conceived of the work, why he decided on a "jazz ballet," or what input Poole had into the work other than creating the choreography. The *Cape Times* of 16 August tells us that the work is "said to have a universal theme, dealing with the hopes and frustrations of the youth and the struggle between good and evil."[146] With regard to the music, the *Cape Times* further reports that "[Glasser] has provided music based on jazz elements which, he feels, express the spirit of the story and is to be played by the Municipal Orchestra augmented to 50 musicians with the inclusion of jazzmen Cecil Ricca (drums), Bob Hill (double bass) and Alan Gordon (trumpet)."[147] The work was conceived for seventy-seven dancers, of whom thirty-six were young dancers and the rest came from the mature ballet corps within the group. The work premièred on 29 August 1962 and earned positive reviews that praised Mosaval's dancing, Poole's choreography, and Stephen de Villiers's costume design. Glasser's music, however, received little attention other than a few remarks on the fact that the orchestra had to cope with playing jazz. *Cape Times* reviewer Denis Hatfield accused Glasser of impropriety for adapting a solemn chorale into the composition.[148]

In *The History of Ballet in South Africa* (1981), ballet historian Marina Grut provides the reasons she thought the work was successful: "Creating a style which suited the Coloured dancers, it gave them scope for their acting ability as well as successfully reproducing the feel and atmosphere of the Cape, where the Coloureds have their home."[149] Although Glasser's score for this work and an audio recording of the performance have been preserved in the composer's archive, the choreography has not, and one has to rely on the sketchy information provided by newspaper articles about what dance "style" Grut has in mind here. Glasser's score describes the ballet as "music for symphony orchestra and jazz band."[150] Grut states that "it is a great pity that more ballets like this have not been created for these dancers; it would have turned the Group into a unique company in South Africa."[151] Her comment here points to the perceived lack of a distinct dance style, which she deems characteristic of the life of the coloured community living in Cape Town, underlining the way the Eoan Group related to other kinds of music practiced within the coloured community in general. This touches on the aesthetic ideal that the group was aspiring to. It is clear that for opera production at least, Manca was not interested in any deviation from a "true Italian style," and in line with opera production elsewhere in the country at the time, resisted any form of dilution of or change to European performance norms. As described in chapter 1, jazz was not really pursued within the group. In an advertisement for auditions for Eoan's following opera season (published in April 1962), it becomes clear that the practice of popular music was also not welcomed by the management of the group. The advertisement invited singers to audition for operatic roles but specifically stated "no rock and roll singers."[152] Yet *The Square* is one of the few works the group ever produced in which jazz played a role.

There are interesting similarities between the "jazz ballet" *The Square* and the "jazz opera" *King Kong*, produced by Glasser three years earlier. Glasser is an eclectic composer who composed in a wide variety of tonal and posttonal styles in the Western art music tradition, yet at the same time heavily invested his energies in indigenous music and jazz. He was closely involved with *King Kong* over a three-year period (1958–1960), and it was perhaps conceptually an easy step from a "jazz opera" to a "jazz ballet," both of which were unusual formats in South Africa at the time of creation and were conceived for and with black and coloured artists. Both productions reflected on life on the streets where many black and coloured people lived (the townships of Johannesburg and District Six in Cape Town), and neither was politically outspoken in the way that became common in antiapartheid activism after the rise of black consciousness. In between these two productions, Glasser also recorded his musical *Paljas*, with artists such as District Six jazz singer Maud Damons and Eoan singers Gerald Arendse and Esther Parkins, with choreography created by Eoan dancer Gwen Michaels. Other artists who took part in *Paljas* were Blue Note singers Chris McGregor and Dudu Pukwana and the jazz singer Thandie Klaasen.[153] Harry Bloom, who wrote the text for *King Kong*, also wrote the text for *Paljas*. A comparison of the content, choreography, and music of *King Kong*, *Paljas*, and *The Square* renders a fascinating insight into these early forays into cross-cultural, jazz-based South African productions.

As a result of this collaboration, Stanley Glasser ran into trouble with apartheid authorities, in an event that caused him to flee South Africa and settle permanently in the United Kingdom. Glasser had an extramarital affair with District Six jazz singer Maud Damons, who sang for *Paljas*. The affair continued throughout the production of *The Square*, and Damons is said to have been at rehearsals with Glasser, although she did not take part.[154] Having been caught in flagrante by a police officer near Rhodes Memorial in Cape Town some months after the production, the couple were allegedly arrested on contravening the Immorality Act of 1950.[155] After being released on bail, Glasser and Damons allegedly crossed the border to Botswana and fled to the United Kingdom via Tanzania. According to Peter Voges, an Eoan ballet dancer who took part in *The Square*, the affair was "an open secret"; everybody in the group knew about it but nobody discussed it openly.[156] In London the couple separated; Glasser settled as a lecturer in music and Damons went on to have a career as a jazz singer.[157] The incident illustrates, on a level other than funding or administration, how the inevitable interracial personal relationships resulting from Eoan performances were conducted in adherence to legislative demands. Where apartheid norms were flouted, the consequences were dire.

After *The Square*, Eoan's ballet section experienced a decade-long slump in activity, and by the late 1960s the group's annual productions were advertised as "opera seasons" rather than "opera and ballet seasons." It was only in the mid-1970s, when opera activities started to decline, that dance presentations again became part of the group's performance seasons.

In October 1962 the Second Arts Festival came to a close when the group presented Johan Strauss's operetta *Die Fledermaus*. The principal roles were sung by Joseph Gabriels as Gabriel von Eisenstein, May Abrahamse as Rosalinde, Faried Nordien as Alfredo, and Patricia van Graan as Adele.[158] The plot of *Die Fledermaus* is "about a rich husband and wife who each try to deceive the other and who find each other out at the end."[159] The music of this operetta is easy to listen to, melodious and playful, and the work's popularity rests on "mistaken identities, flirtations at a masked ball, elegant frivolities and confusions of all kinds that provide a hilarious vehicle for some of the most captivating music ever written."¹⁶⁰ This production, too, was met with much approval. The reviewer for *Cape Argus* reflected that "a more successful note on which to end the group's 1962 arts festival is difficult to imagine" and praised the finesse with which the group performed the work: "I have not seen principals give a more disciplined performance than last night. The unobtrusive manner in which the equally disciplined chorus supported the principals to give the impression of absolute unity was remarkable."¹⁶¹ Eoan had performed at least nine operettas in the course of the 1950s. Except for W. S. Gilbert and Arthur Sullivan's *Mikado*, none of those works remain in the classical canon today or have experienced repeat performances by the group. *Fledermaus*, too, was performed by the group only once, but thanks to photographer Cloete Breytenbach's having captured this performance on camera, the memory of this production secured a place in the archived history of the group.

In the same month Joseph Gabriels (aged twenty-five at the time) took part in the Mimi Coertse Singing Competition, which was managed by the University of Pretoria. Mimi Coertse was a South African soprano who was the principal female vocalist and coloratura at the State Opera in Vienna, a position she held for seventeen years from 1956 onward. Back home she became a household name in white society and was revered by the opera fraternity, and the competition was a prestigious event that made headlines in local newspapers. The prize money of R800 was to go toward furthering a promising student's studies in opera abroad.¹⁶² In her biography, *'n Stem vir Suid-Afrika*, Coertse remembers that Gabriels was in her opinion the best applicant for the prize during that year's competition, but the authorities would not allow her to award the bursary to him because he was coloured. She then decided not to award the prize at all.¹⁶³ *Die Burger* carried a brief article on the incident stating that the bursary would not be awarded that year, but stopped short of naming Gabriels or explaining why it was not awarded.¹⁶⁴

### AN HONORARY DOCTOR

In hindsight, it is clear that 1963 brought to a close Eoan's most productive years as an arts company, a time during which the group also produced its best-quality opera, drama, and dance. From 1964 onward difficulties on several fronts started to build up, which in time undermined the group's morale and artistic output. This forced the group into a slow but steady descent toward the cessation of opera production some fifteen years later. These dif-

FIGURE 3.5. Manca conducting in City Hall during a rehearsal. Photo by Cloete Breytenbach.

ficulties included chronic lack of funding, increased limitations on accessing venues and other public spaces, and the continuing compromised nature of their musical education. Furthermore, the group's growing political complicity and subsequent loss of credibility among its own community added to the loss of valued artists from its midst and the deterioration of human relations between management and members of the organization.

For Manca, however, the period culminated on a high note when in June 1963 he was awarded an honorary doctorate in music from the University of Cape Town "in recognition of his work for the cultural progress and upliftment of the Coloured Community."[165] Manca had joined Eoan in 1943 and had now been with the group for twenty years. The event received ample coverage in *Alpha*, a magazine issued by the Department of Coloured Affairs (DCA) for a coloured readership.[166] The article indicates that Erik Chisholm initiated the award and also read the recommendation during the graduation ceremony.[167] The event had great significance for Manca because it demonstrated institutional and public recognition of his stature as a musician and provided tangible evidence that he had been accepted in white opera circles. In years to come he never failed to use his title. (See the photo of Manca conducting, figure 3.5.)

EOAN'S BEST OPERA SUCCESS • 95

Such recognition, however, remained absent for Eoan's artists, and their aspirations for professional recognition were dealt another blow when the PACs were established in 1963. The PACs secured state funding and professional career opportunities for white artists only, and Eoan's artists were excluded from taking part in or benefiting from any of their productions on racial grounds. Although the Cape Performing Arts Board (CAPAB), the Cape Province manifestation of this initiative, only started producing opera on a significant scale in the late 1960s, and Eoan probably outdid CAPAB's productions in these years, the exclusion of coloured artists from this prestigious artistic initiative had a negative impact on the morale of the group. For years to come the disappointment over the lack of acknowledgment or recognition by white opera circles of Eoan's singers and the absence of equal opportunities for the artists would permeate the discourse documented in the Eoan Group Archive. Throughout the years, the existence of CAPAB served as a painful reminder that Eoan's artists were not recognized by the state as on a par with their white counterparts.

In September 1963 Eoan's drama section presented an indigenous play, *Behind the Yellow Door*, by the South African playwright Flora Stohr, in the Little Theatre in Cape Town, featuring Mable Kester, Valerie Geduld, Allie Sydow, Mabel Canterbury, and Clifford Rinquest.[168] The play was directed by Robert Mohr, who had also worked with the group in *Die Fledermaus* the year before. This three-act play dealt with the life of a coloured family in Athlone and commented directly on the consequences of apartheid in everyday lives. The story illustrates, among other themes, the disappointment of a coloured boy who is denied the opportunity to study veterinary science because he is coloured. The work incorporated songs and musical formats from the coloured community. The main character of this play, Ahlie, is cast as a singer for the Golden Dixies, a hugely popular music troupe of the time.[169] Reviewer Ivor Jones described the work as "excellent entertainment," "unpretentious," and "mercifully free from messages concerning domestic problems," yet as was the case with Eoan's production of *The Square*, the reviewer noted that the success of the play lay in "members of the Eoan Group [playing] roles not completely alien to their observation and experience."[170] Both these indigenously created works contained the politically driven subtexts of impoverishment and disempowerment, yet these themes were not foregrounded in the performances. Instead, the comical and entertaining elements were favored. After this production, however, the drama section too became inactive and did not produce any plays for a decade.

A number of artists who had a significant influence on the group's output had also left the group in the course of this year. The dancer Didi Sydow (the daughter of Ismail and Carmen Sydow) left for England, where she started training with the Royal Ballet. Funds for her studies were supplied by the group, but although the plan was for her to return to South Africa to invest her expertise in the group, this never happened. Sydow married an Australian citizen and settled in England.

Two of Eoan's principal sopranos also left the group during 1963. Ruth Goodwin finally decided to leave on political grounds. Her husband was a trade union leader who had been harboring political reservations about her participation in the group for a number of years. Abeeda Parker, the shining star of Eoan's 1962 Arts Festival, for whom Manca had such high hopes and for whom he envisaged a stellar career, had also stopped singing. According to other group members, she got married and was forbidden to continue a career as opera singer, bringing her short and spectacular career to an abrupt end.[171]

Finally, on 19 December 1963 the baritone, Lionel Fourie, passed away at the age of thirty-eight.[172] This was a major blow for group members because Fourie was a strong leader, willing to clash with superiors for the sake of his principles.[173] However, it is for his voice that he is mostly remembered today. In an obituary, Manca wrote that "Lionel Fourie's beautiful baritone voice in addition to being powerful, had a bell-like and smooth velvet quality which one never tired to hear. [His] untimely death has cut short the career of an artist who, under the aegis of the Eoan Group, would have reached international fame. His passing away is not only a great loss to the Eoan Group, but to the whole of South Africa and so today we mourn for our colleague Lionel Fourie."[174]

FOUR

## Scala Is Scala and Eoan Is Eoan: The Struggle to Breathe

1964–1971

> Your sacrifice shall be rewarded,
> And in days to come you will be proud of so great a love.
> —GERMONT, Act 2, *La Traviata* by Giuseppe Verdi

### THE EOAN GROUP TRUST

In 1964 an important structural and managerial change took place when the Eoan Group Trust was launched in an attempt to address the group's growing financial difficulties. Despite the group's high productivity and many successes since 1956, it became clear that Eoan needed a more solid financial foundation to stay afloat and fulfill its mandate of cultural upliftment in the coloured community. Although Eoan had been financially self-reliant since 1957 (except for the annual grant of ZAR2,000 received from the Municipality of Cape Town), the disappointing financial results of the 1962 Second Arts Festival and further financial restraints imposed during 1963 and 1964 proved that the group's productions were not as profitable as its management had hoped they would be, despite operating on a shoestring budget.[1]

In 1963 financial guarantees were granted by the state for white arts production when the Performing Arts Councils (PACs) were instated. With this initiative opera production in the country was at long last able to operate on a fully professional level, in which artists could be employed in paid positions and long-term financial security guaranteed consistent production. However, these arts councils were for whites only; being excluded from this opportunity on racial grounds, Eoan's bid to become a professional arts company was dealt a significant blow. In the coming decade promises of a similar body for the coloured community from which the group could benefit were repeatedly made by the government, promises the group and its management had high hopes for but that in the end proved to be empty.[2] Thus the group was formally always regarded as "amateur," a stigma it was never able to rid itself of and that caused much bitterness and resentment toward the world of mainstream (read *white*) opera production.

It is not clear whether the Eoan Group Trust was launched to function as a financial alternative to the PACs, but it operated separately from the Eoan Group, with the aim of acting as a financial guarantor and to assist in raising funds for Eoan's activities.[3] The trust consisted of prominent and well-to-do white citizens who supported the group. Among them were the then mayor of Cape Town, W. J. Peters, and the deputy mayor, Walter Gradner; the lawyer, theater producer, and future mayor of Cape Town, David Bloomberg; the chairman of Shell South Africa, L. C. V. Walker; a director of the Rembrandt Group, J. J. Piek; and in later years also the Afrikaans poet Dr. I. D. du Plessis, who held a senior position at the Department of Coloured Affairs (DCA).[4] Members of the trust deposited money into a bank account whose interest supported a financial guarantee for the group.[5]

The trust, however, was another manifestation of white custodianship of coloured interests, with no representation by anyone from the coloured community. Although the trust certainly had the best of intentions for the group, the body never questioned or challenged existing interracial relations as stipulated by apartheid policies. There may have been well-to-do coloured people interested in making significant financial contributions to the Eoan Group Trust, yet the modus operandi of the trust clearly illustrates that this structure followed existing patterns of white patronage and that no attempt was made to stimulate coloured self-empowerment on a managerial level. Until 1970, no coloured person was part of the trust, irrespective of whether that person could contribute financially.

In a speech held at the trust's inauguration, the chairman of the Eoan Group, Ismail Sydow, put into words the financial burden the group had to deal with:

> Up till now, the Eoan Group managed to keep its head above water in so far that the Music Section has provided the main income and so financed the non-revenue-producing sections. However, there is, in the world, no Welfare, Educational and Cultural organization which is completely self-supporting and not in need of subsidies. Particularly is this so in the field of opera. All over the world, opera is heavily subsidized by governments, municipalities, industries, commerce, private organizations and persons and by specially

established guilds. Therefore, it is a miracle that the Eoan Group has not only been able to carry on but also achieve the already well-known and excellent results.[6]

Even after a decade of prolific opera production and tremendous popularity among the white opera-loving public in the Cape, the logistical limitations and difficulties of the conditions in which Eoan members and the production teams had to function, many due to apartheid, did not abate. In fact, conditions steadily worsened. Sydow used the occasion to highlight these, reminding trust members that the group continued to build its excellent reputation despite the limited time available for rehearsals, the lack of opportunities and infrastructure for professional development, the huge financial strain on individual artists, and the familial sacrifices that members had to make in order to participate in the arts.[7]

It was also clear that the group continued to believe that it could stay clear of politics. Sydow stated during this speech that according to its constitution, "the Eoan Group has always been and is completely NON-POLITICAL [emphasis in original]. Our activities are purely concerned with welfare work and our aim is for the cultural development, uplift and progress of our people."[8] The reality of the group's circumstances, however, was quite the opposite. Decisions made by politicians sanctioned the segregation of coloured artists from the world of professional opportunities and painfully affected their personal and public lives on all levels. Yet participating in opera production and mastering its technical and artistic requirements was also the vehicle to personal achievement and in some cases to stardom, all of which elevated them above their daily realities. The "thundering applause" after each performance counted as a sense of recognition from the (white) public that was otherwise lacking. Engaging the politics of the day with the premises on which the group members practiced opera would come at the cost of giving that up. Moreover, at a time when concepts such as democracy and self-governance by the coloured population had been absent for generations, the acceptance of another's authority was compounded by the hierarchical structures inherent in opera production.

Accepting white benevolence had by this time become standard practice, as "white money" had funded most arts-related activities since the inception of the group thirty years earlier. This is reflected in the tribute to Manca with which Sydow concluded his acceptance speech, which is indicative of the standing Manca had within the group:

Last but not least, on behalf of the Eoan Group and the whole Coloured Community, I take this opportunity of paying a very special tribute and offering our most grateful and heartfelt thanks to a man of faith, vision, determination, indomitable courage and humility—I refer to our beloved Honorary Musical Director, DR JOSEPH MANCA [emphasis in original].

For over twenty-one years, Dr. Manca has unselfishly devoted all his available time and efforts to the welfare and cultural progress of my people. No sacrifice is too much for him, no request or demand has been refused. He has not cared for his family, his children nor has he spared himself both spiritually and physically on behalf of the Group.

His guidance, his love of humanity, his deep understanding of the problems of my people, his outstanding administrative abilities and his artistic and cultural contribution, have been the major factor in bringing into world prominence the achievements of the Coloured People in the sphere of art. This dedicated man has often publicly defined his labour of love as a "Mission in Music". I unhesitatingly say that this is true in every sense and that the field of his mission is universal, but the temple of his artistic worship is the Eoan Group.[9]

Sydow's heartfelt tribute reflects much of Manca's character and his motivation. It is clear that Manca approached his work with Eoan with missionary zeal, illustrated by the number of personal sacrifices he was willing to make and the sacrifices he consciously drove Eoan to make in order to achieve his goals. One cannot but wonder what Manca's goals really were: working toward uplifting coloured people or living out the dream that he, as an amateur musician and accountant, could present Cape Town with grand opera? Or were they a combination of both? And regarding Manca's political consciousness, did he choose to be naive, did he lack political savvy, or did he actually believe that the apartheid model of separate development was a plausible option? Or was parading Eoan's cultural abilities his display of resistance to an unjust system? Perhaps he just tried his best under the circumstances.

From conversations with various former members a more negative picture emerges, one that portrays Manca as a man who was covetous of his position as cultural director of the Eoan Group and enjoyed the limelight that came with it.[10] According to Peter Voges, May Abrahamse, and Tillie Ulster, Manca insisted on conducting all performances himself, apparently at the expense of better-qualified conductors from within the group.[11] Dan Ulster, for instance, who had studied conducting with Enrique Jorda at the College of Music at UCT and was said to be an excellent conductor, was never allowed to conduct the orchestra in Eoan's opera performances.[12] Ulster left the organization in the late 1950s and revived the Spes Bona Orchestra, an amateur orchestra comprising coloured musicians who accompanied classical music productions at Battswood College.[13] Gordon Jephtas, too, often complained in his letters to May Abrahamse that Manca had a tendency to pretend to be a master of music while, in Jephtas's view at least, Manca's musical capacities were limited. Jephtas did, however, note that many opera directors in Europe displayed similar tendencies. On one occasion he complained about artists "who imagine themselves greater creative geniuses than the composers whose music they are singing, and wanting to change everything at will. All rather like Manca, just a lot of notes, near enough to what has been written and then voice, voice and more voice. Perhaps, when I have learnt that the so-called professional world is largely [full] of Manca-types who delight in preening themselves before audiences, life will be more tolerable."[14]

In order to prepare for the 1965 opera season, no productions were held during 1964, although the Eoan Group choir took part in a production of Jerome Kern and Oscar Hammerstein's musical *Showboat* in the Alhambra Theatre in Cape Town in March 1964.[15] This production, staged by the Johannesburg Operatic and Dramatic Society, was on tour throughout the country, and since it required a choir representing African American workers, Eoan's choir was chosen for the Cape Town performances. It is also one of the few productions the group took part in that was not strictly an Eoan production. The story of this musical concerns personal suffering caused by racial intolerance and has an African American, Joe, as one of the main characters.[16] In his historical overview of the Johannesburg Civic Theatre, where this production was staged, J. Brooks Spector reflects on the unusual choice of this musical in apartheid South Africa and argues that the work was specifically chosen by the Johannesburg Operatic and Dramatic Society as a racially integrated production. The Maori bass from New Zealand, Inia Te Wiata, was brought to South Africa to sing the role of Joe. According to Brooks Spector, Te Wiata was officially classified as coloured under apartheid legislation, but by virtue of having a Scandinavian grandmother, he was reclassified as white in order for him to be allowed to participate with white singers.[17]

Since Te Wiata was regarded as a coloured person, Manca also tried to co-opt him to sing with Eoan as a guest artist. In a letter to David Tidboald, at the time director of the Cape Town Municipal Orchestra, Manca mentioned that he was going to travel to the United States and Europe on a grant from the United States-South Africa Leader Exchange Program.[18] While in the United States he planned to "contact various internationally famous

American Negro Opera Stars and Artists to visit South Africa and appear as Guest Artists in the Eoan Group Opera and Ballet Season in March 1965."[19] It is not clear whether he did go on this trip or how wide he cast his net to find opera singers who fitted the racial requirements, but this initiative did not come to fruition. The only document found in the Eoan Group Archive relating to the matter is a letter from Te Wiata in which the singer wrote that he didn't know which Verdi roles he could sing with Eoan.[20]

In the larger political context, 1964 presented a watershed moment in the history of the country when Nelson Mandela was sentenced to life imprisonment during the protracted Rivonia trial. Mandela and nine others were accused of committing sabotage to overthrow the apartheid government.[21] It is during this trial that Mandela delivered his historic speech at the opening of the defense declaring the courts of South Africa invalid and apartheid legislation draconian. He was imprisoned for the next twenty-seven years, during which he became a symbol of the oppressed in the country. In the same year a number of racially mixed suburbs in the vicinity of Cape Town, such as Wynberg, Constantia, Kenilworth, Vasco, Goodwood, and Rondebosch, were declared white residential areas, and thousands of people classified as coloureds were forcibly removed from their homes and relocated to the Cape Flats under the Group Areas Act.[22]

Within the coloured community in the Cape, the heterogeneity of this racial grouping was at the time further articulated in increasingly pronounced differences between social strata or classes, resulting in the continued undermining of political unity in the community. With regard to Eoan, it is safe to say that those participating in Western art formats such as opera, ballet, and drama, as well as the coloured public who attended their performances (few as they may have been), aspired to, if not belonged to, the coloured petty bourgeoisie. This situation may have been different in the 1940s and 1950s, but the association of class with opera production became more pronounced over time. As a result of the National Party's Coloured Preference Policy, which created protected employment of skilled coloured labor, unskilled coloured labor became increasingly poorer. This widening gap resulted in alienation between the coloured petty bourgeoisie and the lower strata of coloured society.[23] Richard van der Ross wrote at the time that "those in the upper strata, aspired to be assimilated with the white middle class."[24] Soon the coloured upper class also eschewed the Eoan Group.

The lack of political unity within the coloured constituency at the time is illustrated in the floundering of its political movements, such as the NEUM, the CPC, and various others that came and went throughout the 1960s. The absence of a strong and unifying political force added to the marginal status the coloured community occupied politically, and it was only when joining forces with the black consciousness movement of the 1970s that they were able to effectively work toward political change.

### THE SIXTH OPERA SEASON

The year 1965 was exceptionally active for Eoan's music section. As usual, Manca planned on a big scale for the season, which he hoped to conclude with a tour to Europe and the United States. In a letter to Cape Town municipal conductor David Tidboald, Manca wrote that Eoan planned to produce at least seven operas and add two new ballets for its next season.[25] These grand plans materialized only in part, and the group's sixth opera season was held in March and April, consisting of four operas; for the first time since 1956, no ballet productions were included as part of the season. Manca's plans to tour abroad were also downscaled to a local tour, and Eoan's second tour of the country took place from June to August, encompassing Johannesburg, Durban, East London, and Port Elizabeth. During the tour the group gave a total of forty-nine performances. In the course of that year its existing repertoire was augmented with three new operatic works—Giuseppe Verdi's *Il Trovatore* and Gaetano Donizetti's *L'Elisir D'Amore*, which were performed during the Cape Town season, and George Bizet's *Carmen*, which was added to the tour program—bringing the total number of works from the operatic canon performed since 1956 to eight operas and one operetta.[26]

The season opened on 18 March and comprised two operas from the group's existing repertoire, Verdi's *La Traviata* and Puccini's *La Bohème*, as well as the first two new productions mentioned above. All operas were directed by Alessandro Rota, who from this year onward not only produced all of Eoan's operas, but also took responsibility for much of the vocal training of principal singers.[27]

The season ran until 17 April, comprising thirty-one performances: one every weekday evening as well as a matinee and evening performance on Saturdays.[28] In a press release, Manca continued to claim, even after a decade of opera production, that Eoan's artists had almost no musical education, no exposure to opera as an art form, and no knowledge of Italian, despite the fact that the group had been performing Italian opera for almost a decade:

The operas will be sung in the Italian language and produced and presented in the Italian tradition. Here again, the immense talents and versatility of our Coloured people come to the fore. It is almost incredible that here are artists who have never seen Italian Opera, have a limited or no knowledge of music, have not had vocal training and cannot speak the Italian language and yet are able to perform opera of a high standard.[29]

These condescending half-truths were accompanied by Manca's lofty idea that Eoan was on a par with opera houses in the West: "This is indeed an ambitious programme equal to seasons presented by the more famous Opera Houses in Europe. Nevertheless, the Eoan Group is proud to bring to Cape Town these very popular operas which are some of the favourites of most opera lovers."[30]

Even though Manca was meticulous in the preservation of all documentation regarding the administration of the group, the artistic and musical side of his personality is virtually absent from the archive. He never seems to have written down why, for instance, he chose to perform Verdi's *La Traviata* so often, and nowhere is there any letter or note discussing the vocal forces he had at his disposal (other than audition reports, which seldom describe voices in more than two words); the quality of the principal singers' voices; or, as one might expect, on what basis he chose the repertoire that was performed at that particular time. Such choices, however, were not arbitrary. Manca's decision to teach the group three new works in the course of 1965 most probably happened in discussion with Alessandro Rota, with whom Manca had worked closely since the 1930s and whose artistic insight he must have trusted. A newspaper advertisement dating back to 1956 illustrates that Manca had already decided a decade before what repertoire he envisaged the group performing. His choices at any particular moment were presumably also based on practicalities such as how much time was available for the group to learn a new work, which singers he had at his disposal, and the popular appeal of a musical work. A fifty-fifty split between new works that had to be learned and repeat performances of repertoire the group was familiar with emerges as a pattern with regard to the repertoire presented in opera seasons, but this still reveals very little about artistic concerns that may have influenced Manca's choices.

Eoan's production of *Il Trovatore*, with which the group opened the season on 18 March, cast Joseph Gabriels in the role of Manrico, Vera Gow as Leonora, Sophia Andrews in the role of Azucena, Benjamin Arendse as Count di Luna, and Susan Arendse as Ines. As usual Eoan's wardrobe mistress,

FIGURE 4.1. Wardrobe Mistress Carmen Sydow in action. Source: Eoan Group Archive.

Carmen Sydow, oversaw the making of the costumes for this production (see figure 4.1). Reviewers and the public were generally in awe of Joseph Gabriels's voice, which "brought the house down," while *Die Burger* praised the lyrical quality of his voice and his excellent intonation, pronunciation, and acting, stating that his musical abilities could be deemed on a par with any tenor performing in Europe or the United States at the time.[31] Sophia Andrews's voice and acting were described as "a revelation" and "an outstanding mezzo-soprano voice," while Vera Gow's "throbbing performance" in the role of Leonora also impressed reviewers.[32] However, light criticism was made of the rest of the cast, stating that the singers did not seem to understand the meaning of the text they were singing and that the vocal quality of some of the principals was inadequate. The reviewer of *Die Burger* also criticized Manca, stating that his tempo choices were unconvincing and his indecisive conducting resulted in many wrong entries by soloists and the orchestra.[33]

*L'Elisir D'Amore* was the second new work on offer during this season, showcasing the tenor Gerald Samaai making his debut in the role of Nemorino and soprano Patricia van Graan partnering as Adina. The choice of this opera buffa confirms Manca's favoring of comic opera alongside the group's other Italian romantic repertoire, a trend confirmed with the addition of Gioacchino Rossini's *Il Barbiere di Siviglia* to Eoan's list in 1969 as well as the many musicals the group performed over the years.

*L'Elisir D'Amore*'s combination of a comical love story with beautiful music that includes the famous and well-loved tenor aria "Una furtiva lagrima" was a delight to Cape Town's audiences, who continued to show their appreciation for Eoan with "prolonged applause."[34] Both principals, Gerald Samaai and Patricia van Graan, received favorable comments from reviewers.[35]

After the season was over, many letters expressing appreciation were received from the public, although responses from individuals on either side of the color line indicated important differences with regard to reception. Erik Chisholm, dean of the College of Music and avid opera composer and producer, wrote to Manca on 19 May 1965:

> Dear Dr. Manca,
> 
> I should have dropped you a line much earlier than this to tell you how much my wife and I enjoyed your thrilling performance at the opening night of *Il Trovatore*.
> 
> I thought the whole performance a triumph. My sincerest congratulations for the wonderful opera season you and Eoan group have just completed: I cannot begin to tell you how much I admire your courage and achievements.[36]

However, a letter from a coloured woman, Mrs. R. Smith, expressed quite different sentiments. She wrote to Manca that "the overwhelming success of the show made up for the hurt that filled me towards those who cannot accept us as part of the human race."[37] At the very least such responses indicate that Eoan's activities were experienced with a deep sense of ambivalence.

During the first decade of Eoan's performance history, a number of soloists established themselves as principal singers. Among them were sopranos

May Abrahamse and Ruth Goodwin, mezzo-soprano Sophia Andrews, tenor Joseph Gabriels, and baritones Lionel Fourie, Benjamin Arendse, and Robert Trussell. In the course of the 1960s a second generation of principals started to emerge, due in part to the departure or death of some of the early principals. Of the initial group, Sophia Andrews, Joseph Gabriels, Benjamin Arendse, and Robert Trussell sang leading roles in the 1965 season, while May Abrahamse did not sing at all due to a throat infection. Although some of the younger principals had been singing minor roles in 1962, for many the 1965 season was their first opportunity to shine in major roles, for which most received favorable attention in the newspapers. The new generation of principals that was to dominate the leading roles well into the 1970s included the tenors Gerald Samaai as Nemorino and Martin Johnson as Belcore in *L'Elisir D'Amore*, and James Momberg as Alfredo and the baritone Cecil Tobin as Germont in *La Traviata*. New and upcoming soprano soloists almost entirely replaced the stars of Eoan's previous season, including Vera Gow as Leonara in *Il Trovatore*, Patricia van Graan as Adina in *L'Elisir D'Amore*, Winifried du Plessis making her debut as Violetta in *La Traviata* and Musetta in *La Bohème*, Yvonne Jansen as Mimi in *La Bohème*, and Susan Arendse as Flora in *La Traviata*. During this season Gordon Jephtas was also training and rehearsing with the group.[38] His roles during the season and the upcoming tour were repetiteur, accompanist, and stage conductor, the only nonwhite person ever to fill these positions in Eoan's history.[39] In rehearsal schedules Manca gave him the title "Maestro Gordon" (he was twenty-two years old at the time) and allowed Jephtas the freedom to rehearse with the group whatever section of the music he felt needed attention.[40]

Other companies in Cape Town also staged opera productions during this time. The UCT Opera Company was still very active despite the existence of CAPAB, and during 1964 and 1965 it staged seven productions, among them Verdi's *Othello*, Giacomo Puccini's *Turandot*, Francis Poulenc's *Carmelittes*, and Raffaello de Banfield's *Lord Byron's Love Letter*.[41] Principal roles were sung by, among others, Gregorio Fiasconaro, Désirée Talbot, Clive Morgan, Gé Korsten, Albie Louw, and Sarita Stern.[42] The opera section of the CAPAB was slow to stage productions. At the bottom of Chisholm's letter to Manca quoted previously, he added by hand, "As for CAPAB . . . ??," indicating that in Chisholm's opinion, as far as opera production was concerned, Eoan competed well if not better than CAPAB. In February 1965, two years after the launch of CAPAB and shortly before Eoan's sixth opera season, the company produced its first opera, Bedrich Smetana's *The Bartered Bride*, in which principal roles were sung by Nellie du Toit, Raymond Nilsson, and Gert Potgieter, with Sarita Stern, Jacobus Bouwer, and Deon Knobel in minor roles.[43] The production was held in the Alhambra Theatre, with the Cape Town Municipal Orchestra conducted by David Tidboald.[44] Reviews of this production were very positive, and CAPAB's opera production grew steadily in the following years.

## THE 1965 TOUR

Eoan's second tour through the Republic of South Africa was undertaken from June to August 1965, and as stated previously, included Johannesburg, Durban, East London, and Port Elizabeth.[45] The program for the tour included the operas presented during the opera season in Cape Town, as well as an addition to Eoan's repertoire, Bizet's *Carmen*.[46]

From the start the tour was beset by problems, cancellations, and disappointments. The degree to which apartheid legislation restricted the group's freedom of movement had increased substantially since its first tour in 1960, resulting in many logistical problems and a host of arrangements that could not be finalized before Eoan's departure from Cape Town. On a grassroots level, formal apartheid had by this time made major inroads into areas that formerly were less regulated. Rules with regard to travel, accommodation, and performances during the tour now required that approval be obtained from various government departments, resulting in endless streams of correspondence. As the Eoan Group Archive illustrates, much of the correspondence concerned petitioning to reverse the denial of requests for the group to perform in certain venues and the restriction of the group's travel plans. Exacerbating these difficulties, the only person who stood a chance of convincing white government officials to make allowances within the restrictive regulations was Manca; requests to government departments that were signed by Sydow were refused. Apart from his role as artistic director of the group, Manca was thus inundated with administrative tasks, but he (as a white person) seemed to be the only one who could effectively negotiate permissions for the group's tour. This situation further reinforced the notion of coloured dependency on white custodianship.

On arrival in Johannesburg the group faced a particularly cold winter, and in addition to the effects of the high altitude and dry winter, the company was affected by flu and colds. Joseph Gabriels, for instance, suffered from laryngitis during most of the tour and did not sing. Since he had a national reputation, a number of concertgoers wrote to Manca afterward expressing their disappointment at missing the opportunity to hear Gabriels's voice.[47]

The Johannesburg season was held at the Civic Theatre, and Eoan had to apply for a permit to perform as a coloured group in a hall designated for whites. Eoan was informed that although the group was allowed to perform in that venue, a permit allowing two concerts in front of a coloured public in the same venue was refused.[48] Eoan's letter of appeal was dismissed, and the group eventually presented only one performance in the coloured suburb Coronationville, on 5 July.[49]

Manca's original plan was to extend the tour to (the then) Rhodesia and Mozambique after completing the performances in Port Elizabeth by the end of August, but this also did not happen.[50] As late as 23 July 1965, while Eoan was already on tour in Johannesburg, the Department of Home Affairs advised the group that passport applications for the whole group would be approved, except for its principal male singer, Joseph Gabriels. No reason was provided why his application had been turned down.[51] Despite an urgent appeal to the secretary of home affairs in Pretoria, no favorable answer was received, and this leg of the tour was canceled.[52]

For its performances in Port Elizabeth, Eoan also had to apply for a permit to perform in the Opera House and for coloured people to attend performances. As late as 7 July, while on its way to Durban, Eoan was informed that although its permit had been granted to perform in the Opera House for white audiences, coloured audiences were not allowed "as the Opera House lacks separate facilities for a non-white audience."[53] The department further added that should Eoan "find a less contentiously situated hall where adequate separate provision for non-white audiences exist, Eoan may submit another application to stage one or more performances by the Group before a non-white (other than Bantu) audience."[54] The facilities in question were separate entrances as well as toilets. Knowing that no other venue in Port Elizabeth existed that could accommodate an opera performance, the group found this situation particularly difficult. Ismail Sydow again wrote an urgent letter of appeal, addressed to the secretary of coloured affairs in Cape Town:

> If there is to be no performance to non-whites (other than Bantu) in Port Elizabeth, the Group's relations with the coloured population of Port Elizabeth are likely to be prejudiced. I would particularly like to point out

that there is no suitable hotel accommodation for the cast and I am accordingly obliged to arrange accommodation for 62 non-white members with private families in Port Elizabeth and I very much fear that if I have to advise the coloured population of Port Elizabeth that there will be no performance of any of our operas for them I may not secure the necessary accommodation and will accordingly not be able to perform in Port Elizabeth at all.[55]

In a letter to Murray Bisset (an Eoan Group trustee), Manca reflected on the host of problems the group had experienced: "When I started out on this tour I was fully aware of the many difficulties and handicaps both Ismail and I would have to face, but it seems that on this occasion they have been more than thousandfold."[56] Coloured attendance at performances on this tour was also considerably lower than in 1960, illustrating the degree to which Eoan's tarnished political reputation had spread throughout the coloured community in the country. Bisset also received a letter from Hymie Udwin, who assisted with arrangements in Johannesburg, that illustrated the extent to which the coloured community withdrew support: "Non-European support was negligible. It is not for me to enter into the whys and wherefores of the obvious boycott, but this attitude is surely tragic."[57] The lack of coloured attendance at concerts in Durban was even discussed in the newspaper—"A rift has developed between the Coloured people of Durban and the Eoan Group"—although in this article Sydow put the blame on the government's late granting of a permit for coloureds to attend the performances.[58]

Reviews of the tour's performances were generally positive. In Johannesburg soprano Winifred du Plessis impressed reviewers with her rendition of Violetta in *La Traviata*, which she sang alongside Gerald Samaai's Alfredo. The local newspaper reported: "What amazing purity of intonation and certainty of pitch the young Cape Town soprano, Winifred du Plessis, has in the difficult role of Violetta!"[59] Another reviewer added that "her mezzo-voce and pianissimo is delightful. Her technique is of such quality that the colour of her voice stays the same in all registers. It is like a silver thread spun throughout her range."[60] Many other newspaper reviews carried laudatory headlines, such as "Another Outstanding Opera," "Triumph for Cape Town Violetta," "A Colourful Trovatore," "Eoan at Its Best in High Comedy," and "Il Trovatore Gives Us a Star."[61]

Yet for the first time in Eoan's performance history, a production was met with some serious critique, too. The production of *Carmen* was less successful, and one critic even stated that it "smacked all too coyly of musical comedy rather than Bizet's fiery portrayal of Espana."[62] The Eoan Group Archive

FIGURE 4.2. Alessandro Rota, Gordon Jephtas, and Joseph Manca discussing a production. Photo by Cloete Breytenbach.

also contains a four-page document, presumably drawn up by the producer, Alessandro Rota, or the repetiteur, Gordon Jephtas (see figure 4.2), containing commentary on the group's inadequacy in creating a lively and charged atmosphere for this production. It comments, for instance, on inappropriate acting and bad singing by principal singers and notes that Vera Gow was unconvincing in portraying a sexually aggressive and bad-tempered Carmen. The report concluded that the entire production had to be acted and sung with much more vigor, pace, and excitement in order to be successful.[63] These conditions were apparently not met, and the group never attempted a repeat performance of *Carmen* in Cape Town, making it the only opera in the repertoire that Eoan never sang in the Cape Town City Hall.

Notwithstanding the many logistical problems resulting from the prohibitive apartheid laws, the lack of coloured support, and a number of critical reviews, Manca regarded the tour on the whole as another artistic success. Financially, however, it was a disaster and landed the group in major financial difficulties.[64] The overdraft on Eoan's bank account by year-end amounted to ZAR34,374. Manca wrote that "regrettably, in spite of the great artistic success of this tour, financially it proved to be a loss—a most inexplicable fact."[65] As if to soften the blow, he added:

> Until 1965 the Eoan Group has had to finance itself from its own work and it has been and still is a very onerous undertaking to meet the growing financial requirements of an organisation such as the Eoan Group which in addition to being a Cultural Institution is also a welfare organisation. In this respect the Eoan Group is "unique" and must be, if it is not already, one of the few organisations in the world which can present an annual opera season without financial subsidies. This can only be achieved due to the unselfish dedication of its Directors, Workers, Artists and members.[66]

It is clear from documentation in the archive that it had become impossible to meet the spiraling financial demands of an ambitious and ever-growing opera company with the ZAR2,000 annual grant the group received from the City Council and the meager profits made from ticket sales. Although the Eoan Group Trust had been launched in order to stabilize Eoan's finances, consistent and sufficient financial support had not materialized, and the task of obtaining funds remained squarely in the hands of Manca and Sydow. Financial support from the coloured community was nonexistent, and during a special meeting at the end of 1965, Eoan decided to reapply for financial assistance from the DCA.[67] From 1966 onward, Eoan was granted financial support, and in so doing the group became further entangled in an ever-tightening political web that, in retrospect, cost it dearly. From this time onward, the group also complied with apartheid regulations and annually applied for a permit to perform its opera season in the City Hall to mixed audiences, submitting to the political compromise it had refused to make in 1957.[68]

## EXIT DISTRICT SIX

Eoan's acceptance of government funding had immediate implications, highlighting the growing divide between management decisions and the day-to-day experiences of the coloured citizen. The fact that the government now exercised firm control by providing funding is illustrated by Eoan's performance of *La Traviata* as part of the 1966 Republic Festival in Cape Town, celebrating the fifth anniversary of the Republic of South Africa.[69] Manca described the event in his customary superlatives, seemingly in awe of the exclusivity of this performance, characterized by the attendance of high-ranking (white) officials and invited guests: "As its contribution towards the celebration for the 1966 Republic Festival, the Eoan Group presented the

Italian Opera *La Traviata* to an invited Non-White audience. This presentation was under the aegis of the DCA and the performance was graced with the presence of the Minister for Coloured Affairs, the Hon. Mr. Marais Viljoen who after the performance came back stage and personally thanked the Eoan Group Artists for the magnificent performance."[70]

In the same year the Group Areas Act was extended to District Six when the entire suburb, housing more than sixty thousand people, was declared a white area in February. Although forced removals, affecting Eoan members as well as the group's support base within the coloured community, had been ongoing for a number of years, the zoning of District Six as a white area hit at the heart of the coloured community. In hindsight it is clear that the destruction of District Six carried the symbolic significance of the destruction of a place the coloured community identified as "home," the repercussions of which are still felt today. Within the following decade all of District Six's inhabitants, as well as Eoan's headquarters at 302 Hanover Street, had been moved to the Cape Flats and the houses flattened by bulldozers.

Manca's disregard for the effects of this situation on group members is astonishing, as is his seeming lack of understanding or empathy. Nowhere in the archive can one find evidence that Manca ever entertained the idea that apartheid was wrong, that the system disempowered and dehumanized group members, or that the system had a detrimental effect on the morale of the group or its artistic standards. Even subtle textual phrasing, choice of words, and references between the lines are completely absent. His writing continues to be littered with convoluted phrases of praise and ambition, with occasional references to the fact that the system was inconvenient with regard to practical arrangements. Although Manca as a person may not have been prone to the expression of personal feelings, especially not on paper or in formal correspondence, nowhere does one find any trace of empathy for those who were affected by draconian apartheid legislation. Neither is there any evidence of an awareness on his part of his privileged position as a white person. In fact, the deafening silence in the archive with regard to anything that questioned apartheid and the way its power relations played out in the group is testimony to the repression of the lived experience of its members. The gap between the reality of the political environment and the premises on which Eoan was managed is starkly illustrated by management's incomprehension with regard to dwindling support for the group. Not only did many Eoan members lose their homes when District Six was earmarked for white occupation, but Eoan itself had to give up its premises in Hanover Street, and many supporters and

FIGURE 4.3. Ismail Sydow. Source: Eoan Group Archive.

members had left the organization by this time. The same strangely out-of-touch register was sounded by the Eoan Group chairman, Ismail Sydow (see figure 4.3), when he lamented in his chairman's report for the 1966 annual general meeting (AGM): "I now appeal to all our ex-groupers, our foundation members, our dancing girls, drama members and all music and choir members to return to the fold—the Eoan Group is one big family and we rejoice in the return of our prodigal brothers and sisters."[71]

It is moments such as these that make one wonder why Eoan's members continued to participate in opera production at all and what it meant to them in their personal circumstances. In a letter written to May Abrahamse in August 1966, Gordon Jephtas provided a perspective that speaks to this. Although Jephtas seldom commented on politics, he was acutely aware of his position as a disenfranchised artist, not only as a coloured person in South Africa but also as a foreigner in Europe. At this stage he was attending Italian-language studies in Perugia, Italy, and was pondering whether he should come back to South Africa and work with Eoan's singers or stay in

Europe to see if he could manage a career there. Although he was aware of the growing divide between himself and many singers in the group with regard to artistic expectations, he wrote that "deep down, the only responsibility that I feel strongly, is an allegiance to the singers. Speaking purely objectively, I think they have so much talent which can produce worthwhile results and realizing just how much this music-making means to them in the midst of oppression makes me want to continue working with them—if only to produce these few hours of escape from the brutality of the reality. Perhaps this is the strongest link that is pulling me homewards."[72]

Jephtas did return to South Africa on several occasions throughout the 1960s and 1970s and worked with some of Eoan's principal singers, but besides the lack of job opportunities at home, the artistic ethos within the group proved to be a great source of frustration for him. From the correspondence with Abrahamse it is clear that the greatest of these frustrations was Manca's stunted artistic sensibility and what Jephtas regarded as the inflated self-images of both Manca and a number of principal singers. Of Manca's comparisons between Eoan and La Scala or "the famous opera houses of Europe," referred to previously in this book, Jephtas commented that "it wouldn't cost Manca anything to think that he is on par with La Scala. But Scala is Scala and Eoan is Eoan. One cannot compare cognac with coca-cola, because even though both are drinkable, they're not nearly the same."[73] Furthermore, throughout his correspondence with Abrahamse, the phrase "Manca-mentality" was used to refer to insufficient preparation for concerts and lack of musical finesse, circumstances, Jephtas added, that were rather common in Europe as well. He ended the letter by stating that "perhaps my greatest disappointment in the group has been that Manca never was the sort of person I could turn to with my purely musical problems and in-comprehensions."[74]

The Eoan Group Archive may be voluminous, but it also has significant discontinuities. It is only from 1966 onward that we find minutes of Eoan's executive committee meetings and AGMs. These documents are rich sources of behind-the-scenes information that provides overviews of its problems, reflects the attitude of management toward key issues confronting the group, summarizes earlier decisions, and between the lines, gives an indication of issues that were considered out of bounds for discussion. The minutes of the 32nd AGM, held in September 1966, are particularly rich in this regard, and much can be gleaned regarding future plans for the group as well as concerns regarding the group's standing within society.[75] From the chairman's report, written by Ismail Sydow, it emerged that plans had been afoot for some time to restructure the group with the aim of focusing on education in the arts on a broader scale. The idea was to start a ballet, drama, music, and opera school; launch a boys' club; start pottery, sculpture, and painting classes; add more nursery classes; and introduce business education as a course that could be attended by the (coloured) public.[76] At this point the group was aware that it would have to give up the Ochberg Hall in District Six, and plans were announced that new premises in Athlone had already been allocated to the group by the Cape Town municipality. The group knew that it would have to relocate to the Cape Flats and planned to start afresh by implementing the new education initiatives. Although the minutes do not mention how and where the group planned to obtain funds to pay for a new building or where it would be sourcing funds to afford the "qualified teachers" it hoped to employ, the concern for much-needed education and job creation is apparent. The minutes further state that the establishment of a new center would "provide 1) the creation of professional careers for our many artists, 2) serve as a training college, and 3) employment for our people in the promotion of the performing and non-performing arts and the general uplift of our community."[77] Within the greater context of apartheid as a disempowering superstructure, these laudable initiatives were, however, doomed to fail.

The minutes furthermore serve as a reminder of the activities of the group that did not necessarily reach the newspapers. An important part of Eoan's mandate was to function as a welfare organization, and the group had been running nursery schools since its inception. Throughout the years this activity remained part of Eoan's mission and was reported on at each AGM. The group also had branches all over the peninsula where ballet was taught and where group volunteers and parents worked tirelessly for "the promotion of ballet among our children."[78] On the production level, ballet performances had suffered a slump since the 1962 production of *The Square*, despite the fact that ballet used to be a core activity of the group throughout the 1940s and 1950s. The minutes report that thousands of children had received elementary ballet training via the Eoan Group, but most of them had disappeared from the group. A similar scenario applied to the drama department, which had its last show in 1963.[79] The dominance of the music section with regard to output and subsequent income is clearly stated in these minutes, and praise is heaped on this department and its achievements.[80]

The precarious state of the group's finances received much attention in the report. Although it was clear that the group could not continue functioning on the dwindling revenue from the music section, management's decision to reapply for funds from the DCA at the end of 1965 had to be justified to members at this AGM. The report attempted to do this by emphasizing the educational goals of the group rather than its arts production and stated that the financing of education was the responsibility of the government. However, it stubbornly ignored the fact that the group was primarily perceived by the government as well as the coloured community as an arts organization and that the bulk of its funding applications was earmarked for opera production. This situation is an illustration of the difficulties that arise when a humanitarian organization morphs into an arts company without sufficient acknowledgment by management that its goals have in reality changed and that former structures will not suffice. The lack of funds was further compounded by poor support from the coloured community: "The great lack of support given us by our community is notoriously well known. Appeals for funds fall on deaf ears; members of our teaching and professional section not only do not support us, but openly oppose us in our voluntary labours for the advancement of our people."[81] Here, too, it is clear that Eoan's management took cognizance of the lack of community support but failed to acknowledge what caused such withdrawal, and the steps taken to remedy the financial situation (i.e., applying for funds from the DCA) exacerbated rather than alleviated the withdrawal of community support. Sydow's reference to those in the teaching profession in the preceding statement is significant. Tertiary education possibilities for coloureds were restricted during the apartheid era, and many educated people ended up in the teaching profession. The Teacher's League of South Africa (TLSA), a body representing mainly coloured teachers, had for many years been openly critical of Eoan. A number of Eoan singers happened to be teachers as well. Cecil Tobin, one of the group's principal baritones, was a school principal, while tenor Gerald Samaai was a teacher. In an interview, Samaai described the impossible situation that everyone who worked in government institutions, including all teachers, were in. His colleagues at work said to him, "you are accepting the grant from Coloured Affairs, so we don't support you anymore."[82] He would in turn question the source of their salaries, which were also paid by the DCA. They felt they had no option and were forced to accept this situation. Despite the logic of his counterargument that the Eoan Group was similarly forced to accept funding from the DCA, it did little to convince liberal-minded teachers that Eoan needed government funding in order to produce any of the arts.[83] The TLSA remained critical of the group throughout the apartheid era. In hindsight, one has to question whether it would have been possible to salvage the group's reputation within the community without risking a complete cessation of activities. Eoan's acceptance of government funding during the 1940s and early 1950s had already tainted its reputation, and despite its financial independence between 1957 and 1965, the stigma stuck. Sydow's words at the inauguration of the Eoan Group Trust, namely that no arts organization in the world operates without subsidies, was the hard reality the group had to deal with and illustrates the impossible situation the group was in. Of this Samaai said that "we had to take the grant, otherwise we couldn't have performed anything. [We] knew that should [we] not take it, it's a slow death."[84] In reality, however, taking the money was also a "slow death."

On 6 September 1966, South Africa's prime minister and the architect of apartheid, Hendrik Verwoerd, was assassinated by a parliamentary messenger, Dimitri Tsafendas.[85] Newspapers of the 1960s bear witness to the steady rollout of apartheid legislation and the painful rupture of South African society at the hands of that system. Plentiful evidence can be found of racially integrated sections of society that were suddenly forced apart and where the burden of loss was carried by the coloured community. This pertained not only to housing in residential areas, which had been racially mixed for decades, but also to activities such as sports and recreation. The *Cape Argus* of 23 March 1965, for example, reported that "because of the government's clampdown on multi-racial sports meetings, the Western Province Cycling Union (a non-White body) will be without the usual White officials when it holds its championships on Saturday and Coloured cyclists will not begin their races to the sound of the customary starter's pistol."[86] The sport of boxing was clearly a racially integrated sector that did its utmost to stay that way. A few days later the *Cape Argus* reported that "last minute permits were issued today authorizing non-Whites and Chinese to attend a boxing tournament between well-known South African and overseas African boxers at a venue in a White area in Durban."[87] Unequal remuneration within the teaching profession was discussed in an article on the same page: "Coloured teachers with the same qualifications as White teachers could not yet be paid the same salaries."[88] The evils of apartheid have been elaborated on in many narratives before this one, but a cursory read-through of the newspapers of the time confirms how legislated racial segregation disempowered and impoverished South Africans who were not white.

## THE SEVENTH OPERA SEASON

In May 1967 Ismail and Carmen Sydow traveled to London to visit their daughter Didi.[89] Four years earlier Didi had been sponsored by the Eoan Group to study ballet in London; by this time she had a professional dancing career with the Royal Ballet. They also met with Gordon Jephtas, who was studying at the London Opera Centre at the time. During this time Sydow wrote several letters to Manca that have been preserved in the archive. From these letters it is clear that one of Sydow's main objectives for this trip was to convince Jephtas to return to South Africa and join Manca in directing the group for the upcoming season. At the time, Manca was almost sixty years old and had been hoping that Jephtas would become his successor as Eoan's musical director. It seems that both Manca and Sydow were at this time verbally informed that a Council for Culture and Recreation was to be created for the coloured population as an equivalent to the whites-only PACs. It is clear from the correspondence that they anticipated an institution with equal state funding and the possibilities for professional careers for Eoan's singers, a situation in which they would need an artist of the caliber of Jephtas. It also seems that they thought, however naively, that such a council would be the end of their financial troubles. Sydow reported to Manca that Jephtas had many opportunities in England, had been offered a six-month position in Cardiff, Wales, and was not yet in a position to return home to the Eoan Group. Sydow explained the failed negotiation to Manca on 5 June:

> I told Gordon that he must think very hard and carefully about his future and that if he came home the future will be secured forever and that he will earn the same money but with a better position. He does understand but he feels as long as he is here he can learn a lot more. However, after a long talk with him by Didi, John, Mrs. Sydow and myself the whole of yesterday, he has asked us to give him the chance to go to Cardiff.[90]

When Jephtas's decision not to return to South Africa was final, Sydow wrote to Manca on 29 June 1967. The tone of this letter is endearing and (ironically) indicates that these two men from different races had a long-standing and strong bond that included their single-minded conviction that there was only one way for the group to survive into the future: opera production in the way it had been done so far. The letter also illustrates that Sydow anticipated Manca's disappointment at not getting his way:

Dear Brother Yusuf,[91]

I must tell you that everything as far as the Group's future is concerned seems very bright, although one thing did not come out the way I wanted. That is for Gordon to come with me, but God knows best, he alone will give us Gordon at the right time. Gordon is going to be to you what you want him to be to you and the Group. In the mean time for a year we will have to be patient and wait, I assure you that you will have your greatest wish because Gordon will come with a vast knowledge that will bring the Group up to a very high standard. Not that it is not high already, but he will be able to help you to build it so that it will be ready for the Arts Council. Please believe me when I say that you will get everything that you wish for the group, only be patient and let us wait one more year.

Please work hard on the forthcoming opera season and have faith. It is going to be an all-round successful season. God wants you to make this last struggle alone so that he can be proud of you and after this God will give you help by giving you young Gordon, fully capable and qualified to carry at least half of your burden.[92]

Apart from Manca's obvious need for support in his position as musical director of Eoan, the letter suggests that he had begun to find the responsibility for Eoan's artistic performances a heavy burden; the letter even suggests that Manca was nearing the end of his tether.[93] This stands in sharp contrast to how former members remember the issue of Manca's succession. Virginia Davids and Phillip Swales, principal singers for Eoan during the 1970s, are among the many former members who are of the opinion that there were no contingency plans at all.[94] Yet references to Jephtas as Manca's successor appeared in the press as early as 1958.[95] Despite Manca's wish to see Jephtas as his successor, neither he nor others within the organization conceived of Manca's position in a more differentiated way by, for instance, entrusting administration or finance to someone other than the artistic director. Manca controlled most of what was going on in the group, including administration, finance, and artistic direction, and seems to have micromanaged group activities to such an extent that former members recalled that without his permission, nothing happened.[96] It is clear from the archive as well as from interviews with former members that no other person within the group was ever seriously considered for the position, and nobody was trained to take over managerial or administrative responsibilities. In the minds of Manca and others within the group, Jephtas probably embodied that mythical person, the artist who would keep the "glory days" of opera production alive and would solve all their problems through his perceived musical excellence. Yet in practical terms, no actual measures were put in place to provide the infrastructure for a smooth transition. In his letters to May Abrahamse, Jephtas indeed emerges as a highly skilled and sensitive artist who had superior abilities, yet whose weakness was routine administration.

Sydow's other mission during this visit to Europe was successful. He held meetings with the Bernard van Leer Foundation in The Netherlands, from whom he was able to secure a donation of R34,000 toward the building costs for the Joseph Stone Auditorium in 1969.[97]

Eoan's seventh opera season was held in September 1967 in the Cape Town City Hall. The program comprised three operas: Puccini's *Madame Butterfly*, Verdi's *La Traviata*, and Donizetti's *L'Elisir D'Amore*.[98] This time, all works were repeat performances of repertoire the group was familiar with. Vera Gow made a triumphant appearance as the star soprano, although reviews also praised the other principal singers, such as May Abrahamse, Winifried du Plessis, Patricia van Graan, Sophia Andrews, and Susan Arendse. Judging by the reviews, the group had lost none of its enchantment for the white, opera-loving public. Hans Kramer wrote in the *Cape Times*:

> On Saturday night salvoes of applause punctuated the performance at the City Hall of Verdi's *La Traviata*. Taking into consideration the tremendous overall achievement, which Capetonians have come to expect of the Eoan Group, this night was Vera Gow's, whose tragic Violetta was, without a doubt, one of the best operatic performances seen here.
>
> In Vera Gow the Eoan Group has a star of the first order. Her pure and beautiful soprano at all times was a pleasure to listen to, for its sustained quality throughout an arduous role, which makes the greatest demands, even on the seasoned performer. Her acting was of rare and natural quality, matching the singing to perfection. This performance will long linger in the memory.[99]

Kramer reviewed the entire season for the *Cape Times* and stated that the group's production of *L'Elisir D'Amore* "won rousing acclaim from another capacity audience" and *Madama Butterfly* has become "one of the group's finest achievements."[100] *Die Burger* was of the opinion that May Abrahamse and Benjamin Arendse possessed the "scarce talent" of singers who can also act and reported that, due to public demand, Eoan's opera season was yet again extended for another few weeks.[101] Principal tenor James Momberg's rendition of "Una furtiva lagrima" from *L'Elisir D'Amore* was singled out as one of this season's main attractions.[102]

### RETURN TO MUSICALS

During the late 1960s the group returned to the production of musicals. Before Eoan's first opera performance in 1956, the group had been performing operettas and musicals, and the lighter genres of opera had been popular with the group over the years. Its first operetta was a production of *A Slave in Araby* in 1949, which starred May Abrahamse as a very young soprano. During the 1950s nine more followed: *Hong Kong* (performed in 1950), *The Maid of the Mountains* (1951), *The Gypsy Princess* (1953), *Magyar Melody* (1954), *Zip Goes a Million* and *The Mikado* (both in 1956), *Maritza* (1957), *Rose Marie* (1958), and *Rio Rita* (1959). In 1962 the group produced the operetta *Die Fledermaus*, and in 1964 the members sang the chorus parts for the Cape Town production of *Showboat*, which was produced by the Johannesburg Operatic Society and was on tour throughout the country. However, the shift from light opera to serious opera in 1956 was an important step in Eoan's artistic aspirations to become an opera company.

During the late 1960s and early 1970s a number of important American musicals became part of Eoan's repertoire. During this time the Cape Town lawyer and theater producer David Bloomberg became actively involved with Eoan and its productions.[103] Not only was Bloomberg a trustee on the Eoan Group Trust, but he was also able to secure the performing rights to three American musicals for Eoan, despite the cultural boycotts that were in place against South Africa. Thus the group added more artistic "firsts" to its already impressive list of cultural achievements, as it was the first South African group in the country to perform *Oklahoma!* (in January 1967), *South Pacific* (in March 1968), and *Carmen Jones* (in September 1970).

Bloomberg had close ties with theater producers in the United States and persuaded the New York producer Stanley Waren to come to Cape Town to direct Eoan's South African premiere of Richard Rodgers and Oscar Hammerstein's *Oklahoma!*[104] Waren's wife, Florence, a dancer who originated from Johannesburg, was responsible for the choreography. The composer Rodgers and librettist Hammerstein II had created a string of musicals for production on Broadway during the 1940s and 1950s, works that have enjoyed huge popularity and continuous performances all over the world ever since. *Oklahoma!*, first produced in 1943, was the duo's first collaborative effort. Hammerstein was an old hand in the industry and was the librettist for other musicals that Eoan had performed in earlier years (*Rose Marie* and *Showboat*). The story of *Oklahoma!* concerns the cowboy Curly McLain (sung in Eoan's production by Martin Johnson) and his love for the farm girl Laurey Williams (sung by Patricia van Graan), while a secondary romance develops between Will Parker (sung by Rupaire Koopman) and his flirtatious fiancée, Ado Annie (Winifried du Plessis). A standard feature of Broadway musicals is the inclusion of a number of dances, and *Oklahoma!* was no exception. Florence Waren's choreography received special attention in reviews.[105]

The musical was to be performed in the Alhambra Theatre in the city center, which had a capacity of two thousand seats. The Alhambra was, however, a "whites-only building," and no permission was given for coloureds to attend these performances. Bloomberg tried to negotiate on behalf of Eoan, because this issue clearly influenced the morale of the group. In a letter to Manca, Bloomberg wrote:

> I am not allowing the matter to rest there and am causing urgent representations to be made to the Honourable W. A. Maree, Minister of Community Development. In the interim I think it is important that news of the permit being refused does not leak out. There will be far greater chance of the Minister reversing the Department's decision if it can be shown that this will not be an embarrassment to the Department. Also, there is no reason for members of the Group to become depressed unnecessarily.[106]

However, despite Bloomberg's influential position, the minister did not reverse his decision, and Eoan had to schedule performances for the coloured public elsewhere. In the end eleven performances were scheduled between 19 and 28 January for the white public in the Alhambra and two for the coloured public in the Luxurama in the coloured suburb of Wynberg (fifteen kilometers [over nine miles] outside of town), on 31 January and 1 February.[107] *Die Burger* described the production as "ambitious" and "enjoyable."[108] The critic for the *Cape Argus*, Owen Williams, had some reservations, stating that "at times they seemed a little inhibited and that they could have given more rein to their natural verve. In general one can say that their singing was far superior [to] their acting."[109]

Besides producing *Oklahoma!* with Eoan during this year, Waren also worked with other (white) theater productions, and upon returning to the

United States he described his experiences in an article titled "Theatre in South Africa." His observations concerned the effects of the artistic isolation in which local theater in all of South Africa was operating and the fact that "government policy is not helping to foster an indigenous drama dealing with South African problems."[110] About Eoan, he noted that the group members were "particularly talented" but that their "development is hindered by lack of professional contact with Europeans and by lack of playing opportunities."[111]

The following year, Manca asked Bloomberg to produce *South Pacific* with Eoan in March 1968. For Bloomberg this was his first musical production, and it turned out to be the biggest financial success of Eoan's entire production history.[112] As was the case with *Showboat*, the plot of this musical centers on the issue of racially mixed relationships and the problems caused by prejudice against such unions and their resulting offspring. The story concerns an American nurse (Nellie Forbush, sung in this production by Vera Gow) stationed on a South Pacific island during World War II. She falls in love with an expatriate French plantation owner (Emile de Becque, sung by Benjamin Arendse) but struggles to accept his French Polynesian children. Another romance, between an American lieutenant (Luther Billis, sung by Allie Sydow) and a young woman from Vietnam (Bloody Mary, sung by Sophia Andrews), explores the lieutenant's fears of the consequences should he marry his Asian sweetheart.

The musical was performed in the Alhambra Theatre in the city center, and all ten performances sold out. No permission was given for coloured audiences to attend, despite Bloomberg's best efforts. This production also was moved to the Luxurama Theatre in Wynberg for seven performances for the coloured public, after which it moved back to the Alhambra for another five performances for the white public. According to Bloomberg, about fifty thousand Capetonians had seen the musical by the end of that season.[113] The reviews were even more enthusiastic than for previous Eoan productions. Owen Williams of the *Cape Argus* wrote: "It was a splendid piece of work, one of the milestones in Cape Town theatre history. It is a lavishly mounted, beautifully sung, crisply directed version of this Rodgers and Hammerstein work, one of the classics among American musicals. For one thing, it tells a strong story, and unashamedly, it has a message. The story is of love, the message is of the evils of race discrimination."[114]

The "message" to which Williams referred illustrated the absurdity and inconsistencies of the South African political system and its administration at that time. While no permission was given for the coloured public to attend performances in the Alhambra, the lyrics of some of the songs exposed intolerance across racial borders. The issue of racial prejudice is candidly explored throughout the musical, most controversially in the song "You've Got to Be Carefully Taught." The irony and potentially explosive content of these songs seem not to have registered with government officials responsible for state censorship, despite some of them having attended the performances, and illustrated that government was not really interested in the content of arts production, only in the skin color of those who were onstage or those who were in the audience.[115] In his autobiography, *My Times*, Bloomberg lamented that the message of the song had made no impact on officialdom. A planned tour of this musical to Johannesburg was stillborn when the government refused permission for Eoan (as a coloured cast) to perform in the Civic Theatre, the only venue at the time that could stage the production.[116]

Reviews throughout the run were extremely positive, with Vera Gow and Sophia Andrews emerging as star entertainers of this production, and Benjamin Arendse, Martin Johnson, and Allie Sydow being given credit for their performances. Terry Herbst of the *Cape Times* described the production as a "hit which the Eoan Group will remember as the show that helped restore its artistic reputation in the field of musical comedy."[117] Ben de Kock of *Die Burger* lauded it as a triumph that pointed to the genre that actually suited Eoan best.[118] Although the reviewer does not elaborate on this statement, it does beg the question whether he thought opera as a genre did not really suit the group and why he thought so.

The rehearsal schedules for this musical illustrate the grueling practice routines the group had grown accustomed to over the years. Practice sessions were scheduled for every weekday evening from 7:45 p.m. to 10:00 p.m., Saturday afternoon from 2:30 p.m. to 5:30 p.m., and Sunday from 3:00 p.m. to 6:00 p.m. Starting six weeks before opening night, on Monday, 8 January 1968, rehearsals ran until Wednesday 28 February without a single day's break. The rehearsal schedule in the Eoan Group Archive also includes this comment: "NO-ONE MUST MISS REHEARSALS."[119] Bloomberg had much admiration for the members of the Eoan group and noted: "It was difficult to appreciate that those who were attaining professional standards were by day ordinary workers in the city. While some were teachers, the majority were maids, messengers, labourers, factory hands and clerical workers, yet all were imbued with the same spirit—to give of their best and achieve excellence."[120]

The political landscape of the time was strangely quiet. Today it is easy to forget how effectively the apartheid government suppressed resistance against the status quo and quashed any sign (on the surface at least) of rebellion. The African National Congress and the Pan Africanist Congress were banned, their leaders were jailed or in exile. and media coverage of antiapartheid activities was heavily censored. Books expressing alternative political or societal ideas such as communism or socialism were generally not available; if they did appear, censors removed them from book stores. Among white society the political Left was almost nonexistent, and the party that opposed apartheid in government structures, the Progressive Federal Party, only came into existence a decade later. However, following the 1968 student rebellions in Europe and the United States, a similar uprising occurred on the University of Cape Town campus, in response to the government's interference when a lecturer appointed to UCT's Social Anthropology Department was fired because he was black.[121] Small as this uprising was in numbers, it was the first of a growing student resistance that over time spread to other universities and intensified in the decades after this event. It is important to keep in mind that during this time Eoan continued to engage with opera and other Western art forms in a society where apartheid law and order and a fake and strange sense of calm were maintained at any cost.

Following Eoan's successful production of *South Pacific*, the eighth opera season was planned for October 1968. The program this time was to include Verdi's *La Traviata* and *Rigoletto* as well as a new addition to the repertoire, Rossini's *Il Barbiere di Siviglia*.[122] On the organizational side, matters did not go smoothly. Manca had just experienced a very satisfactory season of Eoan's *South Pacific* in the Alhambra Theatre and tried to negotiate some performances of the opera season in this venue. The Alhambra was a "whites-only venue," and a permit had to be obtained to perform there. Eoan now also had to apply for a permit to perform for mixed audiences in the City Hall (see an example, figure 4.4). Due to the possible change in venue, the performance dates for the opera season were revised several times. The Eoan Group Archive also holds copies of an unusually large number of letters Manca wrote to Eoan members regarding absenteeism from rehearsals, while members in return complained of heavy workloads and limited time.[123] It was also at this time that many members were relocated to the coloured suburbs of Athlone, Bonteheuvel, and Heideveld, which were all approximately fifteen kilometers (over nine miles) away from District Six. Traveling the extra distance for rehearsals became an added burden, as the majority of members did not own cars and had to rely on public transport. Rehearsing at night after a full day's work became much more difficult.

G.P.-S.735381—1966-67—100-150. S.    G.C. 188

REPUBLIEK VAN SUID-AFRIKA.  REPUBLIC OF SOUTH AFRICA.

Lêer No.
File No. 32/1/4584/4

DEPARTEMENT VAN GEMEENSKAPSBOU.
DEPARTMENT OF COMMUNITY DEVELOPMENT.

## PERMIT.   06352

[Artikel 18 van die Wet op Groepsgebiede, 1957 (Wet No. 77 van 1957)].
[Section 21 of the Group Areas Act, 1966 Act No. 38 of 1966]

Uitgereik op las van die Minister/Minister se gedelegeerde* handelende ingevolge 'n delegasie van bevoegdhede
*Issued by direction of the* ~~Minister~~ *Minister's delegate* acting under a delegation of powers in terms of section twenty-two of
kragtens artikel *negentien* van die Wet op Groepsgebiede, 1957 (Wet No. 77 van 1957).
*the Group Areas Act,* 1966 *Act No.* 38 *of* 1966

1. Uitgereik aan
   *Issued to*
   
   MEMBERS OF THE COLOURED GROUP AS INDICATED IN PARAGRAPH 4.

2. Doel waarvoor uitgereik to lease and occupy on 26th, 27th & 31st August, 1968;
   *Purpose for which issued*
   1st, 3rd, 7th to 10th, 16th to 18th, 21st 22nd, & 30th September 1968;
   1st, 3rd, 5th to 13th, 16th to 31st October, 1968; 1st & 2nd Nov. 1968,
   for the purpose of rehearsing and presenting three operas during the
   Eoan Group's 1968 Opera Season.

3. Beskrywing van grond of perseel
   *Description of land or premises*
   
   CITY HALL, CAPE TOWN.

4. Voorwaardes waaraan hierdie permit onderworpe is
   *Conditions to which this permit is subject*
   
   (a) The number of Coloureds that may be admitted to the operas each night shall not exceed the number of seats allocated to those Coloureds who attend the Municipal symphony concerts;
   
   (b) The seats allocated to Coloureds who attend the Municipal symphony concerts shall be used by the Coloureds who attend the operas.
   
   (c) Separate entrances, exits, ticket boxes and toilet facilities shall be used by Whites and Coloureds.

5. In die geval van 'n verkryging van onroerende goed of die okkupasie van grond of 'n perseel verval hierdie permit
   *In the case of the acquisition of immovable property or the occupation of land or premises this permit will lapse if the*
   as die betrokke onroerende goed nie verkry of die grond of perseel nie ingevolge die permit geokkupeer word binne
   *immovable property concerned is not acquired or the land or premises occupied in terms of this permit within*
   _____ vanaf die datum hiervan nie.
   *from the date hereof.*

Plek       KAAPSTAD/CAPE TOWN            Gemagtigde Uitreikingsbeampte.
*Place*                                  *Authorized Issuing Officer.*
Datum      27-5-1968
           DEPT. OF COMMUNITY DEVELOPMENT
           DIE STREEKVERTEENWOORDIGER
           PRIVAATSAK/PRIVATE BAG 9027
           THE REGIONAL REPRESENTATIVE

*Skrap wat nie van toepassing is nie.
Delete whatever is not applicable.

FIGURE 4.4. Example of a permit issued to Eoan for performing to mixed audiences. Source: Eoan Group Archive.

One week before the season was due to start, Manca, Rota, and Sydow decided to cancel the season altogether. This course of action was unprecedented in Eoan's history and symptomatic of larger underlying problems. In a letter to the town clerk, Sydow explained that the organizers felt the cast was insufficiently prepared and that a bad performance would be worse than no performance at all. He further elaborated that their preparations had been hindered predominantly by illness experienced by principal artists and chorus members throughout the winter.[124]

The financial consequences of the cancellation of the season were serious. The group had lost approximately ZAR10,000 in pre-box-office expenditures, which not only plunged the organization into debt yet again, but also left it with few financial resources for future activities. A letter from the Eoan Group Trust to the Eoan Board clearly shows that the relationship between the two bodies was compromised by the cancellation of the opera season. The role of the trust was to act as financial guarantor of the group, and in the event of serious problems the final responsibility lay with the trust.[125] The letter indicated that the trust and the board had agreed on strategies for the group to try to generate its own income and that the trust felt the board had not honored this agreement. The trust duly complained of not being consulted in the decision to cancel the season and pointed out the grave financial repercussions:

> Arising from the Group's lack of liquidity and the prospect of a substantial overdraft building up before any significant revenue is likely to accrue, the Committee expressed strong views on the recent cancellation of the 1968 opera season. It was also the view of the Committee that they should have been consulted before the decision was taken, not because the Trust wishes in any way to interfere in the Group's running of its own affairs, but because of the grave financial implications of the decision.[126]

### THE EIGHTH OPERA SEASON

To address the financial overdraft caused by the cancellation of the opera season in 1968, in March the following year Eoan presented a program of operatic concerts, Opera for All, starring its principal singers in arias from various operas. Eoan seems to have performed better than ever, with Vera Gow's rendition of well-known arias from *La Traviata* earning her much praise in the press. (See the picture of her as Violetta, figure 4.5.) Gordon

Jephtas had been with Eoan for some months during its training period in 1968, and it was clear from a review that the members' singing benefited from his input.[127] Elsa Winckley's review in the *Sunday Express* of 30 March 1969 was very complimentary, demonstrating that Eoan continued to be admired and well supported by Cape Town's operagoing public. Judging by reviews, the underlying financial and political problems appear not to have had too direct an impact on the group's performances:

> It is astonishing that this company has managed to remain such a welded unit during the formative years. Much credit for this must go to its dedicated musical director and conductor, Dr. Joseph Manca, and its producer Alessandro Rota.
>
> In true prima donna fashion was Vera Gow's singing of "E Strano" and "Ah Fors è Lui" from La Traviata—her voice has matured in quality and her poise greatly increased. Even more remarkable is the progress of Patricia van Graan, whose singing of "Una Voce Poco Fa" from The Barber of Seville fully invited the thunderous applause she received.[128]

By this time Gow's reputation seems to have extended to opera circles in other provinces of the country as well, and in June 1969 she was invited to sing with the SABC Symphony Orchestra in Johannesburg. The local newspaper described Gow as "one of South Africa's outstanding Coloured sopranos."[129]

For the eighth opera season the group returned to the Cape Town City Hall. The season comprised four operas: Verdi's *Rigoletto, La Traviata,* and *Il Trovatore,* and Rossini's *Il Barbiere di Siviglia*. Rehearsals with principal singers started in April.[130] The principals for this season included Gerald Samaai, James Momberg, Ronald Theys, Charles de Long, Cecil Tobin, Vera Gow, Josephine Liedemann, Yvonne Jansen, Susan Arendse, Sophia Andrews, and Patricia van Graan.[131] The performance of *Rigoletto* had to be canceled shortly before the season opened due to the sudden death of the principal baritone, Robert Trussell, who had been singing as soloist with the group since 1956.

Adding Rossini's *Il Barbiere di Siviglia* to Eoan's repertoire confirmed Manca and Rota's predilection for comic opera. This two-act opera buffa, composed in 1816, is based on a French play by Pierre Beaumarchais, a work that has served as a topic for operas by other composers, most notably Giovanni Paisiello's opera *Barbiere di Siviglia* (composed in 1782).[132] Beaumarchais wrote a trilogy of plays on the life of Figaro, of which the first is the topic of Rossini's opera, while the second play, *Le mariage de Figaro,* was used by Mozart for his opera *Le nozze di Figaro* (composed in 1786).[133]

FIGURE 4.5. Soprano Vera Gow as Violetta. Source: Eoan Group Archive.

Both operas have proven to be great masterpieces of comedy in music, and after two centuries, their continued popularity on modern opera stages attests to their greatness.

Eoan's rendition of this opera received high praise from reviewers, with Martin Johnson in the role of Figaro being foremost in receiving accolades. The *Cape Argus* reported that "while the production was remarkable for its excellent casting, it was Martin Johnson whose personality and voice dominated the stage from beginning to end. His rich baritone voice and natural acting ability were combined with the happiest of results."[134] Similarly, Patricia van Graan as Rosina was praised by the *Cape Times* as "delectable and vocally and histrionically outstanding," while of Gerald Samaai the reviewer wrote that "in him, the group has a fine light tenor whose clear and flexible voice copes well with Rossini's florid writing. He looks good, is dashing when demanded, and also 'tipsy', martial or imposing."[135] The group's productions of *Il Trovatore* and *La Traviata* were both well received, with Vera Gow as the group's star soprano continuing to build her reputation with the public. Antoinette Silvestri described Gow's voice as "quite exceptional," having a "thrilling quality," and compared her lower register to the "lower tones in the singing of Callas."[136] Sophia Andrews's portrayal of Azucena impressed Hans Kramer so much that he left the City Hall "with the image of [her] commanding personality and impressive voice in mind and ear."[137] Silvestri, however, did not spare the group her criticism when she stated that the production of *Il Trovatore* was exciting yet "disappointing because there were the same voice faults, and a raw quality in the voices."[138]

Manca's ambitions for the group were undiminished, and he addressed the audience about future plans before starting the last performance of this opera season. Ever since Eoan's first opera production in 1956, Manca had wanted to take the group abroad, and on this occasion he seemed to be fundraising for this purpose, opening his speech with the words "as accountant [I am] doing a quick sum to see how much the house will yield."[139] While stating that a lack of funds was the main obstacle preventing the group from touring abroad, he also seems to have achieved a degree of realism regarding the group's artistic strengths, and instead of making his habitual comparisons of Eoan to La Scala, he noted that the group would "not show Europe how to put on opera, they know how to do that, but [we want to] show how we can do it." Furthermore, he was hoping to take the group abroad with a new musical that was to be composed for it, "which would be wholly South African and belonging to the Coloured people."[140] It is not clear how convinced Manca was of the feasibility of such an initiative, but the successful financial spin-offs of the musicals the group had produced the year before most probably gave rise to the idea. No references to this initiative could be found in the archive, but we do know that such a work was never composed, and the group was to wait another six years before it toured abroad.

Manca was held in high regard by government officials at the DCA and was asked to serve on the Council for Culture and Recreation, a governmental body created for the coloured community as an equivalent to the whites-only PACs.[141] In due course, instead of functioning as a supporting arts council, this body merely became the route via which Eoan had to submit its funding applications to the DCA, and the group's wish for equal opportunities and infrastructure with regard to arts production remained unfulfilled.

Little of the apartheid government's policy of "separate though equal development" came to fruition, and the Eoan Group remained solely responsible for obtaining funds for its activities, a situation that never changed throughout its opera-producing years. This was the case despite expectations raised by the creation of the council that Eoan performers would eventually enjoy the same rights and privileges as white artists.

As mentioned previously, the creation of the PACs was a painful reminder of racial discrimination for Eoan's artists. While professional careers were enabled for white performers, Eoan's singers were still unpaid, despite their excellent reputation and their substantial contribution to opera production in Cape Town. Although the group received some funding from the DCA, it had to apply for the money annually and lacked the security of consistent income on which it could budget and plan ahead. In his foreword to the 1969 opera season's program, Ismail Sydow lamented this situation: "Subsidies are the "life-line" of all Opera undertakings, yet in spite of the lack of this life-giving necessity, this truly South African Opera Company has contributed in no small measure towards the presentations of regular annual opera seasons with the resultant growing appreciation of "Opera" in the Republic."[142]

Sydow's use of the phrase "this truly South African Opera Company" is instructive. Eoan felt itself to be a unique South African institution, but in the reconstructed historical narrative presented thus far it is unclear what this understanding was based on. "Truly South African" in this case had less to do with the repertoire (which remained static and overwhelmingly Italian) than with all-coloured (and therefore "truly South African") casts. However, the group's cultural aspirations were directed toward Europe, and support was predominantly from whites rather than coloureds. Eoan existed, in short, on apartheid's terms under white management, co-opted in the functioning of separate groups and structures. Writing from the vantage point of the present, it is also clear that little remained of Helen Southern-Holt's practice of educating and empowering people within the group's structures in order for them to occupy management positions. Coloured self-determination was not on the agenda, let alone encouraged.

During this period music in the coloured community consisted of a wide variety of formats and types that were practiced formally and informally. These included Coon Festivals, dance bands, jazz, choirs, and music at church gatherings as well as the ever-growing entertainment industry. Various coloured musicians attested to the presence of classical music in their homes, which was often blended with other styles in their own music making. The mixing of classical music with popular styles is beautifully described by Vincent Kolbe in Denis-Constant Martin's book *Sounding the Cape*, in which Kolbe explains that "my mama used to sing opera and Jeanette MacDonald, home style, they just sang that because it was the popular tune of the day. [...] My mother bought all these Benjamino Gigli and Arturo Toscanini [records]. She and her friends used to play these ten inch [records] of Jascha Heifetz."[143] However, in order to become an established artist and earn a living, musicians had to progress to the formalized structures of recording facilities, entertainment halls, and clubs, where possibilities existed for generating income. The industry, however, was heavily regulated by apartheid legislation, providing few opportunities for artists of color to operate professionally. As an (amateur) opera company with the ambition to practice professionally, Eoan had no choice but to operate within the formal operatic industry. Yet it was not granted the opportunities or possibilities to do so. At the same time, jazz in Cape Town was a burgeoning musical format with a firm foothold in indigenous music such as *langarm*, *vastrap*, and *sopvleis*, much of which was infused by the Capetonian *ghoema* beat, outstripping Eoan's operatic endeavors in scope and size.[144] Yet here, too, few artists had the opportunity to create sufficient income by making music.

Pointing the way to Eoan's programming of many operatic concerts during the next decade, the Eoan Group Trust advised Manca regarding beneficial financial outcomes of certain types of productions:

> The Group will, I know, wish to prove its ability to stand on its own feet as much as possible and to build up a reserve of funds which will help to finance its classical productions in the field of opera, ballet, etc. I do suggest that the Group's programmes each year should include one musical so as to ensure a regular source of production profit and that "Opera for All" be exploited to the full. It is not a question of giving the non classical precedence over the classical, but merely a matter of using the former as a means to financing the latter.[145]

From 1968 onward, Eoan presented operatic concerts; as time passed, these became more frequent, eventually dominating the operatic endeavors of the group. Named Opera for All, A Night at the Opera, or Gems of the Opera, these concerts were not only economically more viable than full-scale opera productions, but were also much easier to take on short tours. Eoan performed in this format in various towns in the Western Cape throughout the 1970s.

## THE EOAN GROUP CULTURAL CENTRE

Shortly after the close of the eighth opera season, Eoan took up residence at the Eoan Group Cultural Centre, located on Klipfontein Road in the coloured suburb of Athlone. The minutes of a special AGM, held on 26 August 1969, state that the Cape Town municipality had donated 3.25 acres of land in Athlone, and the main financial contributors to the building of the center were the following:

| | | |
|---|---|---|
| The South African Government | ZAR | 120,000 |
| The Joseph Stone Foundation | | 100,000 |
| The Bernard van Leer Foundation | | 34,000 |
| The Eoan Group | | 33,000[146] |
| Total: | ZAR | 287,000[147] |

Little information is available about who led the project or what the credentials or motivations were of its private benefactors. A letter from the Eoan Group Trust to Ismail Sydow suggested that the initial idea was to incorporate the center as part of a cultural wing of the University of the Western Cape, but this did not happen.[148] The why and how of Joseph Stone's contribution remains a mystery to this day. Other than his residential address in Sea Point and his postal address in Somerset West, the archive holds no information about who Joseph Stone was and why he donated such a large amount to the building of the center. According to David Bloomberg, former Cape Town mayor and Eoan Group Trust chairman, Stone was a bookmaker who was not particularly interested in opera or the coloured community, but he was going through a divorce and sought a way of keeping his money away from his estranged wife.[149]

Eoan's relationship with the Bernard van Leer Foundation remains equally vague. The Dutch-based foundation still exists today and according to its website has been donating money to disadvantaged cultural groupings since the 1950s.[150] A policy document in the archive states that the organization's mission was to "enable children and youth, who are impeded by the social and cultural inadequacy of their background and/or environment, to achieve the greatest possible realization of their innate, intellectual potential."[151] The document also states that the foundation had at the time established a branch in South Africa, and it seems that the foundation funded

FIGURE 4.6. The Joseph Stone Auditorium, 1969. Source: Revel Fox Architects.

Eoan for a number of years during the 1970s, despite the international boycotts against South Africa at the time.[152] Apart from the fact that Ismail Sydow visited the foundation in the Netherlands in 1967 and secured the donation, the Eoan Group Archive holds no information about why the foundation donated this amount to the building of the center.

The center was designed by the well-known Cape Town architect Revel Fox.[153] Other than managing a prestigious architectural firm, the motivation for Fox's involvement with the group also remains unclear.

The discrepancy in governmental support for cultural initiatives of the coloured community was demonstrated unequivocally eighteen months later, in May 1971, when the Nico Malan Theatre Complex, a whites-only building, was completed on Cape Town's foreshore. The project cost R11 million and was fully subsidized by the government.[154]

The Eoan Group Cultural Centre, consisting of the Joseph Stone Auditorium (see figure 4.6), several ballet studios, practice rooms, and office space for administration, was inaugurated on 21 November 1969.[155] The ceremony was followed by a short concert in the auditorium. The Eoan Group Trust became the official owner of the Eoan Group Cultural Centre and remains so today.[156] Despite the small budget on which it was built and the scant government support, expectations for the possibilities created by the new center were high. As early as 1966, the minutes of the AGM held in August stated: "The Cultural Centre is to be in the nature of an Academy where all forms of art are to be taught and to be practiced. Its establishment would further provide i) the creation of professional careers for our many artists, ii) serve as a training college, and iii) provide employment for our people in the promotion of the performing and non-performing arts and the general uplift of our Community."[157]

Lofty ideals notwithstanding, the move out of the city center to the Cape Flats had a detrimental impact on the group, and the era during which Eoan was considered an integral part of the cultural activities in Cape Town came to an end. Documents in the archive indicate that after 1969 Eoan was slowly excluded from cultural activities in the city as venues in town became more inaccessible and apartheid legislation made it increasingly difficult for the group to maintain its position at the heart of Cape Town's music scene. Not only had the group's presence in the city been connected with its performances in venues such as the City Hall and the Alhambra Theatre, but its members had frequented venues in town on a daily basis, as rehearsals used to take place in either the Ochberg Hall in District Six, the City Hall, or Delta House in Bree Street, all of which were no more than ten minutes on foot away from other places in the city. Most administrative tasks, AGMs, and committee meetings also took place in the City Hall, at Delta House, or at Manca's home in Sea Point. The move to Athlone clearly illustrates how the forced physical removal of people under apartheid could and did disempower them. Furthermore, the physical shift from the city accompanied the gradual loss of the group's otherwise loyal white support base who, in the spirit of apartheid, were generally loathe to visit Athlone, especially during the evening, when most performances took place.

ONE MORE MUSICAL

During the course of 1970, Eoan gave several operatic concerts in towns further afield in the Cape Province. Minutes of the 1970 AGM mention that the group gave "three concerts, one at Stellenbosch and two at Paarl to members of our own community [which were] met with great success."[158] Eoan's big production for this year took place in August 1970, when the New York–based producer Stanley Waren returned to South Africa to direct Eoan's performance of the American musical *Carmen Jones* by Oscar Hammerstein II.[159] Once again Eoan could claim a "first," as this production constituted a South African premiere. Having staged the Rodgers and Hammerstein musicals *Oklahoma!* (in 1967) and *South Pacific* (in 1968), the group now had three major American musicals in its repertoire. Unlike much of its operatic repertoire, these musicals were all only staged once.

*Carmen Jones* is Hammerstein's 1943 adaptation of Bizet's opera *Carmen* for Broadway, using much of the original music but changing the setting "from Spain to the American South and the American Negro. The gypsy girl, Carmen, is now the Negress, Carmen Jones."[160] The work was an instant success in the United States, with many hundreds of performances being given in the decades following its premiere, including a film adaptation made by Otto Preminger in 1954. Despite the work's continued popularity, Melinda Boyd takes a critical view of the work's claim to be an authentic cultural portrayal. In her discussion of this musical in the book *Blackness in Opera* she writes: "Hammerstein's *Carmen Jones* is about as authentic a representation of African American culture as Bizet's *Carmen* was of Spanish culture—that is to say, not very."[161] Although such concerns were most likely not entertained by Manca at the time, Boyd continues her argument, stating that "scholars need to ask who creates representations of whom, with what imagery and toward what ends," an approach that can productively be applied to the context in which Eoan staged this work.[162] Manca's publicity material stated, not surprisingly, that Eoan's artists fit the requirements for this work particularly well, writing that "if one were to travel around the world it would be difficult to find a cast more eminently qualified to stage a presentation of Carmen Jones than the unique Eoan Group."[163] Although skin color is not explicitly mentioned as the qualifying attribute here, within the context of apartheid South Africa it is clearly implied. However, factually Manca's assumption was incorrect. It may have been true that Eoan's cast fit the representation of African Americans well, but the work had already been performed by African American casts in the United States for more than twenty-five years.[164] Manca's comment can be read as a symptom of an ignorance stemming from the isolation in which the group functioned, yet it also points to Manca's well-versed marketing ploy of capitalizing on the "otherness" of coloureds performing music which, in apartheid South Africa, was seldom performed by people who were not white. For Eoan this was the first time that skin color per se seemed to be a contributory factor to the choice of a work, a claim that cannot be made for any of the group's other repertoire.

On the other hand, the "blackness" of its cast was probably just one of a number of criteria for this choice; the American musical as a genre was hugely popular with the public and a format in which the group had previously excelled. This was also not the first time that Eoan had performed a work with racial overtones. The musical *South Pacific*, which the group had performed in 1968, has as a central theme the issue of mixed-race relationships and the existence of racial prejudice.

This time, performances were held for coloured-only audiences in the Joseph Stone Auditorium in Athlone and at the Luxurama in Wynberg, both venues located in designated coloured-only areas. Permission had to be obtained for white newspaper critics to attend the performances in order to review the production. The invitation letters to newspaper reviewers explained: "I have to advise you that permission has been obtained from the Department of Community Development for the official theatre critics who belong to the White race group."[165] From this one can conclude that newspaper critics were predominantly white and that journalism covering the arts was controlled by whites.

FIVE

*Slow Death: On Twilight and Loss*

1971–1980

> A poor, lonely woman abandoned in this teeming desert they call Paris!
> What can I hope?
> What should I do?
>
> —VIOLETTA, Act 1, *La Traviata* by Giuseppe Verdi

## A CAREER ABROAD

During the 1960s and 1970s a number of Eoan's artists left South Africa to pursue careers abroad. Among them were the tenor Joseph Gabriels, repetiteur Gordon Jephtas, ballet dancer Didi Sydow, and soprano Patricia van Graan. Of these, Gabriels and Jephtas arguably had the most notable success, and these individuals are today remembered by former Eoan members with much pride. A closer look at the two men's attempts to establish themselves in the music industry in Europe and America reveals the sobering side of "a career abroad" and illustrates the reality of how difficult it was for these artists to become professionals internationally.

On 5 February 1971, Joseph Gabriels sang the first major role of his international career when he made his debut at the Metropolitan Opera House in New York in a one-off performance as Canio in Ruggero Leoncavallo's *I Pagliacci*.[1] Gabriels was the first South African opera singer ever to sing at this prestigious venue, and the event was possibly also the finest moment of his career as an opera singer abroad. In hindsight, Gabriels clearly had a longer and more productive career as a singer in South Africa, where he was known in opera circles throughout the country as Eoan's star tenor, sang more roles than he ever did abroad, and was popular with reviewers and the operagoing public. Although he was known as an Eoan opera singer and participated in most of the group's productions between 1958 and 1965, Gabriels built his South African career relatively independently from the

Eoan Group, also singing light music and jazz. After landing his first big role with Eoan in 1959 as the Duke of Mantua in Verdi's *Rigoletto*, Gabriels managed a concurrent career in the entertainment industry, touring with light music groups such as Morris Smith's Golden Dixies Show and singing in music clubs in Cape Town.[2] He even hosted a radio program on the SABC channel Springbok Radio called *The Firestone Programme*, in which he broadcast Neapolitan songs.[3]

In June 1964 Gabriels married Mabel Kester, a long-standing Eoan member from the drama section who had played the role of Sanna in the group's 1963 production of *Behind the Yellow Door*.[4] In 1965 the couple moved to Johannesburg, where Gabriels started lessons with the (white) musician and conductor Edward Dunn, who began teaching him staff notation.[5] While studying in Johannesburg, Gabriels was introduced to a group of well-to-do opera enthusiasts (among them Graham and Rhona Beck, Minna Witkin, and Gwen Clarck), and with financial support from the Schneier family he was able to study abroad.[6] In February 1967 he left for Milan, Italy, after which he never sang in an opera production in South Africa again.

Between 1967 and 1970 Gabriels received tuition from various individual singing teachers in Milan while his wife Mabel worked as an English teacher at the Shenker Institute. Her position supported the family financially throughout this time and in subsequent years, after Gabriels's opera career came to an end. Among his teachers were Otto Mueller and the Italian lyric tenor Giuseppe di Stefano, who had collaborated with Maria Callas and became a family friend of the Gabrielses.[7] In 1970 Gabriels won the Giuseppe Verdi Singing Competition in Busetto (the town where Verdi was born), which gave him the opportunity to sing at various operatic concerts during that year and earned him lifelong membership in the Friends of Verdi Opera Society, Amici Verdi.[8]

Gabriels landed the role of Canio for the New York production via the South African consul in Milan, Malcolm Smith, and his Italian (opera-singing) wife, Elda Ribetti, who had connections to Rudolf Bing, the general manager of the Metropolitan at the time.[9] According to the soprano Emma Renzi—the first South African to sing at La Scala, who boasted a stellar career in Europe for three decades—the decision to contract Gabriels for this performance was politically motivated. In her opinion, his technique and skill as a professional singer had not matured enough to withstand the criticism leveled at singers in the New York environment. She felt that influential players in the opera industry wanted to make a political statement by promoting a disenfranchised, coloured singer from the Cape Flats on one of the world's most prestigious stages.[10] Furthermore, the role of Canio required a dramatic tenor, while Gabriels was a lyric tenor. Gabriels physically resembled the famous tenor Enrico Caruso, who had an international reputation for his role as Canio in *I Pagliacci*, and the *New York Times* at the time also referred to Gabriels as "the South African Caruso."[11] The Metropolitan proved to be a tough stage; Gabriels gave one performance only and was never invited back.

His American debut was reported widely in the South African press, where it received headlines such as "Gabriels in Fine Voice as S. A. Caruso," "Gabriels Wins Praise," "Triumph for Tenor Joseph Gabriels," "Suid-Afrika se eie Caruso!" [South Africa's own Caruso], "Fresh Distinction for S. A. Tenor," and "Joey Triumphs at New York Met Debut," presenting a narrative of an extraordinary performance and standing ovations.[12] The *New York Times* review was more sober. While not discrediting Gabriels as a singer, it stated: "Mr. Gabriels is not a Caruso. His voice is actually on the smallish side, although it carries easily because it is well focused. In other respects, he gave a creditable performance. He phrased musically, carrying some phrases through where other tenors have to make a break. He did not overact, so that his round face and portly figure acquired a feeling of pathos."[13] (See Gabriels as Canio, figure 5.1.)

In the following years Gabriels was contracted to sing roles in specific productions at a few opera houses in Europe but was never employed full time at an opera house and never sang at La Scala, the opera house in his adopted hometown.[14] In 1972 and 1973 the Deutsche Oper am Rhein in Düsseldorf and Duisburg invited him to sing the role of Carlos in Verdi's *Don Carlos*, Pinkerton in Puccini's *Madama Butterfly*, and Manrico in Verdi's *Il Trovatore*, the latter two of which he had sung with Eoan a decade earlier. In July 1974 the English National Opera in London contracted him to sing Carlos again, this time in an unabridged version of this opera, which had not been staged in full since its premiere in 1867. For the London production, the libretto was translated into English and was directed by Colin Graham with Sir Charles Mackerras as conductor. Reviews of this production were not favorable and described Gabriels as "a poor actor," leaving the reviewer with the fear that "during the first two acts [...] we were in for Carlos without the Don," although his performance apparently improved as the opera progressed.[15] Gabriels was replaced with another singer after five performances.[16] This production proved to be his last role in a formal opera production in Europe.[17]

FIGURE 5.1. Joseph Gabriels as Canio in the 1972 Metropolitan Opera House production of Leoncavallo's *I Pagliacci*. Source: Louis Mélançon/Metropolitan Opera Archives.

The fact that Gabriels sang in so few productions during his European career was not for want of trying. Newspaper articles in the South African press reported on two occasions that Gabriels sang auditions throughout Italy as well as England, "all with discouraging results," illustrating how tough it was for opera singers in general to obtain contracts.[18] Getting a role in the tightly knit Italian opera community proved to be equally difficult, so much so that in 1973 the Gabriels family became Italian citizens in an attempt to secure more professional opportunities for him. In a letter to May Abrahamse, Gordon Jephtas also commented on the difficulty Gabriels had experienced in finding work, writing that "I have been very worried and sad that his career had not got off its feet. Evidently, voice is not enough for making a career.

Mutual friends in Milan are always on to me because they think that I am the one who should help and advise. But, I can't advise on how to make a career—he needs a break and with that voice deserves to sing more."[19]

According to his widow, Gabriels smoked throughout his singing career and was diagnosed with emphysema in 1975, prematurely ending his career as an opera singer. He apparently also struggled with the European winters, and from the 1970s until his death in 1998 he spent as much time in South Africa as possible, staying with either his mother or one of his sisters.[20] Throughout these years his wife and their children, Vanessa and Marcello, stayed in Milan, where Mabel continued to support the family through her work as an English teacher.

### CAPE TOWN'S WHITES-ONLY OPERA HOUSE

In Cape Town the 1970s saw the steady decline of opera production by the group. The reasons ranged from the ever-tightening grip of apartheid legislation on the group's day-to-day functioning, to financial constraints, to the forced removal out of the city center to the Cape Flats, to the suffocating effects of the artistic isolation in which the group operated. During this time control over Eoan's activities by the Department of Coloured Affairs (DCA) gradually tightened. In reply to Eoan's application for financial assistance for the 1970–1971 financial year, for instance, the DCA responded favorably and granted the group R3,000, but (for the first time) requested formal representation on the Eoan Executive Committee.[21] Eoan's management duly complied and replied that same month that the "committee further resolved to take immediate steps to provide for the permanent representation of the administration on the Eoan Group's governing body, which is responsible for the management of the whole group."[22] During the annual general meeting (AGM) held on 8 December 1970, Eoan's constitution was indeed amended to allow for representation of the DCA on the executive committee.[23]

In May 1971 Eoan took part in the festivities that celebrated the ten-year existence of the Republic of South Africa, cementing its image as a supporter of the apartheid government. Joseph Manca initially planned three productions for this occasion: an "indigenous musical," an "international musical," and an opera season comprising four operas.[24] The financial estimates for these productions make clear that white and coloured audiences were to be kept separate, with half the performances planned for white audiences in the

Cape Town City Hall and the other half for coloured audiences in the Joseph Stone Auditorium. Not surprisingly, the estimated income from admission fees from whites was double that from coloureds. The documentation also reveals that Manca budgeted professional fees to be paid to singers, dancers, and production staff. Approximately 40 percent of the cost was expected to be covered by the income generated from admission fees and the remaining 60 percent by subsidies from the government.[25] Few of Manca's plans were implemented, and in May 1971 Eoan staged Verdi's *Rigoletto* as well as a number of operatic concerts in the Joseph Stone Auditorium for coloured-only audiences.[26] The coloured community seems to have largely boycotted these performances, and Manca later reported that only fifteen hundred people attended, resulting in poor box office income.[27] No reviews of any of these productions could be found in the newspapers of the time.

As part of the Republic Festival in the Cape Town city center, the Nico Malan Theatre, a new, state-of-the-art performance complex, was inaugurated on 19 May 1971. It included a 1,204-seat opera house and various other venues for the performance of theater, music, and ballet and was built at a cost of ZAR11.5 million, funded in full by the government. The theater was declared a whites-only building, provoking much public debate and protest. Although Eoan was entirely absent from the happenings in and around the inauguration, public protests illustrated that the group weighed heavily on the conscience of many who enjoyed opera and ballet in the city. Apart from students from the University of Cape Town handing out protest pamphlets outside the venue during the inauguration, an extensive campaign against the color bar imposed at the Nico Malan Theatre was waged by advocate Brian Bamford, who lobbied for a boycott of the inauguration by the Cape provincial parliament.[28] The resistance movement Black Sash joined the protests, picketing on the day of the inauguration in the city center with slogans such as "Culture knows no colour bar" and "Never have so many paid for so few."[29]

Most newspapers reported on the "glitter and dissent" that accompanied the inauguration, which was attended by high-profile politicians such as State President Jim Fouche and Prime Minister John Vorster.[30] The *Cape Times* dedicated its entire editorial column of 19 May to the issue, calling it "an operatic tragedy" that coloureds were barred from a building that "contains within its walls every possible technical advance, set against an artistic background of sophisticated good taste."[31] The article deplored the color bar enforced at the venue, referencing Eoan's achievements: "Culturally the non-White contribution has been direct and spectacular. The Eoan Group has given this city the opportunity to see and hear live opera beyond the scope of anything which could have been achieved in Pretoria. And Joseph Gabriels was triumphantly received by the New York Metropolitan."[32] The article even boasted that Cape Town's political track record "compared well" to other cities such as Pretoria and Bloemfontein, which were deemed conservative. The editorial also named a number of coloured individuals who were deemed likely visitors to the building, had there not been a ban on coloureds. These included the academic Richard van der Ross, the politician Tom Swartz, the poet Adam Small, and the cricketer Basil D'Oliviera.[33]

In a telling display of the frustration, bitterness, and anger many coloureds experienced at the time despite the "good intentions" of white liberals, the poet Adam Small entered the fray in a scathing attack on the above-quoted editorial, illustrating his political sensibilities, his awareness of the complicity of white liberals with apartheid, and his reservations about the Eoan Group:[34]

> Your [editor] goes on and on and, in well-known fashion, gives the Coloureds a pat on the back. You mention the famous "non-White contribution," recognition of which, in the matter of this farce of the Opera House (of course you do not call it that), would secure for South Africa the position of the true cultural "outpost of the Western world"! (Is colonialism, really, not yet over?)
>
> You mention the Eoan Group (still singing Italian opera, I see, while, in so far that they are Coloured, they should be singing indigenous protest); you mention Joseph Gabriels; you compare Cape Town's liberal tradition with Pretoria's and Bloemfontein's wickedness (as if Cape Town's liberal tradition ever existed beyond the level of nice, rather nice, master-and-servant relationships; and you go on even to pat me on the back. [. . .] May I ask you please not to take my name in vain?
>
> For, you see, the truth is that someone like myself feels sorry for the mass of White South Africa whose will lies behind this Opera House farce (and the uncountable other farces of its kind in South Africa) and this mass includes the bulk of the Opera House "boycotters." You see you have no need to speak on our (Coloured) behalf, for people like me stand above this; we look down on it. I have to tell you, unfortunately, that I pity even you, in spite of your good intentions towards me and the likes of me. In short, the time for Coloureds to "look up at" Whites and to aspire to White status is over.[35]

Small's letter is quoted at length here because it displays great dignity and articulates the outrage and frustration of the coloured community that did not support Eoan. It also resonates with a number of issues of coloured identity discussed in the introduction to this book, specifically the legacy of slavery so entrenched in the coloured community's history, which can be traced in the managerial structures of the Eoan Group. Earlier that month the *Cape Times* had published a speech by the well-known Afrikaans clergyman and antiapartheid activist Beyers Naudé, who discussed the rising activism within the coloured community against the ingrained submissiveness on which apartheid as a system thrived. He stated that "in less than a year the Coloured people of South Africa have shed their traditional submissive attitude towards White people. They have suddenly emerged with a new consciousness of human dignity, a new aggressiveness to claim what is theirs, by right."[36]

For Eoan's artists, though, it seems that singing opera (or dancing, or acting) gave them a sense of dignity. Sophia Andrews, former mezzo-soprano soloist of the group, described it as follows: "Every performance was a milestone. Just to get on there and sing over that orchestra. It's something that you cannot give to anybody and that you live with for the rest of your life."[37] Yet their singing continued to chain them to the power relations within the group, in which subjugation, if not to management then to the group's motto of service, was expected. Furthermore, the hierarchical structure inherent in much of Western art music, wherein singers and musicians abide by the authority of the conductor, did not encourage Eoan's artists to question Manca. The shedding of a subservient attitude by Eoan's members only became evident some years later, when it allegedly contributed to Manca's resignation in 1977.

In 1971 access to the Nico Malan Theatre for Eoan (whether as artists or audience members) remained impossible. The Afrikaans newspaper *Die Burger* published an interview with Nico Malan, the man after whom the building was named, in which he was asked if he did not feel that the Eoan Group should be allowed to perform in the building. The article included four paragraphs of Mr. Malan's evasive and meandering response, ending in a vague and noncommittal reply that in time, Eoan should be able to perform there. However, the lifting of the color bar at the Nico Malan Theatre did not occur until March 1975.[38] Some form of protest also came from David Poole, the coloured-turned-white ballet dancer who, as a result of his reclassification as white, now headed the Cape Performing Arts Board's (CAPAB's) Ballet Section. Poole had apparently publicly stated that he hoped the Nico Malan Theatre would soon open its doors to all races. He was reprimanded by the provincial administrator and asked formally to apologize, which he did by stating that he was sorry to have upset the official, but he refused to withdraw his comment on the color bar.[39]

# THE NINTH OPERA SEASON

In July 1971 Manca submitted the following year's budget requirements to the DCA. In his report accompanying the budget he discussed, among other things, the chronic lack of professional training:

> Despite the fact that for at least the past twenty years the Eoan Group artists have been performing Oratorio, Operettas, Musicals and Opera without any real and serious knowledge of music, it speaks much for their inherent talents that they have achieved so much and been in the forefront, specially of opera.
>
> For many years, it was deemed necessary to establish a Music School where the artists would be taught the theory and rudiments of music, sufficient enough for them to read musical notation. For some reason or another, this much needed requirement did not come about. However, it was finally decided to introduce this pressing need and so the establishment of the Music School was planned to commence this year.[40]

In line with Manca's comments, the limited possibilities for vocal training were reorganized. Manca's fellow Italians, Alessandro Rota and Olga Magnoni, had been responsible for voice training since the 1960s, but poor attendance and lack of discipline were apparently common, and all trainees now had to sign a contract binding them to regular attendance, punctuality, and the strict control of singers who performed at occasions not related to Eoan's activities.[41]

The group's 1971 opera season was held in October. The program included Giuseppe Verdi's *Rigoletto* and *La Traviata* and Pietro Mascagni's *Cavalleria Rusticana*, as well as an addition to the repertoire, Leoncavallo's *I Pagliacci*. The season was staged in the Alhambra Theatre on the northern side of the city, and permission was obtained to allow the coloured community to attend. In a new move to engineer racial separation and avoid racially mixed audiences altogether, the permit stipulated that performances for whites and coloureds were to be held on separate evenings, eleven performances for whites and three for coloureds.[42]

Leoncavallo's *I Pagliacci* was the last new work the group ever took on, bringing its tally of operas performed since 1956 to eleven. Shortly after its completion in 1892, this opera was paired with Mascagni's *Cavalliera Rusticana* (composed in 1890) in what became known in the opera world as "Cav and Pag." These operas were often performed as a double bill, and for Eoan's ninth opera season, they were treated as such. Both operas are relatively short works, composed in the *verisimo* style, which "presents everyday people, especially the lower classes, in familiar situations, often depicting events that are brutal or sordid."[43] For Eoan's production, Canio was sung by Charles de Long, Nedda was shared by May Abrahamse and Patricia van Graan, and Silvio was sung by Ronald Theys.

The season opened on 18 October with "Cav and Pag." Stalwarts May Abrahamse as Nedda in *I Pagliacci* and Sophia Andrews as Santuzza in *Cavalliera Rusticana* earned much praise in the press. Roy Pheiffer of the *Cape Times* reported that "the honours were shared with equal brilliance by the leading ladies," describing Andrews's voice as "rich in resonance, especially in the lower register and dramatically suited to the most taxing parts of the score. Hers was a resounding success." He was equally impressed by Abrahamse's "grace and utter conviction in her singing" and wrote that "her refined and sensitive interpretation was the highlight of a generally most convincing presentation of this opera."[44]

Over the years Eoan had many star sopranos, but it was Abrahamse who remained consistently involved with the group, from her debut in 1949 in the operetta *A Slave in Araby* to Eoan's last performance of *La Traviata* in 1975, and continued as a singing teacher for a younger generation of Eoan singers in the 1990s. Although she worked in an administrative function at the *Cape Times* newspaper in the 1950s, she became a housewife and mother to two daughters after marrying Jonathan Rushin and pursued her operatic career from home.[45] As mentioned previously, she had a close friendship with repetiteur Gordon Jephtas, with whom she shared a lifelong commitment to and fascination with opera, much of which is documented in their exchange of letters between 1962 and 1990.[46] Due to Abrahamse's isolated position as a coloured singer in apartheid South Africa, Jephtas did much training by letter and cassette tape from Europe, and he was closely involved in Abrahamse's performance of Nedda in this 1971 production. Apart from discussing matters such as her decision whether or not to accept the role, Jephtas did a fair amount of coaching. His advice was often very technical and detailed, and he always felt it imperative for her to not only sing the music but also act the character onstage. The following example illustrates his advice on how to portray Nedda's character and feelings through movements:

> Now that you've studied [the role] for nearly a month you should have it under control. You're dead right about the details: sexy movements of the arms on the chords before "o che bel sole", and the duet scenes. Remember, the move-

ments must be young and arrogant; that is quick movements with the head for example, and Nedda listens a great deal and must re-act to whatever she hears and how she hears it. She is not sophisticated nor elegant – remember I told [you that] Callas' Violetta was a whore and though Nedda is not exactly that, she is not Tosca nor Leonora. Have you been able to do anything about Nedda's face? You must, that's as important. And the words? Check yourself on pronunciation, [remember] double consonants. Single vowels [are] all long, and understand every word. [Having] the sense is not enough.[47]

Jephtas's admiration for Abrahamse is palpable throughout their correspondence. The letters illustrate that "flattering newspaper critics" did not impress her and that she continuously worked toward improving her singing, yet remained humble throughout her life.[48] According to Jephtas she was the only singer in the group who really understood what it meant to be a professional opera singer.

Eoan had performed *Cavalliera Rusticana* a number of times before (in 1958, 1959, and 1960), during which productions May Abrahamse sang the role of Santuzza and Sophia Andrews sang Lucia. Yet for the 1971 production Andrews was cast as Santuzza. Benjamin Arendse sang the role of Alfio, as he had done a decade before; Vera Neethling sang Lucia; and Virginia Damons sang Lola.[49] The recasting of Andrews in a soprano role is an example of how Eoan's principals were sometimes required to sing roles that did not suit their "fach." This role is best suited for a dramatic soprano with a range reaching two octaves above middle C, yet Andrews was a mezzo-soprano. Despite this, she carried it off well enough, and reviewers were greatly impressed with her ability to make her voice project over the orchestra and create a darker sound in her lower register. According to Andrews, even the role of Lucia, which she had sung a decade before, did not suit her voice comfortably because its range was too low.[50]

In 1971 Eoan was able to restage its production of *Rigoletto*. After two failed attempts in 1968 and 1969, the production was staged during the Republic Festival celebrations in May and again during the ninth opera season in October. Legend has it that the singers were haunted by "the ghost of Lionel Fourie," who had sung *Rigoletto* in the group's 1959 production; they claimed that he roamed the stage during the performance.[51] Despite this, the *Cape Times* reviewed the production favorably, lauding principal singers Gerald Samaai as the Duke of Mantua, Freda Koopman as Gilda, and Ronald Theys as Rigoletto. Smaller roles, Phillip Swales as Sparafucile and John van der Ross as Monterone, received equal praise. The only singer who had taken part in the original production twelve years earlier was Sophia Andrews, cast in the role of Maddalene; as always, she received a well-deserved positive critical response.[52] The famed ghost of Lionel Fourie may have been the cause for reviewer Pieter Kooij of *Die Burger*'s comment on strained and jittery acting by just about all the principals.[53] This time, however, Eoan's production of *La Traviata* was not that well received. *Die Burger* was of the opinion that Vera Gow's Violetta was the only redeeming part of the production, criticizing not only the singers, but also the choir, decor, and out-of-tune playing of the orchestra.[54]

Budget overviews from this time show that Eoan's principal singers and other support staff were to receive honoraria for their services during the opera season, with only choir members receiving no financial compensation at all.[55] Minutes from executive committee meetings indicate that such honoraria were often donated back to the group.[56] Tracing the budgets drawn up by Manca as well as the audited financial statements of the group over the years, it comes as no surprise that they tell the story of a hierarchy based on race. To this day the absence of financial compensation for Eoan's artists features in most interviews with singers, and references to the issue in archival documentation as well as press statements from the time are common. Although an attitude of "selflessness" and "work without pay" seemed to have been the rule during the early years, it is clear that this changed with time. The archive, for example, contains a letter from Manca written shortly after the 1956 Arts Festival in which he returned a paycheck for his services during the festival and in which he stated that he wanted no compensation for what he did for the group.[57] By the early 1970s the picture was rather different. The minutes of the finance committee meetings of 1970 reveal, for instance, that shortly after settling in the Eoan Group Cultural Centre, the group purchased a car, which was used to transport Manca to and from his house in Sea Point on a daily basis, with Sydow as chauffeur.[58] The 1970–1971 budget also shows that despite being a pensioner benefiting from forty years' employment at the Cape Town City Council, Manca budgeted a salary for himself at twice the amount that the administrator and chairman of the board, Ismail Sydow, received.[59] On top of this, Manca also made provision for a salary for the "conductor" of the group's productions, a position he always filled.[60]

In budgeting a substantially higher salary for himself than for Ismail Sydow, Manca was not doing something unusual. The labor market had a tradition of paying whites more than coloureds, regardless of their level of skills or job description. Equal remuneration for white and coloured workers of the same educational level was frequently discussed in the newspapers during this time. The *Cape Times*, for example, reported that the government was still considering legislation that would entitle coloured teachers to the same remuneration as white teachers.[61] *Rapport* reported that coloured mechanics as a rule earned between R40 and R55 per week, while the average salary for a white mechanic was R65.[62] The Cape Chamber of Commerce was reported to be contemplating offering coloured factory workers pensions, annual bonuses, and medical aid for the first time ever.[63]

The nonpayment of Eoan's singers and other artists furthermore stands in stark contrast to the motto of "upliftment" of the coloured community that management had been preaching for years and on which it prided itself. By this time Eoan had been teaching and performing ballet for thirty-five years and producing opera for fifteen years, yet the much-vaunted "upliftment" stretched only as far as singing or dancing, while the financial realities of the everyday world of Eoan's artists and members remained unaddressed.

## SUCCESSION

By this time Manca had been with the Eoan Group for twenty-eight years and had health problems, so the hunt for a successor was all the more urgent. Due to apartheid legislation, the scope of suitable coloured candidates was exceedingly limited, and many efforts were made during this time to obtain new staff. In a meeting held on 28 July 1971, the executive committee decided formally to approach Ismail Sydow's daughter, Didi Sydow, to become Eoan's ballet director and Gordon Jephtas to become assistant cultural director.[64]

In August 1971 Ismail Sydow traveled to Europe to visit his daughter in England and Gordon Jephtas in Italy to personally discuss these requests with them. This time both agreed to return to South Africa to work with Eoan, although certain conditions had to be met. Didi Sydow had become a British citizen and was married to an Australian, and she requested permission in writing from the South African government for her and her husband to have unrestricted entry to and exit from the country. Furthermore, her husband was white, and she requested written consent that they "may live together as man and wife while in South Africa."[65] The archive does not hold correspondence pertaining to the government's answers to these requests, but she never took up the position, and one can safely assume that such consent was not given.

FIGURE 5.2. Repetiteur Gordon Jephtas in conversation with Ismail Sydow in London. Source: Eoan Group Archive.

Gordon Jephtas's main concern was that he wanted to be in a position to conduct any orchestra for Eoan's productions, irrespective of whether members were white or not.[66] Written consent for this took a full two years and came in the form of a permit granted on 15 October 1973. In line with apartheid's ideology of separate development, the approval was formulated as follows:

> I have the pleasure in advising you that the Honourable the Minister of Community Development has approved of the issue of a group areas permit, subject to withdrawal at his pleasure, enabling Mr. Jephtas to conduct all orchestras playing at performances by the Eoan Group as well as at rehearsals. The Minister has at the same time expressed the wish that as the Coloured community is itself musically talented it will develop its own Eoan Group orchestra in the near future.[67]

From a letter written by Jephtas to Abrahamse early in 1974, it appears that Sydow had visited Jephtas and informed him that the South African government had finally given permission for him to conduct an orchestra consisting of white musicians. (See the picture of Jephtas and Sydow, figure 5.2.) Jephtas had been abroad for eight years by this time and was less than flattered by the whole affair. For him, subservience to white authority was clearly not acceptable any longer, nor was the idea that white musicians are by default good players. He commented to Abrahamse: "Big deal indeed to conduct some shitty white orchestra. You know, for me, to be frank, the word white is not operative, but what I'd like to know is how good these bastards are? What matters is the music and not this 'white must be good' mess."[68]

In these years the group's repertoire had become standardized, and operatic concerts such as Gems of the Opera became regular items in its performance schedule, providing much-needed income. These concerts were less expensive to produce, were generally well attended, and showcased Eoan's principal singers performing popular arias. After *I Pagliacci*, no new works were added to the repertoire. The feelings of excitement, hopeful expectation, and general amazement that had accompanied Eoan's productions in the years prior to 1970 appear to have been replaced by routine, as concert after concert was given in a floundering attempt to resuscitate the exuberance of past experiences. Apart from a number of operatic concerts in 1972 and 1973, no opera seasons were held, creating an unprecedented three-year gap between the ninth and tenth seasons.[69]

Documentation dating from this period focuses predominantly on schedules for operatic concerts, problems and worries regarding funding, maintenance of the Eoan Group Cultural Centre, matters of permission to perform in white venues, and future plans.[70] It is also clear from the documentation that the political situation was worsening as the control exercised over the group by the DCA increased and political tolerance toward the group by coloured society deteriorated.

Despite the revenue earned from the many operatic concerts, by early 1972 Eoan's financial affairs were in dire straits. A closer look at budgetary documentation from this time provides a glimpse of the ongoing financial constraints the group had had to deal with for years. Its costs for the 1971–1972 financial year stood at ZAR128,000, of which the group had generated just over half by itself.[71] Of the remaining ZAR63,000, the DCA had already committed ZAR35,000. The Eoan board requested additional financial support for the shortfall of ZAR28,000 from the DCA but soon afterward decided to reduce its annual staff costs by another ZAR3,000, bringing down the budgeted shortfall to ZAR25,000.[72] In reality this meant paying even less to regularly appointed staff. By the end of March 1972, the DCA had allocated only ZAR5,000 toward the shortfall, bringing the group's total grant to ZAR40,000 and leaving its bank account R20,000 in the red, with no guarantees for funds for the next financial year.[73] Manca's ambitious funding application to the DCA of the year before, requesting a new teaching block, also rendered no results. In a letter of 23 March 1972 to the Eoan Group from Mr. F. L. Gaum, the then commissioner of the DCA, the condescending tone is unmistakable:

> I should again like to point out that the Administration does not have at its disposal unlimited financial resources. It is, therefore, sine qua non that the Eoan Group itself should undertake its affairs within its financial limits and it should not rely on the Administration to meet its shortfall. Whereas the White community has hitherto been the main support of the Group, the question of a greater financial contribution and better support from the Coloured Community arises. It would appear to be necessary, should further financial aid be granted, that stricter control be exercised over the expenditure.[74]

In its reply to the DCA, the Eoan Group Trust referred to the issue of coloured support, stating that "the overall problem of [Eoan's] popularity amongst its own community is a very thorny problem which I feel is somewhat beyond our capabilities."[75]

## LOSING THE CAPE TOWN CITY HALL

In January 1973 the Eoan Group was informed by the Cape Town City Council that the City Hall was to be renovated to its original architectural design of 1905. In practice, this meant that the curtains were to be removed from the stage and the area where the orchestra used to sit was to be filled with permanent seating for the audience. It was also made clear that the venue, after renovations, would no longer be suitable for the production of operas or musicals. Since the city now had a modern opera house (for whites only), the council did not deem necessary a secondary venue for opera production. For Eoan this meant that the City Hall could no longer host its operatic endeavors and that future productions in the city had to happen elsewhere. The Alhambra Theatre on the northern side of the city, where the group had performed previously, was also not an option because the council had closed this venue in 1972, and it demolished the building in 1974. For Eoan this was a huge blow. The City Hall had been its artistic home since 1937, when the group's first ballet productions took place there. It was in this venue that Eoan evolved from a choir to an opera company, and it was home to the group's greatest operatic triumphs. After thirty-five years, Eoan lost the venue that had stood as a symbol of racial coexistence and tolerance in the heart of the city.[76]

The City Council in turn proposed that the Green & Sea Point Civic Centre be used as an alternative to the City Hall because it had the necessary facilities to accommodate separate entrances and seating arrangements for coloured and white racial groups. The logistics were explained in detail to the group by the town clerk, who "produced a sketch of the Centre, showing suitable separate amenities for both White and Coloured Sections of the Community. Both the Communities would enter from the Main Road to Sea Point and provision was possible for the Coloured Community to occupy one section of the seating in the same pattern as in the City Hall."[77] (See the sketch in figure 5.3.) However, the new venue was situated about five kilometers (about three miles) to the west of the city, while the Group Areas Act forced the coloured community into areas approximately twenty kilometers (over twelve miles) northeast of the city. Since most of Eoan's members and artists depended on public transport, this meant that they had to travel longer distances after a day's work, adding to the already heavy financial burden they were experiencing. In a rare display of emotion, Sydow wrote in his report to the Eoan Executive:

> Fellow members, I regret I have to present such a gloomy report to you in connection with one of our more important activities. There is nothing we can do to continue to perform before both sections of the Community at the same time in the same venue. It would be a great tragedy were the Eoan Group not to present opera, operettas and musicals in the future. This would be a great blow to the many talented members of our community, who would have no outlet to express their natural artistic achievements to the people of our country. What has the Eoan Group done to receive this form of treatment? We have always been law abiding and endeavoured at all times to carry out our motto: "WE LIVE TO SERVE!"[78]

Sydow's report also mentioned that Manca continued to hunt for sponsorship from within the coloured community but reported that his efforts were all but fruitless. He had appealed to more than fifty coloured industrial and commercial firms for financial assistance, but the outcome was the receipt of one single donation with the value of R15.[79] The burden of Eoan's financial requirements was clearly a heavy responsibility left in the hands of Sydow and Manca alone, and they faced an unenviable predicament: the DCA seemed

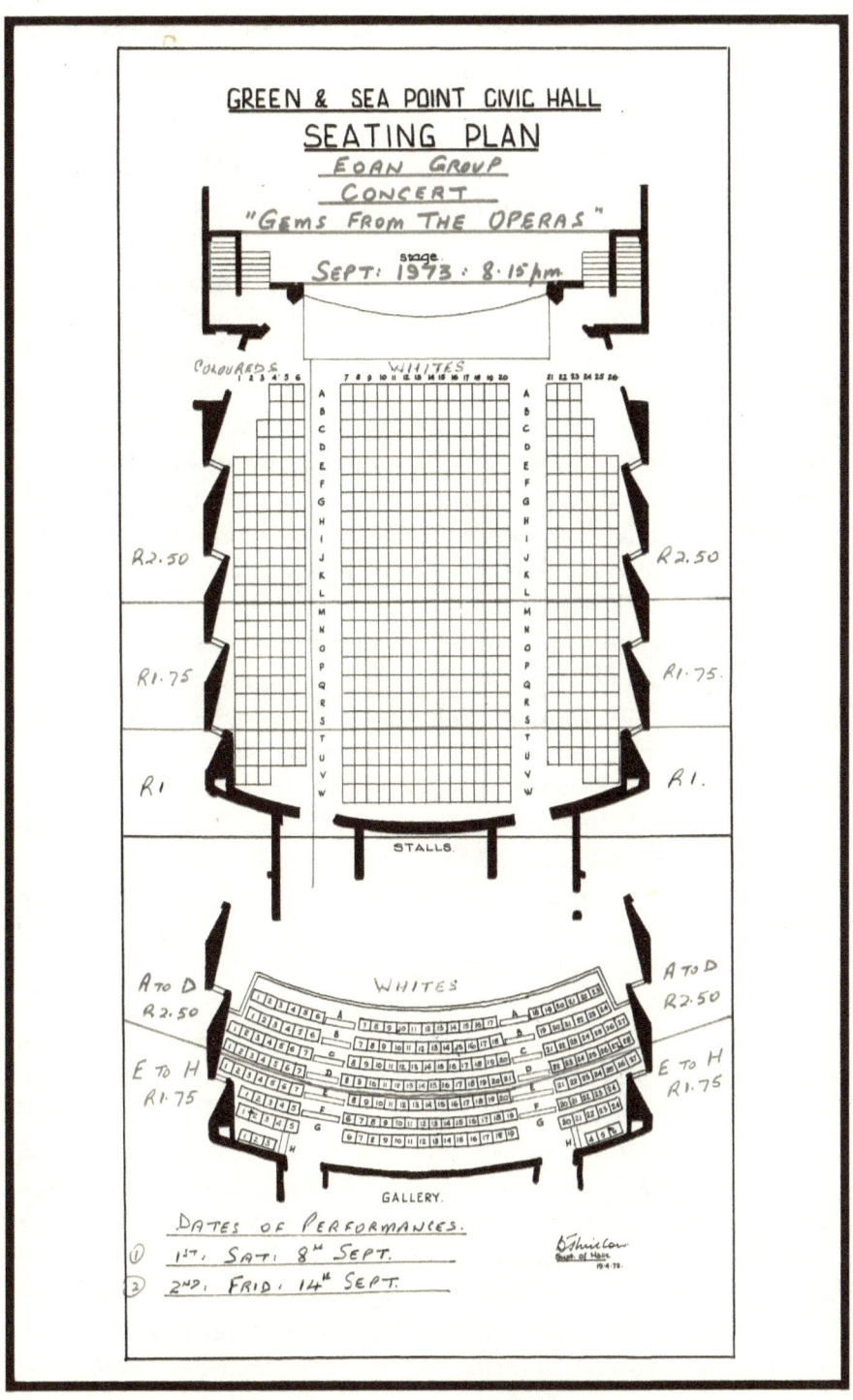

FIGURE 5.3. Seating plan of the Green & Sea Point Civic Centre, showing designated seating for whites and coloureds. Source: Eoan Group Archive.

indifferent to their needs, the Eoan Group Trust's initial generosity had diminished, and the coloured community was clearly not interested in supporting Eoan.

## THE ERIKA THERON COMMISSION

The minutes of the 36th AGM, held in November 1973, noted that the Eoan Group was asked to participate in the Commission of Inquiry into Matters relating to the Coloured Population Group, set up by then prime minister John Vorster and headed by Erika Theron, a retired professor of social work from Stellenbosch University.[80] The mandate given to the commission was to investigate the progress made by the coloured community since 1960 in the social, economic, and political spheres as well as local governance, sports, and culture. The commission was also tasked to identify factors causing hindrances in these areas and any other related issues.[81] A copy of the questionnaire that Manca filled out for this enquiry in March 1974 revealed decreased support for Eoan from the coloured community. Section 6 of the questionnaire showed a drastic decline in membership, as Eoan's almost 2,000 members in 1960 had now dwindled to a mere 370.[82] Section 18 of the questionnaire inquired about mixed or separate audiences, and Manca answered as follows: "When the Eoan Group performs before separate audiences, houses are generally poorly attended. The public tends to boycott separate performances. When performing to both sections of the public, houses are generally full."[83] Manca maintained that attendance at Eoan's performances had remained constant since 1960, but added that "from 1965 [onward] Coloured and White support showed a drop in attendance."[84]

The questionnaire extensively investigated the issue of venues. Manca confirmed that the suitable venues for opera production were those situated in white areas. The fact that Eoan had little access to those venues caused many logistical problems for the group, such as permits for which Eoan had to apply, the separate seating for whites and coloureds, and the long distances Eoan's artists had to travel. This was particularly problematic at night when artists, who were as a rule dependent on public transport, had to return home after concerts. The facilities at the Joseph Stone Auditorium also came under attack from Manca: "The Joseph Stone Auditorium is absolutely inadequate to meet the requirements for Eoan Group activities."[85] Having seen what the government was willing to make available to white singers, Manca most likely compared the Joseph Stone Auditorium to the Nico Malan Theatre, stating that the Eoan Group Cultural Centre had insufficient and inadequate facilities for rehearsals of opera, choral singing, and ballet and that no studios for voice production classes were available. He listed the shortcomings of the center, voicing his displeasure in no uncertain terms:

No stage facilities.
No proper dressing rooms.
No suitable toilets.
Complete lack of equipment necessary for a proper theatre such as the Nico Malan.
The Joseph Stone Auditorium is only partially equipped.
Seating capacity is too small.
Area not suitable for legitimate theatre lovers.
Too dangerous for members of the public.
South Africa has no *real* opera house or theatre for Coloured persons.[86]

Sydow's cover letter to the Commission of Inquiry on 7 March 1974 indicated that the professional body for arts and culture for the coloured community, which had been promised since 1967, had after seven years still not materialized. CAPAB, which made professional artistic careers for whites possible, had been in existence for eleven years and had access to a building that was constructed at a cost almost forty times that of the Joseph Stone Auditorium. It also appeared that some of Eoan's artists were able to get paid employment at cultural organizations elsewhere and were therefore no longer willing to sing without compensation for Eoan. Manca wrote to the DCA, keeping up appearances that the arts and culture body would certainly be established:

> In connection with the Eoan Group's future plans for the presentation of opera, the professional body about to be established by the Council for Culture and Administration should assist the Eoan Group financially to invite well-known overseas Coloured artists to participate in the Eoan Group presentations.
>
> Due to the fact that artists taking part in all presentations by the Performing Board receive remuneration, especially Capab in the Cape, the Eoan Group now finds great difficulty in obtaining the voluntary services of performing artists, choristers, producers, décor and costume designers, and all personnel concerned with the organization, administration and technical aspects of the theatre business.[87]

## THE 1974 OPERA AND BALLET SEASON

The 1974 season was held in March and consisted of five performances of Gioacchino Rossini's *Il Barbiere di Siviglia* and two operatic concerts. For the first time in more than a decade the group's ballet section contributed to the season with two presentations.[88] Eoan had no option but to present its season in the Green & Sea Point Civic Centre and had to apply for a permit to perform to mixed audiences in this venue. Permits had to be obtained from the Department of Community Development and were issued to the municipal body that governed the venue at which such performances were to be held. In the case of Eoan, applications for any venue in the city and its suburbs were channeled via the City Council, which governed the venues in which Eoan regularly performed. Correspondence between the City Council and the Department of Community Development about this permit illustrates the degree to which the coloured community was deemed an "undesirable" presence in white areas. A complaint appears to have been lodged at the department that should Eoan's performances in Sea Point be open to the coloured public, an influx of coloured individuals into the white residential areas, accompanied by unfavorable behavior, was feared. In response to this the council wrote to the department that the venue in question was on the outskirts of the area, where there were no residences, and argued that coloured patrons of the opera were "cultured, respectable people, who are able to pay the comparatively high prices for seats and who go home after the performance immediately."[89] The subsequent arrangements for the separated movement of coloureds and whites in the building is described in this letter as follows: "The main entrance from Main Road, the assembly foyer and the central and right hand seating of the Hall would be reserved for Whites. Entry for non-Whites could be through the Minor Hall from the completely separate forecourt of the building complex and the Minor Hall could also serve as a foyer for non-Whites. There would be thus complete separation of the races and no points of friction."[90]

The permit was granted on 25 April 1974. Apart from the regular conditions regarding amenities such as separate entrances, ticket boxes, toilet facilities, and seating, a new condition had been added to the permit: "No social mingling shall be allowed between Whites and Coloureds."[91] Although it is impossible to say how this regulation was to be policed, it starkly illustrates the extent to which the government endeavored to control society and tried to keep racial groups apart.

Reviews of the performances continued in similar vein as in previous years, praising the group for its "high standard," "spirited Rossini," and "hard work."[92] The *Cape Times* review attested to the continued support by white patrons: "Last night saw a tremendously vital and appealing production by the Eoan Group of the Barber of Seville. The Green & Sea Point Civic Centre was well filled by an enthusiastic audience which appreciated Joseph Manca and Alessandro Rota's production of Rossini's masterpiece for its light dramatic touch and good pace."[93] For this production May Abrahamse sang the role of Rosina, Ronald Theys was cast as Figaro, Gerald Samaai sang the role of Nemorino, and Martin Johnson was cast as Bartolo, all of whom got a nod from the reviewer for "effective singing."[94] The *Argus* even argued that "Cape Town has reason to be grateful to the Eoan Group for its latest operatic offering," describing Abrahamse's rendition of Rosina as "a role she portrayed with superb artistry. She uses her rich soprano voice to excellent effect particularly at top range which comes over with vibrant power when necessary and lyrically delicate when required."[95] The Gems of the Opera concert on 18 March, however, received some criticism for a perceived lack of communication among soloists, orchestra, and conductor.[96] The ballet productions also received good reviews, with credit given to dancers such as Ruth Fry, Achmat Ockards, and Henry Paulse for their dancing and choreography.[97]

In October 1974 Manca received yet another accolade from the white intellectual community when he was awarded a gold medal by the Afrikaans organization Suid-Afrikaanse Akademie vir Wetenskap en Kuns (South African Academy for Arts and Science) for his cultural and educational work among the coloured population and his contribution to opera production in South Africa.[98] The Akademie, as it was called for short, was launched in 1909 with the aim of encouraging and cultivating scholarly and cultural endeavors in the Afrikaans language.[99] Although it started out in the first half of the twentieth century as an organization striving for the growth and expansion of a fledgling language, its position was substantially empowered with the rise of the National Party by 1948.[100] Aided by the system of apartheid and its white Afrikaans-speaking support structures, it became a prestigious and influential organization during the apartheid years. Within the resistance movement and among the many people on the receiving end of apartheid, however, the Akademie was synonymous with white domination, and Manca's acceptance of this prize reinforced the group's reputation as an organization that supported and condoned apartheid.

To celebrate the event an operatic concert was held in October in the Joseph Stone Auditorium, and the medal was presented to Manca by Professor Beukes, the chairman of the Akademie at the time. Sydow thanked the Akademie: "The Eoan Group is proud of being associated with the Akademie on this unforgettable occasion. The very generous gesture of Die Akademie marks yet another milestone in the history of our beloved country and the Eoan Group is deeply recognizant of the importance of this memorable occasion when we all, as true South Africans met and enjoyed each other's company irrespective of race, colour and creed."[101] Sydow's acclamations of Manca and by implication of apartheid organizations such as the Akademie or the DCA are baffling. Serving as Manca's assistant throughout the years, he clearly believed in everything Manca deemed good for the organization and seems never to have questioned the power structures on which the organization functioned or the effects apartheid had on himself or the group. The quote is indicative of the extent to which Sydow continued to admire and support Manca despite the fact that they apparently often fought with each other, even in front of group members.[102] Sydow and his wife Carmen (who was Eoan's wardrobe mistress throughout this time) were born and bred in District Six, and as much as everyone else in the coloured community, they suffered great personal and collective losses at the hands of the system. Being close to Manca and having intimate knowledge of the administration of the organization, Sydow cannot but have witnessed how the system suffocated the group and its artistic endeavors over time. On the one hand, one can argue that Manca's control over the group guaranteed Sydow the influential position that he occupied, a position of relative privilege he surely was loathe to let go of. Yet such an opinion does not account for the lifetime of energy and dedication he brought to the group. His position must have given him a sense of fulfillment and meaning, explaining to some degree his support of the status quo.

### EOAN'S LAST OPERA SEASON

In 1975 Manca's dream for Eoan to tour abroad eventually came to fruition when the group was invited to participate in the 1975 International Festival of Youth Orchestras and Performing Arts, held in London and Aberdeen in the United Kingdom.[103] That year proved to be the group's last active year as an opera company, producing its season in February and March, taking part in the Cape Town Festival in April, and for the first and only time, touring abroad in August and September.

The final season was held from 26 February to 8 March. The program consisted of Verdi's *La Traviata* as well as two ballet productions, on 6 and 8 March, respectively. The ballet productions each included a Spanish, classical, and modern ballet, all of which were choreographed by Eoan's own dancers. The principal singers for this season were May Abrahamse in the role of Violetta, Gerald Samaai as Alfredo, Ronald Theys as Germont, John van der Ross as Baron Douphol, Keith Timms as Grenvil, Josephine Liedemann as Annina, and Sybille Adams as Flora. The principal dancers included Lydia Johnson, Henry Paulse, and Dick Jaffer.[104] The season was again held at the Green & Sea Point Civic Centre. During the season Eoan also held various operatic concerts in the coloured residential areas of Elsies River, Bellville South, and Athlone.[105]

Eoan's production of *La Traviata* received mixed reviews, with May Abrahamse for once being less favorably received. The reviewer was of the opinion that she "lacked the brilliance and sparkle required in [the] grand opening, and [that] her range of expression seemed limited in this act," although in the second act she "showed her mettle [where] Violetta's indignation, pride, anxiety, distress and resignation were effectively conveyed."[106] Ronald Theys as Germont was also not spared when the reviewer noted that, despite his pleasant voice, "he failed to react in any way to Violetta's changing moods." The stage set and orchestral accompaniment were equally criticized as unhelpful and unsupportive.[107] *Die Burger*'s review was full of praise, describing Abrahamse's rendition of "Ah Fors'e'Lui" in the opening scene as the highlight of the evening and complementary to the lyric capacity of Gerald Samaai's voice as well as Ronald Theys's strong voice.[108] Similarly, the dance presentations for this season received good reviews from *Die Burger*, stating that the evening was most enjoyable, with the modern ballet as a highlight and excellent dancing and choreography by Henry Paulse, Lydia Johnson, Dick Jaffer, and Achmat Ockards.[109]

Glowing reviews notwithstanding, being an Eoan artist could not have been easy at the time. Lack of money continued to be the most pressing problem, not to mention the continued artistic and social isolation, the politics of the day, and the strict hierarchy within the managerial structures of the group. Although some of the dancers were teaching at the group and therefore received a salary, most artists still had to combine a working life (which in many instances was far removed from the artistic world) with operatic singing or dancing, resulting in rehearsal schedules that included practices on every weekday evening as well as on weekends. For some the commitment to and love for their art still seemed to function as a powerful motivator. Ballet dancer Lydia Johnson, for example, explained that "dancing was for me what was important, the love of the art. That's why I'm still involved with it [to this day], you go to the extreme, and you don't worry about travelling and money. At one time the Eoan group had no money to pay us a salary for a couple of months and we went on teaching, you know, we went every day and we did it until Mr. Sydow could get money again and then he paid us."[110]

Manca and Eoan's artists were at the time of course not aware that this would be their last opera season, but fate had it that Verdi's *La Traviata* happened to be their first opera production, in 1956, and also their last production, in 1975, starring Abrahamse as Violetta on both occasions. The group had mastered, among other music, a repertoire to eleven operas and three musicals from the standard canon, of which most were repeated in intermittent seasons. *La Traviata* was performed during ten seasons in the course of twenty years and served as a signature of sorts throughout the group's performance history.[111] In the introduction to the *Cape Times* review of Eoan's performance on 17 February 1975, the reviewer wrote that "La Traviata must count as one of the most difficult operas in the repertoire. It demands expertise of a high order from the principal characters, and most experienced performers find difficulty in maintaining pace and interest. The Eoan Group must therefore be congratulated for a production that was generally successful."[112] The work certainly requires superior musical and technical mastery; combined with its spectacular display of the voice as an instrument and its ever popular love story, the opera never fails to impress. Although other operatic works may fulfill the same criteria, the group was by that time very familiar with the work; combining this with the availability of experienced principal singers who had mastered these roles for years already, its repeated performance by the group is not difficult to understand. Eoan's many successful performances of this demanding work stand to this day as a monument to the achievements of a disenfranchised organization.

In 1975 legislation was passed that lifted the ban on coloured attendance at and participation in productions at the Nico Malan Theatre.[113] The debate had been ongoing since the inauguration of the theater in 1971, and the press reported on the issue intermittently. The Eoan Group's existence and its decades of arts production were often used in arguments against the ban. Most vocal in the campaign was Brian Bamford, who had lobbied in the provincial parliament to boycott the opening in 1971 (his attempt was unsuccessful at the time) and continued to raise the issue in the ensuing years.[114] In February 1973 the *Argus* published a letter by Bamford in which he explained the legislation that enabled the ban to come into place and identified the administrator of the Western Cape, the highest political position in the province, as the person who could easily change it all. In the introduction to this article he stated unambiguously the sobering reality that "no non-white may enter its portals as a performer or patron, but only as a workman or foreign diplomat."[115] He furthermore argued that the founding of the Performing Arts Councils (PACs) and the erection of buildings such as the Nico Malan Theatre were actions taken by the government because it "observed somewhat enviously" the successes and standing ovations that the Eoan Group had earned since the 1950s.[116] Although this claim has also been made to the current author by other group members during interviews for this book, the reasons for the founding of the PACs were in fact more varied. Although government certainly took notice of Eoan, it was evident that opera production in the country as a whole was burgeoning and in need of strong central administration and proper funding.[117] However, apartheid legislation pertinently excluded other races from the structures or benefits of the PACs.

Not all in government supported the ban. In February 1973 the *Argus* also ran an editorial that discussed the condemnation of the ban by former minister of community development and at the time South African ambassador to Italy, Mr. Blaar Coetzee. He is reported to have said that the ban was doing South Africa "great harm" and that the legislation was unnecessary and unjustifiable.[118] The editorial stated that "even the most ardent of apartheid theorists—the ones who claim that their principles are not racially based but stem from the contention that separation is 'natural' for those with different backgrounds and different interests—find it hard to argue that enthusiasts for opera experience enjoyment in some peculiarly separate way if they are of different races."[119] Apparently this comment cost Coetzee his job; he was forced to resign shortly afterward.[120]

The lifting of the color bar was accompanied by yet more controversy, as the government initially insisted on opening the building for coloureds on certain days only, causing another furor in the press. The process surrounding the unbanning aggravated the already strong resentment against the building within the coloured community. After the ban was lifted, many coloureds for years refused to go to the Nico Malan Theatre.[121] In theory, the removal of the color bar at the Nico Malan Theatre opened the door for Eoan to perform opera or ballet in its capacity as an independent arts company and for its artists to participate in CAPAB productions, whether as singers, dancers, or actors. In reality, however, Eoan performed only once in the Nico Malan (during a fund-raising concert for its tour to the United Kingdom), and participation in CAPAB's productions by Eoan members had to wait until 1980.

In February 1975 the Cape Town City Hall also was declared open to all races.[122] Although Ismail Sydow commented in the press that the group was "naturally very pleased," this relaxation of apartheid legislation was a hollow victory for Eoan because the venue was in any event no longer able logistically to accommodate its opera productions.[123]

### EOAN TOURS ABROAD

During this period the Eoan Group was preoccupied with preparations for its UK tour, marked by a busy rehearsal schedule, a host of administrative matters, and a desperate scramble for funds. The initiative to approach the Festival Foundation in the United Kingdom had been taken by Sydow some time earlier when he visited his daughter, Didi, in London in December 1972. A meeting with the foundation was set up via Bruce Pinkard (Didi Sydow's husband), and Sydow managed to convince the festival organizers to guarantee Eoan's participation.[124] At this early stage the Eoan Group was already placed on the official list of organizations taking part in the 1975 Festival.[125] The official invitation, received on 11 February 1974, set out the scope of the tour:

> The Festival Foundation cordially invites 35 members of the Eoan Opera Group to attend the 1975 International Festival of Youth Orchestras which will take place from 4th–15th August in Aberdeen and from 15th–17th in London. The Eoan Group will give one main performance in Aberdeen and another in a neighboring Scottish town as well as participating in the two gala evenings, one in Aberdeen and one in London.
> 
> We, the International Festival of Youth Orchestras Foundation, guarantee to pay for the 35 members of the Eoan Group's full board and accommodation. The Festival Foundation will also be responsible for covering the cost of the Eoan Group's transport from Aberdeen to London on 15th August.[126]

With its lodging and transportation inside the United Kingdom paid for, Eoan only needed sponsorship for the group's airfares and other costs such as loss of wages for those singers who had to take unpaid leave from their daytime jobs, pocket money for their time abroad, and freight costs for shipping costumes. Additional funding also had to be raised for an extra two weeks of training for the group at the Opera Centre in London after the festival. Through Sydow, Eoan applied for sponsorship from South African Airways, in a letter dated 20 September 1974: "[The festival organizers] replied that the Eoan Group's participation in the Festival sounded very interesting and exciting not only from the cultural aspect but more importantly from the point of closer understanding of the activities of various countries thereby promoting closer human relationships between the youth of the world."[127] The budget for the tour amounted to ZAR45,000, of which the group was able to contribute approximately ZAR15,000 from fund-raising concerts.[128] The bid for sponsorship from South African Airways was unsuccessful, and it was only in April 1975 that Sydow could confirm that the DCA (yet again) had promised to meet the shortfall in the group's expenses, provided that Eoan approached as many other institutions as possible to raise funds.[129] In June Sydow applied for additional funding from the Municipality of Cape Town. This letter too explained the purpose of the festival, in terms that contrasted starkly with the circumstances and political atmosphere in which Eoan was trying to produce opera locally. Just two years earlier, the permit that had allowed Eoan to perform in the Green & Sea Point Civic Centre had gone so far as forbidding social mingling between the white and coloured races.[130] Sydow now described how the aim of the festival was to counter racial segregation on just those terms: "The Festival brings together with a common cultural purpose youth from different countries, varying socio-economic backgrounds, different religions, races and even opposed political ideologies, and encourages a harmonious, co-operative and creative period of living together, with music as the common interest and motivation. A major aim of the Festival is to foster good relationships and international understanding amongst the youth of different countries and to promote respect and tolerance for one's fellowman."[131]

Since this was a youth festival, those chosen to travel abroad had to be under twenty-six years old. The full company consisted of a choir comprising twenty-six singers under that age; four guest soloists (tenors Ronald Theys and Gerald Samaai and sopranos Vera Gow and May Abrahamse); six of Eoan's dance teachers (Lydia Johnson, Ruth Snyders, Achmat Ockards, Bedroenisa Watson, Henry Paulse, and Dick Jaffer); and six administrative staff members, including Joseph Manca and his wife, Minnie, Ismail Sydow and his wife, Carmen, Eoan's voice trainer, Alessandro Rota, and Eoan's accompanist, Regina Devereux.[132] To raise funds for the tour, the group gave six additional operatic concerts: two in Cape Town (of which one was in the City Hall and the other in the Nico Malan Theatre, Eoan's first and only performance in that venue); one in Stellenbosch; and on the group's way to Johannesburg to catch its flight to the United Kingdom, one each in Bloemfontein, Johannesburg, and Pretoria.[133] The week before Eoan's departure, the group traveled 1,000 kilometers (about 621 miles) by bus to Bloemfontein in the Free State, where it gave a concert in the Bloemfontein Town Hall on 25 July. Sydow described this event: "This represents a great break-through for the Coloured Community. Never before in the history of South Africa have Coloured People been allowed a) to appear in the Orange Free State, and b) to stay in the same hotel with White persons."[134] On 26 July the group traveled another 500 kilometers (about 310 miles) to Pretoria and gave its last fund-raising concert at the University of South Africa in Pretoria. This too was described as "another break-through" with regard to racial matters.[135] On 28 July the group departed for London from the then Jan Smuts Airport outside Johannesburg.

During the festival Eoan performed various opera choruses from its existing repertoire, with and without soloists. The group was accompanied by the Young Person's Symphony Orchestra from Scotland, which Manca conducted.[136] (See Manca conducting the Eoan Group choir, figure 5.4.) The festival in Aberdeen was held not only to display musical talent, but also to focus on training. The ballet participants attended classes in London, and Dick Jaffer was given the opportunity to fly to Madrid, Spain, for training in Spanish dance. After the festival the group stayed in London for another twelve days, during which members received training in acting, movement, dialogue, and makeup at the London Opera Centre, where they were trained by, among others, Gordon Jephtas. The group also presented a concert at the Theatre Royal in Drury Lane.[137] On 27 August the group was invited to a reception hosted by the South African ambassador in England at the South African embassy; the group then returned home on 30 August.[138]

The National Youth Orchestra of South Africa, consisting of white musicians only, also participated in the festival. The two groups were apparently unaware of each other's existence until they met in Aberdeen; according to Winfried Lüdemann, who at the time was a member of the Youth Orchestra, most orchestra members were completely surprised that a coloured opera group such as Eoan existed. The South African participation in the events did not occur without controversy; according to Lüdemann, antiapartheid demonstrations took place outside the concert hall where both groups were

FIGURE 5.4. Manca conducting the Eoan Group Choir. Source: Eoan Group Archive.

performing. During the festival informal sports events were organized, and the Eoan singers and Youth Orchestra musicians played soccer together on one team against Poland.¹³⁹

### THINGS FALL APART

The group's tour to the United Kingdom seems to have infused great energy into the group, especially in the ballet section, whose teachers had the opportunity to receive additional training in their respective disciplines (Spanish dance, classical ballet, and rock and jazz dance). Shortly after the group's return, the newspaper *Rapport* ran an article focusing on the dance section only, describing members' experiences in the United Kingdom and their subsequent enthusiasm for the future.¹⁴⁰ During the tour young mezzo-soprano Judith Bailey had so impressed the principal conductor at the festival Claudio Abbado that he facilitated a two-year study period for her at La Scala in Italy. Bailey took up this opportunity in the course of 1976.¹⁴¹ In February 1976 *Rapport* reported that the opera director from the Morley College in London,

Andrew Downie, had visited Cape Town to negotiate a possible production with Eoan. Downie had attended the group's performance in Drury Lane the year before and was apparently eager to work with the group.[142] In the same month Sydow received recognition from the Cape Tercentenary Foundation for his work with the Eoan Group. He became the first person of color within the group to receive institutional recognition for his years of dedication to its cultural activities.[143] Manca, too, had many plans, and in July 1976 he reported to the DCA that during the financial year 1977 Eoan would "endeavour to present an Opera Season or production of a musical in either the Nico Malan Opera House or the Baxter Theatre."[144]

The mid-1970s were very turbulent years politically, especially for those living in coloured and black residential areas. Resistance groups grew in numbers, and mass mobilization in schools, colleges, and universities, as well as residential areas, became a daily reality. On 16 July 1976, the Soweto uprising took place. Approximately 10,000 people marched in protest against the forced introduction of Afrikaans as a medium of instruction in schools. The protest was brutally quashed, causing the death of 176 people and up to 1,000 people wounded, among them many children. By August antiapartheid protests and subsequent violence had spread to the Cape townships of Langa, Nyanga, and Gugulethu, as well as coloured residential areas. Unrest at the University of the Western Cape (a university for coloureds only) led to several arrests, and in September a mass strike by coloured workers against apartheid legislation paralyzed the Cape Town city center.[145] A year later, on 12 September 1977, Steve Biko, the leader of the Black Consciousness movement, was killed in detention.[146]

With Manca as gatekeeper to the Eoan Group Archive, documentation dating from this period contains no evidence whatsoever of any of these circumstances or any resistance to apartheid among group members. It is therefore difficult to gauge to what extent the unrest influenced the functioning of the group and the daily activities of the artists. The archive does tell us that during the course of 1976 the group continued rehearsing, and that it presented a few operatic concerts as well as a number of ballet presentations.[147] The ballet section seems to have had large numbers of students, and in October 1976 *Rapport* published the names of 146 dancers who had passed ballet exams.[148] But Eoan was not the only ballet academy active in the area. A new ballet school, the Silverleaf Dance School, sprang up independently from Eoan, touring Europe and the Middle East and presenting a number of concerts in the Nico Malan Theatre, an opportunity the Eoan Group had thus far not utilized.[149]

Paging through the documentation in the archive as well as articles published in the newspapers, it seems that, on paper at least, the group's spirits were high, with continued music and dance activities. Major expansion plans existed, accompanied by Manca's customary superlatives about the group's future plans. Noted problems were the lack of subsidies, education, and performing opportunities for artists. However, in November 1977, in a move that seemed to take Eoan's members by surprise, Joseph Manca resigned as director of the group.[150] At the age of sixty-nine, he had been with the group for thirty-four years. The official reason given for his resignation was ill health, but although he had been suffering from heart problems for a decade, it was evident that more was amiss. In an interview many years later, May Abrahamse explained that nobody in the group was formally informed of his resignation, and when she tried to find out what was going on, her inquiries were met with indifference. She said: "Nobody knew anything; nobody could tell [me] anything. So everybody just said 'O, Manca retired.'"[151] Significantly, there was also no opportunity for Eoan members to say goodbye to Manca or to make any formal gesture of thanks or commemoration for the many trials and triumphs that they had shared in the course of more than three decades. Manca is said to have avoided contact with group members in the years following this abrupt exit; when he died in October 1985, his family apparently requested that Eoan members not attend his funeral.[152]

Under-the-surface power struggles seem to have been going on for some time. But to this day it is difficult to find out exactly what happened, since former members are still reluctant to discuss the issue. It is evident from interviews conducted in the course of this research project that despite his shortcomings, members had always respected Manca and that they (perhaps unconsciously) knew that without him, there would be no opera production. Manca's daughter, Ruth Grevler, later said: "I just know that something happened. I wish I knew what it was, I would really love to know what it was and who it was, but I just know it caused my father his downfall."[153] Not having the facts, one is tempted to speculate, and plausible reasons arising from interviews include Manca's authoritarian style of management, his refusal to allow any talk on politics, the lack of acknowledgment for Eoan's artists, allegations of the misappropriation of funds, the rise of black consciousness among the coloured community, and the fact that Manca was indeed growing old and needed to be replaced. His resignation, however, left the organization floundering, and his departure was clearly experienced as a traumatic break. In an interview with Bruce Heilbuth, published in *Scenaria*, David

Bloomberg, who had had a long association with Eoan and was a trustee member, stated that "my biggest worry about the future of the Group is not financial but directional. Joseph Manca's going has left a wide gap. They knew it was coming eventually and for years they have tried to find someone who could take his place. Jephtas might have been the answer, had he been available. No, the main problem is to find a new driving force to co-ordinate and train the Group."[154]

The disintegration of organizational structures within the group accelerated when Sydow too resigned, in February 1978, after having been with Eoan for thirty-six years. During this time he had served as chairperson of the group from 1963 until 1977. The reason given for his resignation was, like Manca's earlier resignation, ill health.[155] Sydow's wife, Carmen, who had been wardrobe mistress since the early 1950s, resigned as well and left Eoan with her husband.[156] With the sudden exit of three individuals who for more than thirty years had taken the main responsibility for Eoan's administration and functioning, confusion seems to have reigned, resulting in much talk, the airing of grievances, and few solutions. The extent of unhappiness and dissent was even reported in an article in *Rapport* that outlined some of the trouble.[157] The article reported that Sydow had allegedly announced the dissolution of the entire music section shortly after Manca's resignation, a seemingly unilateral decision that enraged the singers. Other complaints related to the alleged underutilization of the Joseph Stone Auditorium, problems with funds, and the lack of performing opportunities.[158] The minutes of the executive committee meeting held on 3 May 1978 recorded that three more members of Eoan's management resigned: Mr. M. Modak, Mrs. S. Gierdien, and Eoan's voice trainer, Olga Magnoni. Outgoing members felt Manca and Sydow were undeservedly attacked, and during his resignation speech Modak referred to "the ingratitude and utter unfairness reflected in the recent attacks against Mr. Sydow and Dr. Manca."[159] Other than confirming that strife indeed existed between Eoan's management and its members, this also illustrated an inability to engage with the conflicts that seemed to have been simmering for years. The minutes state that no replacement had yet been found for Manca, but the ballet dancer Dick Jaffer was appointed as new wardrobe master.[160]

In order to find a successor for Manca, it was agreed that May Abrahamse (then secretary of the group) would again write to Gordon Jephtas "to try and see how he felt about the group and if he would at all consider coming to South Africa to aid the group if the necessary funds were available to suitably employ him."[161] In August 1978 Sydow's position was filled by Veronica Allan, who was appointed Eoan's new chairperson, but no treasurer or artistic director is mentioned on the list of executive committee members during that year.[162] In the meantime, Eoan continued to apply for annual grants from the DCA and received ZAR20,000 for the financial year 1977–1978.

After the departure of Manca, the activities of the music section slowed down significantly. The group's efforts to engage the services of Gordon Jephtas as artistic director finally paid off when he agreed to take up the position on a contract basis in 1979. Jephtas had left the group in 1965 to pursue a career as repetiteur and vocal coach abroad and had since enjoyed considerable exposure to high-level opera production in Europe and the United States. From 1972 onward he experienced significant professional success, with regular contracts at prestigious opera houses in Europe and the United States, where he worked with some of the world's foremost opera singers.[163] Jephtas's letters to Abrahamse reveal that although he always felt a strong allegiance to Eoan's singers, he was acutely aware of the artistic isolation in which the group operated and felt that its performance standards were below par. He also often commented on the lack of renewal within the group with regard to repertoire and felt that many principal singers, as well as Manca, had stagnated.[164] Furthermore, communication between Jephtas and Eoan's management regarding his possible return was a drawn-out and complicated affair. Expectations on both sides were never communicated adequately, and Jephtas's return was always uncertain. As early as February 1970, Jephtas gave some indication of the fraught relationship with Eoan's management in one of his letters:

> Just today I had a letter from Manca (only the second since I left Cape Town). A rift had been created between the two of us and hence relationships have been cool—consequently I left the first move up to him and with time he bit at the bait. Up [until now all communication went] via a 3rd person. So about 3 weeks ago arrives this letter, ostensibly with the pretext of sending me some useless income tax receipt and, I presumed, to fix some idea about me returning. As it was too evasive a letter I wrote back, asking him to state his point of view and then I would decide from there. And [in] the second letter of yesterday I [was] particularly struck by one sentence: "obviously you are better off in Europe, but although you may make a success of your career, [here in Cape Town] you will be involved in the most competitive field of employment"—and in fact, <u>this</u> in itself is just what is attracting me to the European field—competition is what I want. And [the lack thereof] is just [that] in the Eoan Group [which] I dislike most.[165]

This quote and numerous other references regarding his possible return in Jephtas's letters to Abrahamse illustrate the uncomfortable relationship he had with Eoan's management. Despite his reputation as heir apparent to the artistic directorship since the late 1950s, his relationship with the group during his years abroad became increasingly complex. Negotiations for his return had been intermittent since 1965, and Jephtas visited the group sporadically, when he would usually coach the principal singers. However, the conversation between him and Eoan's management seemed to be one of continuous inconclusive demands and evasive answers on both sides.[166] Jephtas clearly had little desire to work under the group's conditions. This pertained not only to the artistic isolation and narrow scope of the repertoire, but also to his growing awareness of the managerial subjugation and racial inequalities he would be subject to if he accepted the position on Manca's conditions. It is no coincidence that Jephtas only returned to the Eoan Group as artistic director after Manca and Sydow had both stepped down.

During Jephtas's tenure in early 1979, he and Abrahamse presented a recital at the Nico Malan Theatre (see figure 5.5). The event took place on 3 March 1979 and was indeed of historical significance because this was the only recital ever presented by an Eoan principal singer at this venue.[167] Abrahamse and Jephtas had been close friends since the early 1960s, and in August 1971 they had presented a similar recital in Durban when Abrahamse resided there.[168] In the intervening years they had tried to negotiate a repeat performance of this recital in Cape Town under Eoan's auspices, but to no avail.[169] Years later Abrahamse elaborated on the issue in an interview for the oral history book *Eoan—Our Story*. Her comments illustrate the divergent artistic sensibilities of Jephtas and Eoan's management: "They wouldn't allow it. No, Mr. Sydow said that they don't do concerts with one person only. He said, no, it must be everybody. And then I said to him, 'But Mr. Sydow, it's another art form'. So he said to me 'Art, what is art?'"[170]

The recital consisted of arias from operas by Verdi, Bellini, Donizetti, and Purcell as well as two Afrikaans songs, "Heimwee" by S. le Roux Marais and "O, Boereplaas" by Johannes Joubert.[171] The pair earned many glowing reviews in the newspapers, and Jephtas's focus on interpretation through acting and the use of the voice seems to have paid off well for this concert. Antoinette Silvestri's review in the *Cape Argus* described the event as a "most dramatic recital at [the] Nico" and commented on Abrahamse's singing of the aria "O Rendetemila Speme" from Bellini's *I Puritani*: "In Elvira's aria Abrahamse in one small gesture allows the sleeve of [her] cloak to fall: it is an

FIGURE 5.5. May Abrahamse and Gordon Jephtas during their recital in the Nico Malan Theatre on 3 March 1979. Photo by Amanda Botha.

infinitesimal touch, yet the whole role, the whole life of the opera is there. She then [gives] a superbly contrasted, rich and tragic interpretation where each gesture and inflection mirrors the state of Elvira's mind."[172]

Silvestri's review concluded by stating what many Eoan members as well as their (mostly white) patrons had been fervently hoping for: "The Eoan Group is entering a new era."[173] However, Eoan's "new era" as envisaged through Jephtas's directorship turned out to last less than five months. His term was fraught with disagreements and differences among him, the Eoan board, and the members, and even before his contract expired Jephtas decided to quit. Much appears to be have been amiss with Eoan's administration during this time. Jephtas resigned via telegram and formulated his reasons for doing so to Eoan's management thus:

> Eoan Executive and members,
>
> I, the willing, lead [sic] by the unknowing have been doing the impossible for the ungrateful. I am cancelling my commitment to Eoan because I will not deal with an amateur and mediocre business manager and not being a social worker I am not capable of dealing with people with no identity, big mouths behind authority's back, lots of talent but no skills. Mediocrity and second class situations have never interested me. You all are now qualified to do anything with nothing.
>
> Gordon Jephtas.[174]

The minutes of the AGM of 25 October reveal that much dissension had existed among Eoan members regarding a number of issues, among others Jephtas's role as artistic director. Besides alleged overspending on the Nico Malan Theatre recital in March, his vision for the music section was to let go of opera altogether and tackle what he felt were artistically feasible projects for Eoan's choir. Furthermore, he wanted to dedicate more focus and funding to Eoan's ballet and drama sections instead of continuing in opera. He was of the opinion that drama and ballet were at the time the stronger attributes of the group and had the capacity to carry the organization through its difficulties into the future.[175] Jephtas had also written an unfavorable report about Eoan's "sense of colouredness." This (confidential) report had been leaked to the press, and his opinions not only deeply offended many in the group but also highlighted the conundrum of the concept of coloured identity.[176]

The conflation of Eoan's opera productions with the coloured population's "desire for assimilation into European culture," as discussed in the introduction to this book, has often led to accusations that Eoan aspired to "whiteness." During the time that he lived abroad (some fifteen years by that time), Jephtas had acquired a sense of pride about being coloured and was dismayed at the group's dependence on white benevolence. The leaked report was discussed in the *Cape Herald*, a newspaper aimed at a coloured readership. It reported that Jephtas "made a call to coloured people to develop 'authentic coloured attitudes'" and that he stressed "the need for coloured people to stop imitating whites and instead to become self-reliant, developing a way of life peculiar to themselves."[177] Within the coloured community these comments had both sides of the political divide up in arms. Eoan Group members were incensed at his accusation that they were imitating whites, and his reference to the group's dependence on funding from the DCA added insult to injury.

In the aftermath of this affair, attention was indeed directed at Eoan's dependence on the DCA, bad press the group could ill afford.[178] Those who grew up in the wave of black consciousness (generally the younger generation and some of the older generation) rejected the idea of coloured identity and viewed it as an apartheid construct. In the same article poet and playwright Adam Small was asked to comment on Jephtas's utterances and was quoted as saying that "culturally and in every other way 'colouredism' and 'coloured-ising' must be rejected." Indeed, Jephtas's remarks "stirred a hornet's nest which [caused] Cape Town's Eoan all sorts of problems in its efforts to shed its 'coloured' image."[179]

The correspondence between Jephtas and Abrahamse shows that Jephtas was not politically outspoken, and these comments illustrate his lack of shrewdness with regard to identity politics at home. He also had had little exposure to the ideas of black consciousness while living abroad. Yet the letters also reveal that Jephtas, for a long time, struggled with a deep sense of shame at being coloured and that being out of the country, he appears to have overcome that. Some of his letters are even signed with the word "Boesman" [Bushman], referencing his Khoi ancestry.[180] He had also rid himself of the attitude of servitude that characterized the early development of the group, and he had no intention of withdrawing his remarks. In a newspaper report in *Rapport* on 11 November 1979, he continued to chastise the coloured community for expecting others to improve their destiny, comments he acknowledged would irk his community.[181] Having worked in New York on a number of occasions, he had come into contact with Arthur Mitchell and the Dance Theatre of Harlem and been impressed by the ethos of this all-black dance company. It was this example that struck a chord with him and bolstered his conviction that a coloured arts company was indeed possible.[182]

The breakdown between Jephtas and the Eoan community can also be attributed to the fact that members had assumed that Jephtas would revive the golden years of opera production in the 1950s and 1960s. Although Jephtas was certainly a talented and skilled musician, his organizational skills were nowhere near as proficient as those of Manca, and on the artistic side his ideas about what Eoan should be performing were not popular. During his tenure Jephtas appointed former Eoan ballet dancer Peter Voges as his assistant, who later summed up the situation well: "The Music Section, which was in the doldrums after the glorious days of Grand Opera, presented a different problem. Gordon Jephtas wanted the Opera 'stigma' to be removed and the choir to sing as a choir and its activities to become more diverse."[183]

After submitting his resignation Jephtas returned to the United States, where he became a sought-after repetiteur in New York during the 1980s. He also had regular contracts with the San Francisco Opera House, the Lyric Opera in Chicago, the Metropolitan Opera House in New York, the New York City Opera, and Utah Opera in Salt Lake City. During the 1980s he coached singers such as Luciano Pavarotti, Beverly Sills, Maria Chiara, Frederica von Stade, Luigi Alva, Monserrat Caballè, Leontyne Price, Marilyn Horne, Neil Shicoff, Teresa Berganza, and Joan Sutherland. He was also involved in productions with directors such as Pier Luigi Pizzi, Tito Gobbi, Kurt Herbert Adler, Richard Bonynge, and the controversial Jean-Pierre Ponnelle.[184] During these years he twice tried to relocate to South Africa for longer periods of time; in 1986 he was contracted by the Performing Arts Council of Transvaal (PACT) in Pretoria as chorus master, and in 1991 he coached singers at CAPAB. However, these ventures were short-lived, and he returned to the United States after both ventures. Sometime during the 1980s he became HIV positive, and he passed away in New York in July 1992.[185]

For Eoan, opera activities had formally come to an end in 1980. Apart from Jephtas's sudden departure, the organization was entangled in a maze of political difficulties and internal divisions, exacerbated by a gap between the older and younger generations. The only way forward for the music section seemed to be the implementation of the ideas Jephtas had put forward, which led to the Eoan choir's alliance with the Gilbert and Sullivan Choir in Cape Town.[186] Rosemary Steward was appointed as conductor and reported that the choir had now broken away from opera music.[187] The Gilbert and Sullivan Society had produced operettas since 1927 and functioned throughout apartheid as a whites-only organization, yet with the thawing of apartheid interracial collaborations such as this one became possible. This new venture, however, was also short-lived, and shortly thereafter Eoan's choir stopped functioning altogether.[188]

Compounding the difficulties caused by the political situation and the lack of artistic resources, the organization continued to be crippled by infighting, distrust, and gossip. In his report to the Eoan board of November 1980, in which he announced his resignation, Voges echoed Jephtas's memorable resignation telegram of a year earlier: "Too many uninformed people stir up needless trouble by spreading malicious gossip with the main aim being character assassination and further with the aim of promotion of personal opinions; and these in turn lack total artistic commitment or value. Where else but in Eoan are so many unqualified people allowed to voice so many unqualified opinions, and sadly receive qualified attention."[189] Minutes of board meetings from this time reflect how infighting and distrust resulted in little other than harsh words and poor decisions.[190]

Political imperatives were belatedly entering into Eoan's decision making. Earlier that year Roy Stoffels, head of Eoan's drama section, compiled a report entitled "Reasons Why the Eoan Group Is No Longer a Viable Arts Project." This soul-searching document articulated the consequences of Eoan's overdue acknowledgment of apartheid politics:

1. Eoan is synonymous with "Coloured Culture."
2. "Coloured Culture" is a political offspring of the government of the day.
3. The young people do not identify themselves with a politically cultivated culture.
4. The history of the Group is riddled with the organization's acceptances of this phenomenon, i.e. being a showpiece of "Coloured Culture."
5. The stigma is indelible because the present generation have been schooled into rejecting Eoan.
6. The scholars who attend at present, often have to keep their membership a secret for fear of victimization from fellow students and also staff.
7. Lack of foresight by previous administrations have caused the Group to evolve a stale image; e.g. a place where opera is done or a place where Indian movies are shown.
8. This staleness has remained and the lop-sided distribution of funds proves this point.
9. Businesses have failed to respond effectively enough to appeals for assistance for fear of damaging their own images. We are therefore wholly dependent on the government subsidy.
10. The Eoan Group (with its charter and aims of its founder) has served its purpose to a particular generation.[191]

Stoffels's report was discussed during a general meeting of Eoan's executive committee, and approximately sixty members attended on 1 June 1980. It is evident from the minutes of this meeting that the report was deemed necessary because the public (i.e., the coloured community) no longer supported Eoan, resulting in empty halls at performances or last-minute cancellations, with more dire financial consequences. The minutes also reveal that members were out of their depth and found it difficult to react constructively to the report. The general feedback was recorded in loose sentences such as "a fantastic piece of work which could not be dismissed"; "a delicate matter required deep and earnest thinking"; "there is hot and cold air and they need to balance"; "too many crumbling memorials"; and "members must re-assess the situation, not rely on the past and be unaware of the present and future."[192] Members of the older generation were clearly upset to be labeled "hot air" and found it difficult to accept the reality of the generation gap as well as the presence of political antagonism in their midst. The fact that politics actually influenced the existence of Eoan so fundamentally came as a rude awakening.[193] The following quote from the minutes illustrates how members, in this example a Mr. Arendse, struggled to come to terms with the situation: "We have been sitting with these problems all the years. All have their personal views, but here we must keep politics out of the Group. [I am] a member because of the love of music, but that does not make [me] a government stooge. We can stick to our principles and continue learning or else stay away."[194]

However, in keeping with the new political awareness, the executive decided that the group would not participate in the Republic Festival planned for 1981 to celebrate the twentieth anniversary of the Republic of South Africa.[195] This would be the first time since 1952, when the group had abstained from participating in the Jan van Riebeeck Festival, that Eoan would take an explicitly politically informed decision resisting the government's wishes.

At the same meeting it was announced that Alessandro Rota, Eoan's voice trainer and producer, had retired from the group. He was now eighty years old. As a longtime friend and colleague of Manca, he had directed Eoan's first opera production in 1956 and had joined the group again as director and voice trainer from 1965 onward. A farewell concert by the group was held for him on 26 November 1980 at the Italian embassy. This concert brought to a close an era of opera production in which Eoan enjoyed the support of opera lovers in the greater Cape Town area.[196]

The slow and painful ebbing away of Eoan's opera endeavors may have led to the cessation of formal opera activities, but it did not result in the death of the organization or the end of the artistic activities of some of its artists. Throughout South Africa's turbulent 1980s, the group continued to function as a cultural organization on a smaller scale. Its drama and dance sections remained active, and occasional operatic concerts were held in an attempt to remember the group's "glorious days of Grand Opera." A number of singers also found professional employment at the (formerly whites-only) Performing Arts Councils (PACs). The first Eoan singers to be employed at CAPAB, in 1980, were tenors Keith Timms and Ronald Theys.[197] In the late 1980s soprano Virginia Davids and tenor Sidwell Hartman also joined CAPAB as principal singers, and both were later employed as singing lecturers at the College of Music at the University of Cape Town, where they still teach.[198] For May Abrahamse, too, professional opportunities became a reality. From 1982 to 1987 she sang as ad hoc chorister at CAPAB, and from 1987 to 1990 she held a permanent position as chorus member with the Performing Arts Council of the Orange Free State (PACOFS) in Bloemfontein. During the course of the 1990s she remained involved with the Eoan Group as vocal coach and served in other administrative capacities for the group until well into her seventies.[199]

The group's circumstances after 1980 were difficult, and reinvention in terms of leadership, cultural identity, and activities remained hampered by internal infighting and the lack of infrastructure.[200] The group was also loath to relinquish its state funding, and it wasn't until 1989 that Eoan renounced its dependence on apartheid state funding.[201] Yet even after taking this bold step, its politically tainted reputation persisted well into the twenty-first century.[202]

# *Postscript*

> Farewell, happy dreams of bygone days
> The roses in my cheeks already are faded.
> Ah, all is over, all is over now.
>
> —VIOLETTA, Act 3, *La Traviata*
> by Giuseppe Verdi

In act 3 of *La Traviata,* Violetta is alone in her room and sings the aria "Addio, del passato," a section of which is quoted at the beginning of this chapter. She bids farewell to the days when she knew happiness, had many friends, and was loved by Alfredo. She is now poor, gravely ill, and rejected by her lover, and she knows she is about to die. Evoking Violetta's fate to describe Eoan's has been a persistent image of this book. Despite the group's unconditional (and unexamined) belief in the transcendent values of opera, singing under the auspices of the system of apartheid undermined the aspirations and the lives of Eoan's opera singers in a profound way. By 1980 the group's opera section had all but disappeared; its reputation among its own community was in tatters; professional (white) opera houses deemed its singers below par; the group's organizational structures were in disarray; and the political environment, sensitized by black consciousness, had rejected them. Comparing Eoan's story with that of the main character in the group's favorite opera introduces the notion of pathos, for which little room is left in the uncompromising and robust nature of political activism on the one hand and the pitfalls of uncritical support for a repressive political system on the other. Yet pathos remains central to how I, as a white scholar of Western art music, attempt to make sense of Eoan's opera performances in apartheid South Africa.

The goal of this book has been to recount the trajectory of the Eoan Group's opera performances in order to create some kind of testament to its remarkable story. Scholarly engagement with the opera performances of this group up to this time has been limited to my own work and that of Juliana Pistorius. It includes a chapter on Eoan in my doctoral dissertation; an oral history book, *Eoan—Our Story*, which I coedited; and a few articles published in South African academic journals.[1] The materials of the Eoan Group Archive have been presorted and will remain stored in boxes in the Documentation Centre for Music at Stellenbosch University (DOMUS) for the time being. Apart from telling this unique story, in which the intersection of race, politics, and opera production in apartheid South Africa come into such sharp focus, the book creates a space in the canon of Western art music scholarship for the history of the practice of opera by a marginalized cultural grouping. Central to this endeavor was to sketch the social and political frame in which Eoan's artists lived and performed and the context in which audiences received their performances.

In the broader public domain in South Africa, the memory of Eoan seems to have disappeared after the cessation of its opera performances. In "Remembering to Forget the Eoan Group—the Legacy of an Opera Company from the Apartheid Era," published in 2014, I discuss how I tried to find glimpses of the group in academic and popular publications between 1990 and 2013 and found almost none. I concluded that even though the group was active and widely known (in the Cape Peninsula at least), the memory of its opera productions had started to disappear from public memory. Thirty years later this neglect reached its defining moment when Cape Town Opera produced Verdi's *La Traviata* in October 2011 and the *Cape Times* music critic, Deon Irish, wrote that the first production of this opera in Cape Town was in 1973 by the CAPAB, a body that catered for white artists only.[2]

One of the reasons Eoan's story has not been recounted in the public sphere since South Africa became a democracy may be the inaccessibility of the archival documentation. Up until 2008, when the archive was transferred to DOMUS, it had been lying untouched underneath the orchestra pit in the Joseph Stone Auditorium (formerly the Eoan Group Cultural Centre) in Athlone since 1969. In a country like South Africa, where institutional infrastructure for archives is sorely lacking, the circumstances of the Eoan archive are no different from many other archives that contain the riches of South Africa's musical heritage. What is clear is that the painful associations of the group's complicity with apartheid constitute the most important reason that its story has been so resistant to ownership and scholarly focus. The euphoria of postapartheid South Africa in the years following 1994 saw an exuberant reclaiming of indigenous cultural heritages, a celebration of the heroics of the struggle against apartheid, and an attempt to right the wrongs of the past. In this context, the exploration of the complicity of an organization within a political system that dehumanized those who were not white is difficult. I would even posit that as a result of the political controversy, there has been an express wish (albeit unconscious) to forget the memory of this group.

Today, more than forty years after Eoan's last formal opera production, there is enough historical distance to engage with an instance of opera production by a group that was viewed by its own community as collaborators. From my perspective as a white academic of Western art music who grew up in apartheid South Africa and benefited from its privileges, Eoan was a disenfranchised group. This book therefore recounts the systematic and relentless way in which apartheid eroded the environment that enabled the group to perform opera. Yet the larger community, disenfranchised by apartheid, rejected its performances, and Eoan did little to voice the community's disenfranchisement.

Eoan exemplified "otherness" to the white opera-performing world in twentieth-century South Africa. At the same time, opera so bedazzled the group that it accepted the ensnarement that came with apartheid funding. From this point of view, Eoan was undone by its members' love for opera. Aryan Kaganof's 2013 film on the group, *An Inconsolable Memory*, described as a "poetic meditation on memory," poignantly reflects on how legislated coloureds performed Italian opera and the painful compromises made to survive apartheid.[3] Kaganof, a filmmaker known for his uncompromising perceptions of South African politics and his predilection for music, was expressly drawn to the dignity of the singers he filmed and interviewed. Of this he said:

> I fell deeply in love with many of the people I interviewed. I fell in love with the complexity of their story and the utter indifference that real life has to political ideologies. There really are no good guys and bad guys in life. *An Inconsolable Memory* is about people whose lives were not easily described as heroic in the bold political sense, and yet, every one of them earned a kind of impossible heroism when they performed on the stage singing those Italian operas. Once the show was over they returned to a world where they enjoyed less than second-class status. To retain dignity under those conditions is an immense task, and it is everything.[4]

The material in the Eoan Group Archive is extraordinarily rich, and the issues that the story of the group's opera productions bring to the table are manifold. Only a few of have been taken up in the course of this narrative, and many remain unaddressed and unexplored. These include disciplinary and methodological concerns regarding the writing of history and the meaning of memory, as well as content-related issues such as the indigenization of opera, coloured agency, and the intricate ways in which "whiteness" impacted coloured identity. Similarly varied are the interpretations of the legacy of the group. For Eoan's artists, their families, and the younger generation of coloured artists who carried the group through the 1980s into postapartheid South Africa, the trajectory and the legacy of the group are probably understood in a more positive and assertive way. Political activists from the past to the present take a more critical and unforgiving view and are irked by a sympathetic approach to the group. From the perspective of opera production, the group's legacy lies in its faith in and dedication to opera as a form of art, the strength of personal values imbued by opera amid a dehumanizing environment, and the belief in furthering their talents despite the circumstances. Since the dissolution of apartheid, opera in South Africa has become a dynamic genre in which a new generation of opera singers from diverse racial backgrounds is able to excel on the local and international stage in what is perhaps the most lasting tribute to the lives and work of Eoan's musicians.

APPENDIX ONE

# *Eoan's Music Productions*

The appendix attempts to list in chronological order the music productions by Eoan's music section that could be traced in the Eoan Group Archive. These include performances of opera, operettas, musicals, oratoria, and (some) operatic concerts. The information is not comprehensive, because the needed details have often not been retained in the archive. Over the years the group was in great demand with the public, and Eoan's soloists and choir performed at numerous concerts, charity functions, church services, fund-raising events, and other occasions. Eoan's principal singers were often invited to sing in towns such as Stellenbosch, Paarl, and Oudtshoorn, as well as further afield in places such as Port Elizabeth and Johannesburg. Smaller productions, such as the children's operettas that were performed during the early years, are also listed but with less detail. This appendix does not list Eoan's other activities, such as ballet or drama productions.

## 1946

| | |
|---|---|
| Date | June |
| Work | *The Redeemer* |
| Composer | Martin Shaw |
| Genre | Cantata |
| Venue | Cape Town City Hall |
| Conductor | Joseph Manca |
| Cast | Joey Daniels (soprano), Kitty Paulse (alto), James Adams (tenor), Andrew Mackrill (baritone), and John Ulster (bass), with John Juritz at the organ.[1] |

## 1947

| | |
|---|---|
| Date | April |
| Work | *The Redeemer* |

| | |
|---|---|
| Composer | Martin Shaw |
| Genre | Cantata |
| Venue | Cape Town City Hall |
| Conductor | Joseph Manca |

| | |
|---|---|
| Date | April |
| Work | *The Messiah* |
| Composer | George Frideric Handel |
| Genre | Oratorio |
| Venue | Cape Town City Hall |
| Conductor | Joseph Manca |
| Orchestra | Cape Town Municipal Orchestra |
| Cast | The Eoan Group choir, with Elizabeth April as soprano soloist.[2] |

| | |
|---|---|
| Date | October |
| Work | *Sherwood* |
| Composer | Christopher Edmunds |
| Genre | Children's cantata[3] |

| | |
|---|---|
| Date | October |
| Work | *Lay of the Bell* |
| Composer | Andreas Romberg |
| Genre | Cantata[4] |

### 1948

| | |
|---|---|
| Date | November |
| Work | *The Rose and the Laurel* |
| Composer | Herbert Walter Wareing |
| Genre | Children's cantata[5] |

### 1949

| | |
|---|---|
| Date | April |
| Work | *The Redeemer* (costumed version) |
| Composer | Martin Shaw |
| Genre | Cantata |
| Venue | Cape Town City Hall |

| | |
|---|---|
| Conductor | Joseph Manca |
| Orchestra | Cape Town Municipal Orchestra |
| Cast | Joey Daniels (soprano), Kitty Paulse (alto), James Adams (tenor), Andrew Mackrill (baritone), and John Ulster (bass), with John Juritz at the organ.[6] |

| | |
|---|---|
| Date | August |
| Work | *A Slave in Araby* |
| Composer | Alfred Silver and Stanley Guise |
| Genre | Operetta |
| Venue | Cape Town City Hall |
| Conductor | Joseph Manca |
| Orchestra | Cape Town Municipal Orchestra |
| Producer | Billie Jones |
| Cast | May Abrahamse and Andrew Mackrill (among others).[7] |

## 1950

| | |
|---|---|
| Date | October |
| Work | *Hong Kong* |
| Composer | Charles Jessop |
| Genre | Operetta |
| Venue | Cape Town City Hall |
| Conductor | Joseph Manca |
| Orchestra | Cape Town Municipal Orchestra |
| Producer | Helen Haughton |
| Cast | May Abrahamse (Jessica), Stan Rinquest (Captain Neville), George Cloete (Lieutenant Tophole), Andrew Mackrill, and Hansie Kronenberg.[8] |

## 1951

| | |
|---|---|
| Date | October |
| Work | *The Maid of the Mountains* |
| Composer | Harold Fraser-Simson |
| Genre | Musical comedy |
| Venue | Cape Town City Hall |
| Conductor | Joseph Manca |
| Orchestra | Cape Town Municipal Orchestra |

| | |
|---|---|
| Producer | Jack Cardew |
| Cast | May Abrahamse (Maid), Victor Benjamin (Baldassare), William Curry (Tonia), Thelma Paulsen (Vittoria), Johan Gorvalle (General Malona), Louise Roode (Angela), and Abe Otto (Beppo).[9] |

## 1953

| | |
|---|---|
| Date | March |
| Work | *Elijah* |
| Composer | Felix Mendelssohn |
| Genre | Oratorio |
| Venue | Cape Town City Hall |
| Conductor | Joseph Manca |
| Orchestra | Cape Town Municipal Orchestra |
| Cast | Ruth Goodwin, Edna Herman, and Edwin Boezala as soloists and the Eoan Group choir, with Leslie Arnold at the organ.[10] |

| | |
|---|---|
| Date | October |
| Work | *The Gyspy Princess* |
| Composer | Emmerich Kalman |
| Genre | Operetta |
| Venue | Cape Town City Hall |
| Conductor | Joseph Manca |
| Orchestra | Cape Town Municipal Orchestra |
| Producer | Ruby Morriss |
| Cast | Leon Dreyer (Niblo), May Abrahamse (Sylva), Gwen Michaels (The Dancer), Benjamin Arendse (Mero), Oliver Calvert (Juliska), William McCleod (Nitch), Douglas Phillips (Count Feri), William Curry (Lord Boniface), Daniel Josephs (Vilmer), Abe Otto (Prince Ronald), Andrew Jansen (Eugene), Thelma Paulsen (Countess Stasi), Gerry Rudolph (Notary), Richard Manuel (Prince Leopold), Louise Roode (Anita), Douglas Cooke (Little), Mary Strydom (Mary), and Barbara Diedericks (Barbara).[11] |

| | |
|---|---|
| Date | December |
| Work | *Bethlehem* & *The Messiah* |
| Composer | John Henry Maunder and George Frideric Handel |
| Genre | Cantata |

| | |
|---|---|
| Venue | Cape Town City Hall |
| Conductor | Joseph Manca |
| Orchestra | Cape Town Municipal Orchestra |
| Cast | Eoan Group choir and soloists.[12] |

## 1954

| | |
|---|---|
| Date | August |
| Work | *Magyar Melody* |
| Composer | George Posford and Bernard Grun |
| Genre | Operetta |
| Venue | Cape Town City Hall |
| Conductor | Joseph Manca |
| Orchestra | Cape Town Municipal Orchestra |
| Producer | Ruby Morris |
| Cast | May Abrahamse, Abie Otto, Douglas Phillips, Louise Roode, and Ferguson Peters.[13] |

| | |
|---|---|
| Date | December |
| Work | *The Messiah* |
| Composer | George Frideric Handel |
| Genre | Oratorio |
| Venue | Cape Town City Hall |
| Conductor | Joseph Manca |
| Orchestra | Cape Town Municipal Orchestra |
| Cast | The Eoan Group choir and May Abrahamse (among others).[14] |

## 1956

The Eoan Group First Arts Festival incorporating the First Opera and Ballet Season.

| | |
|---|---|
| Date | March |
| Work | *La Traviata* |
| Composer | Giuseppe Verdi |
| Genre | Opera |
| Venue | Cape Town City Hall |
| Conductor | Joseph Manca |
| Orchestra | Cape Town Municipal Orchestra |
| Producer | Alessandro Rota |

| | |
|---|---|
| Cast | May Abrahamse and Ruth Goodwin (Violetta), Edna Herman (Flora), Arthur Ackerman (Marchese), Abe Jacobs (Baron Douphol), Robert Trussell (Grenville), Leon Dreyer (Gastone), Ron Thebus (Alfredo), Lionel Fourie (Giorgio Germont), and Linda Rinquest (Annina).[15] |
| Date | April |
| Work | *The Mikado* |
| Composer | Gilbert and Sullivan |
| Genre | Operetta |
| Venue | Cape Town City Hall |
| Conductor | Dan Ulster |
| Orchestra | Cape Town Municipal Orchestra |
| Producer | Marjorie Hill |
| Cast | Joyal Meyer (Yum-Yum), Jane Esau (Pitti-Sing), Miriam Masoet (Peen-Bo), Dulcie Seegers (Katisha), Jean Welff (Nanki-Poo), Jean Merckel (Ko-Ko), Mabel Kester (Pooh-Bah), Joan Daniels (Mikado), and Delia Saffier (Pish-Tush).[16] |
| Date | June |
| Work | *Elijah* |
| Composer | Felix Mendelssohn |
| Genre | Oratorio |
| Venue | Cape Town City Hall |
| Conductor | Joseph Manca |
| Orchestra | Cape Town Municipal Orchestra |
| Cast | Doreen Carelse (soprano), Ron Thebus (tenor), Edna Herman (alto), and Lionel Fourie (baritone).[17] |
| Date | July–August |
| Work | *Zip Goes a Million* |
| Composer | George Posford |
| Genre | Musical |
| Venue | Cape Town City Hall |
| Conductor | Joseph Manca |
| Orchestra | Cape Town Municipal Orchestra |
| Producer | Joyce Bradley |

| | |
|---|---|
| Cast | Olive Calvert (Lilac), Daniel Joseph (Percy), Dulcie Littlefield (Sally), Leon Dreyer (Buddy), Abe Jacobs (Motty), George Ferguson (Connelly), Gerry Rudolph (Jed Harper), Louise Roode (Paula van Norden), and Eddie Canterbury (James van Norden).[18] |

## 1957

| | |
|---|---|
| Date | August |
| Work | *Maritza* |
| Composer | Emmerich Kalman |
| Genre | Musical comedy |
| Venue | Cape Town City Hall |
| Conductor | Joseph Manca |
| Orchestra | Cape Town Municipal Orchestra |
| Producer | Joyce Bradley |
| Cast | May Abrahamse (Countess Maritza), Gerald Arendse (Bella Torok), Daniel Joseph (Prince Koloman Zoupan), Sue Scheepers (Countess Lisa Erody), Shirley Smit (Manja), and Alfred Irwin (Captain Karl Stephan).[19] |

## 1958

The Second Opera and Ballet Season.

| | |
|---|---|
| Date | March |
| Work | *Cavalleria Rusticana* |
| Composer | Pietro Mascagni |
| Genre | Opera |
| Venue | Cape Town City Hall |
| Conductor | Joseph Manca |
| Orchestra | Cape Town Municipal Orchestra |
| Producer | Gregorio Fiasconaro |
| Cast | May Abrahamse (Santuzza), Yusuf Williams (Turiddu), Sophia Andrews (Lucia), Benjamin Arendse (Alfio), and Shirley Smit (Lola).[20] |

| | |
|---|---|
| Date | March |
| Work | *La Traviata* |
| Composer | Giuseppe Verdi |
| Genre | Opera |

| | |
|---|---|
| Venue | Cape Town City Hall |
| Conductor | Joseph Manca |
| Orchestra | Cape Town Municipal Orchestra |
| Producer | Gregorio Fiasconaro |
| Cast | May Abrahamse & Ruth Goodwin (Violetta), Matilda Theunissen & Shirley Smit (Flora), Arthur Ackerman (Marchese D'Obigny), Floris Arendse (Baron Douphol), Robert Trussell (Dottore Grenville), Leon Dreyer (Gastone), Ron Thebus (Alfredo), Lionel Fourie (Giorgio Germont), and Matilda Domingo and Linda Rinquest (Annina).[21] |

| | |
|---|---|
| Date | August |
| Work | *Rose Marie* |
| Composer | Rudolph Frimi and Herbert Stothart |
| Genre | Musical comedy |
| Venue | Cape Town City Hall |
| Conductor | Joseph Manca |
| Orchestra | Cape Town Municipal Orchestra |
| Producer | Billie Jones |
| Cast | May Abrahamse, Gerald Arendse, Benjamin Arendse, Brenda Jaftha, and Daniel Joseph.[22] |

## 1959

The Third Opera and Ballet Season.

| | |
|---|---|
| Date | March |
| Work | *Rigoletto* |
| Composer | Giuseppe Verdi |
| Genre | Opera |
| Venue | Cape Town City Hall |
| Conductor | Joseph Manca |
| Orchestra | Cape Town Municipal Orchestra |
| Producer | Gregorio Fiasconaro |
| Cast | Lionel Fourie (Rigoletto), Ruth Goodwin (Gilda), Joseph Gabriels (Duke of Mantua), Sophia Andrews (Maddalene), Robert Trussell (Sparafucile), Sylvia Lindeboom (Giovanna), Benjamin Arendse (Monterone), Alfred Irvin (Marullo), John Williams (Borsa), Arthur Ackerman (Ceprano), Esther Parkins (Countess Soprano), and Patricia van Graan (Page).[23] |

| | |
|---|---|
| Date | March |
| Work | *Cavalleria Rusticana* |
| Composer | Pietro Mascagni |
| Genre | Opera |
| Venue | Cape Town City Hall |
| Conductor | Joseph Manca |
| Orchestra | Cape Town Municipal Orchestra |
| Producer | Gregorio Fiasconaro |
| Cast | May Abrahamse (Santuzza), Gerald Arendse (Turiddu), Sophia Andrews (Lucia), Benjamin Arendse (Alfio), and Shirley Smit (Lola).[24] |

| | |
|---|---|
| Date | March |
| Work | *La Traviata* |
| Composer | Giuseppe Verdi |
| Genre | Opera |
| Venue | Cape Town City Hall |
| Conductor | Joseph Manca |
| Orchestra | Cape Town Municipal Orchestra |
| Producer | Gregorio Fiasconaro |
| Cast | May Abrahamse (Violetta), Matilda Theunissen and Shirley Smit (Flora), Arthur Ackerman (Marchese D'Obigny), Oliver Kleinsmidt (Baron Douphol), Robert Trussell (Dottore Grenville), John Williams (Gastone), Ron Thebus (Alfredo), Lionel Fourie (Giorgio Germont), and Matilda Domingo (Annina).[25] |

| | |
|---|---|
| Date | August |
| Work | *Rio Rita* |
| Composer | Harry Tierney |
| Genre | Musical comedy |
| Venue | Cape Town City Hall |
| Conductor | Joseph Manca |
| Orchestra | Cape Town Municipal Orchestra |
| Producer | Gordon Rennie |
| Cast | Faried Nordien (Corporal McGinn), Daniel Josephs (Ed Lovett), Clifford Rinquest (Davallos), May Abrahamse (Rio Rita), Gerald Arendse (Jim Steward), Patricia van Graan (Carlotta), and Sophia Andrews (Sevillita).[26] |

## 1960

The Fourth Opera and Ballet Season.

| | |
|---|---|
| Date | March–April |
| Work | *La Bohème* |
| Composer | Giacomo Puccini |
| Genre | Opera |
| Venue | Cape Town City Hall |
| Conductor | Joseph Manca |
| Orchestra | Cape Town Municipal Orchestra |
| Producer | Gregorio Fiasconaro |
| Cast | Joseph Gabriels (Rodolfo), Benjamin Arendse (Marcello), Robert Trussell (Colline), Gerald Arendse (Schaunard), Daniel Joseph (Benoit and Alcindoro), May Abrahamse (Mimi), and Winifred Domingo (Musetta).[27] |

| | |
|---|---|
| Date | March–April |
| Work | *Rigoletto* |
| Composer | Giuseppe Verdi |
| Genre | Opera |
| Venue | Cape Town City Hall |
| Conductor | Joseph Manca |
| Orchestra | Cape Town Municipal Orchestra |
| Producer | Gregorio Fiasconaro |
| Cast | Lionel Fourie (Rigoletto), Ruth Goodwin (Gilda), Joseph Gabriels (Duke of Mantua), Sophia Andrews (Maddalene), Robert Trussell (Sparafucile), Sylvia Lindeboom (Giovanna), Benjamin Arendse (Monterone), Gerald Arendse (Marullo), Samual Amos (Borsa), Arthur Ackerman (Ceprano), Susan Arendse (Countess Ceprano), and Patricia van Graan (Page).[28] |

| | |
|---|---|
| Date | March–April |
| Work | *La Traviata* |
| Composer | Giuseppe Verdi |
| Genre | Opera |
| Venue | Cape Town City Hall |
| Conductor | Joseph Manca |
| Orchestra | Cape Town Municipal Orchestra |

| | |
|---|---|
| Producer | Gregorio Fiasconaro |
| Cast | Ruth Goodwin (Violetta), Matilda Ulster (Flora), Arthur Ackerman (Marchese D'Obigny), Oliver Kleinschmidt (Baron Douphol), Robert Trussell (Dottore Grenville), Samuel Amos (Gastone), Gerald Arendse (Alfredo), Lionel Fourie (Giorgio Germont), and Matilda Domingo (Annina).[29] |

| | |
|---|---|
| Date | March–April |
| Work | *Cavalleria Rusticana* |
| Composer | Pietro Mascagni |
| Genre | Opera |
| Venue | Cape Town City Hall |
| Conductor | Joseph Manca |
| Orchestra | Cape Town Municipal Orchestra |
| Producer | Gregorio Fiasconaro |
| Cast | May Abrahamse (Santuzza), Gerald Arendse (Turiddu), Sophia Andrews (Lucia), Benjamin Arendse (Alfio), and Vera Gow (Lola).[30] |

From June to September 1960 the group went on its first countrywide tour, during which it visited Port Elizabeth, Durban, and Johannesburg. The program for the tour consisted of the four operas that were performed during the Fourth Opera and Ballet Season in March and April in Cape Town. During the tour, the group gave seventy-two performances.

## 1962

The Eoan Group Second Arts Festival, incorporating the Fifth Opera and Ballet Season.

| | |
|---|---|
| Date | March–April |
| Work | *Madama Butterfly* |
| Composer | Giacomo Puccini |
| Genre | Opera |
| Venue | Cape Town City Hall |
| Conductor | Joseph Manca |
| Orchestra | Cape Town Municipal Orchestra |
| Producer | Gregorio Fiasconaro |
| Cast | May Abrahamse (Butterfly), Sophia Andrews (Suzuki), Joseph Gabriels (Pinkerton), Benjamin Arendse (Sharpless), |

                    Samuel Amos (Goro), Robert Trussell (Bonzo), Martin
                    Johnson (Commissario and Yamadori), and Patricia van
                    Graan (Kate Pinkerton).[31]

| | |
|---|---|
| Date | March–April |
| Work | *La Bohème* |
| Composer | Giacomo Puccini |
| Genre | Opera |
| Venue | Cape Town City Hall |
| Conductor | Joseph Manca |
| Orchestra | Cape Town Municipal Orchestra |
| Producer | Gregorio Fiasconaro |
| Cast | Joseph Gabriels and James Momberg (Rodolfo), Benjamin Arendse (Marcello), Robert Trussell (Colline), Martin Johnson (Schaunard), Ernest Janari (Benoit and Alcindoro), May Abrahamse (Mimi), and Vera Gow (Musetta).[32] |

| | |
|---|---|
| Date | March–April |
| Work | *La Traviata* |
| Composer | Giuseppe Verdi |
| Genre | Opera |
| Venue | Cape Town City Hall |
| Conductor | Joseph Manca |
| Orchestra | Cape Town Municipal Orchestra |
| Producer | Gregorio Fiasconaro |
| Cast | Abeeda Parker (Violetta), Vera Gow and Joan Fernandez (Flora), Ernest Janari (Marchese D'Obigny), Martin Johnson (Baron Douphol), Ivan Trezires (Dottore Grenville), Cecil Tobin (Gastone), James Momberg and Faried Nordien (Alfredo), Gregorio Fiasconaro (Giorgio Germont), and Sophia Andrews (Annina).[33] |

| | |
|---|---|
| Date | August |
| Work | *Requiem* |
| Composer | Giuseppe Verdi |
| Genre | Oratorio |
| Venue | Cape Town City Hall |
| Conductor | Joseph Manca |

| | |
|---|---|
| Orchestra | Cape Town Municipal Orchestra |
| Soloists | May Abrahamse (soprano), Sophia Andrews (alto), Joseph Gabriels (tenor), and Robert Trussell (baritone). |
| Chorus | The Eoan Group choir and the Cape Town Choral Society.[34] |

| | |
|---|---|
| Date | October–November |
| Work | *Die Fledermaus* |
| Composer | Johann Strauss II |
| Genre | Operetta |
| Venue | Cape Town City Hall |
| Conductor | Joseph Manca |
| Orchestra | Cape Town Municipal Orchestra |
| Producer | Robert Mohr |
| Cast | Joseph Gabriels (Gabriel von Eisenstein), May Abrahamse (Rosalinde), Faried Nordien (Alfredo), Patricia van Graan (Adele), James Momberg (Dr. Blind), Benjamin Arendse (Dr. Falke), Cecil Tobin (Colonel Frank), Susan Arendse (Prince Orlofsky), Esther Parkins (Ida), Robert Trussell (Frosch), and Peter Abrahams (Ivan).[35] |

| | |
|---|---|
| Date | November |
| Work | *La Traviata* |
| Composer | Giuseppe Verdi |
| Genre | Opera |
| Venue | Stellenbosch City Hall |
| Conductor | Joseph Manca |
| Orchestra | Cape Town Municipal Orchestra |
| Producer | Gregorio Fiasconaro |
| Cast | Abeeda Parker (Violetta), Vera Gow (Flora), Ernest Janari (Marchese D'Obigny), Martin Johnson (Baron Douphol), Ivan Trezires (Dottore Grenville), Cecil Tobin (Gastone), James Momberg (Alfredo), Lionel Fourie (Giorgio Germont), and Sophia Andrews (Annina).[36] |

## 1965

The Sixth Opera Season.

| | |
|---|---|
| Date | March–April |
| Work | *Il Trovatore* |

| | |
|---|---|
| Composer | Giuseppe Verdi |
| Genre | Opera |
| Venue | Cape Town City Hall |
| Conductor | Joseph Manca |
| Orchestra | Cape Town Municipal Orchestra |
| Producer | Alessandro Rota |
| Cast | Vera Gow (Leonora), Sophia Andrews (Azucena), Susan Arendse (Ines), Robert Trussell and Leslie Daniels (Ferrando), Joseph Gabriels (Manrico), Benjamin Arendse and Cecil Tobin (Conte di Luna), Lawrence Hosain (Ruiz), and Markus Cloete (Old Gypsy).[37] |

| | |
|---|---|
| Date | March–April |
| Work | *La Traviata* |
| Composer | Giuseppe Verdi |
| Genre | Opera |
| Venue | Cape Town City Hall |
| Conductor | Joseph Manca |
| Orchestra | Cape Town Municipal Orchestra |
| Producer | Alessandro Rota |
| Cast | Winifried du Plessis (Violetta), Susan Arendse (Flora), Ernest Janari (Marchese D'Obigny), Martin Johnson (Baron Douphol), Robert Trussell (Dottore Grenville), Cecil Tobin (Giorgio Germont), James Momberg (Alfredo Germont), Lawrence Hosain (Gastone), and Sophia Andrews (Annina).[38] |

| | |
|---|---|
| Date | March–April |
| Work | *L'Elisir D'Amore* |
| Composer | Gaetano Donizetti |
| Genre | Opera |
| Venue | Cape Town City Hall |
| Conductor | Joseph Manca |
| Orchestra | Cape Town Municipal Orchestra |
| Producer | Alessandro Rota |
| Cast | Patricia van Graan and Yvonne Jansen (Adina), Freda Koopman (Gianetta), James Momberg and Gerald Samaai (Nemorino), Martin Johnson and Cecil Tobin (Belcore), and Robert Trussell (Dr. Dulcamara).[39] |

| | |
|---|---|
| Date | March–April |
| Work | *La Bohème* |
| Composer | Giacomo Puccini |
| Genre | Opera |
| Venue | Cape Town City Hall |
| Conductor | Joseph Manca |
| Orchestra | Cape Town Municipal Orchestra |
| Producer | Alessandro Rota |
| Cast | Joseph Gabriels (Rodolfo), Benjamin Arendse (Marcello), Robert Trussell (Colline), Martin Johnson (Schaunard), Ernest Janari (Benoit & Alcindoro), Yvonne Jansen (Mimi), Winifried du Plessis (Musetta), and Lawrence Hosain (Parpignol).[40] |

From June to September 1965 the group undertook its second tour of the country, during which it visited Johannesburg, Durban, and Port Elizabeth. The program for the tour consisted of the four operas that were performed during the group's Sixth Opera Season in March and April in Cape Town as well as its first (and only) production of Bizet's *Carmen*. During this tour the group gave forty-nine performances.

| | |
|---|---|
| Date | June–September |
| Work | *Carmen* |
| Composer | George Bizet |
| Genre | Opera |
| Venue | On tour in Johannesburg, Durban, and Port Elizabeth |
| Conductor | Joseph Manca |
| Orchestra | The Theatre Orchestra |
| Producer | Alessandro Rota |
| Cast | Vera Gow (Carmen), Patricia van Graan (Micaela), Susan Arendse (Frasquita), Yvonne Jansen (Mercedes), Joseph Gabriels (Don José), Benjamin Arendse (Escamillo), James Momberg (Il Remendado), Lawrence Hosain (Il Dancairo), Robert Trussell (Zuniga), and Martin Johnson (Morales).[41] |

## 1966

| | |
|---|---|
| Date | May (Republic Festival) |
| Work | *La Traviata* |
| Composer | Giuseppe Verdi |

| | |
|---|---|
| Genre | Opera |
| Venue | Cape Town City Hall |
| Conductor | Joseph Manca |
| Orchestra | Cape Town Municipal Orchestra |
| Producer | Alessandro Rota |
| Cast | Vera Gow (Violetta), Susan Arendse (Flora), Ernest Janari (Marchese D'Obigny), Ronald Theys (Baron Douphol), Jacobus Erasmus (Dottore Grenville), Cecil Tobin (Giorgio Germont), Lawrence Hosain and James Momberg (Alfredo Germont), Lawrence Hosain and John Andrews (Gastone), and Josephine Liedeman (Annina).[42] |

## 1967

| | |
|---|---|
| Date | January |
| Work | *Oklahoma!* |
| Composer | Richard Rodgers and Oscar Hammerstein II |
| Genre | Musical |
| Venue | Alhambra Theatre |
| Conductor | Joseph Manca |
| Orchestra | The Theatre Orchestra |
| Producer | Stanley Waren |
| Cast | Martin Johnson (Curly), Patricia van Graan (Laurey), Lawrence Hosain (Ike Skidmore), Cecil Tobin (Jud Fry), Winifred du Plessis (Ado Annie Carnes), Allie Sydow (Ali Hakim), Yvonne Jansen (Gertie Cummings), Freda Koopman (Ellen), Veronica Jacobs (Aunt Eller), William Abrahams (Slim), Rupaire Koopman (Will Parker), Abraham Lewis (Andrew Carnes), John Andrews (Cord Elam), and Bertram Petersen (Fred).[43] |

| | |
|---|---|
| Date | March 14 (special performance for government dignitaries) |
| Work | *La Traviata* |
| Composer | Giuseppe Verdi |
| Genre | Opera |
| Venue | Cape Town City Hall |
| Conductor | Joseph Manca |
| Orchestra | Cape Town Municipal Orchestra |
| Producer | Alessandro Rota |

| | |
|---|---|
| Cast | Winifried du Plessis (Violetta), Vera Gow (Flora), Ernest Janari (Marchese D'Obigny), Martin Johnson (Baron Douphol), Fred Marthinussen (Dottore Grenville), Cecil Tobin (Giorgio Germont), Gerald Samaai (Alfredo Germont), Lawrence Hosain (Gastone), and Veronica Jacobs (Annina).[44] |

The Seventh Opera Season.

| | |
|---|---|
| Date | September |
| Work | *L'Elisir D'Amore* |
| Composer | Gaetano Donizetti |
| Genre | Opera |
| Venue | Cape Town City Hall |
| Conductor | Joseph Manca |
| Orchestra | Cape Town Municipal Orchestra |
| Producer | Alessandro Rota |
| Cast | Patricia van Graan (Adina), Freda Koopman (Gianetta), James Momberg (Nemorino), Martin Johnson (Belcore), and Cecil Tobin and Ernest Janari (Dr. Dulcamara).[45] |

| | |
|---|---|
| Date | September |
| Work | *Madama Butterfly* |
| Composer | Giacomo Puccini |
| Genre | Opera |
| Venue | Cape Town City Hall |
| Conductor | Joseph Manca |
| Orchestra | Cape Town Municipal Orchestra |
| Producer | Alessandro Rota |
| Cast | May Abrahamse (Madam Butterfly), Sophia Andrews (Suzuki), Lawrence Hosain (Lieutenant Pinkerton), Benjamin Arendse (Sharpless), Allie Sydow (Goro), Ernest Janari (Bonzo) Ronald Theys (Commissario), John Andrews (Prince Yamadori), Freda Koopman, and Sybil Adams (Kate Pinkerton).[46] |

| | |
|---|---|
| Date | September |
| Work | *La Traviata* |
| Composer | Giuseppe Verdi |
| Genre | Opera |
| Venue | Cape Town City Hall |

| | |
|---|---|
| Conductor | Joseph Manca |
| Orchestra | Cape Town Municipal Orchestra |
| Producer | Alessandro Rota |
| Cast | Vera Gow (Violetta), Susan Arendse (Flora), Ernest Janari (Marchese D'Obigny), Ronald Theys (Baron Douphol), Jacobus Erasmus (Dottore Grenville), Cecil Tobin (Giorgio Germont), Lawrence Hosain and James Momberg (Alfredo Germont), Lawrence Hosain and John Andrews (Gastone), and Josephine Liedeman (Annina).[47] |

## 1968

| | |
|---|---|
| Date | March |
| Work | *South Pacific* |
| Composer | Richard Rodgers and Oscar Hammerstein II |
| Genre | Musical |
| Venue | Alhambra Theatre, with additional performances for coloured audiences in the Luxerama in Wynberg. |
| Conductor | Joseph Manca |
| Orchestra | Cape Town Municipal Orchestra |
| Producer | David Bloomberg |
| Cast | Vera Gow (Nellie Forbush), Sophia Andrews (Bloody Mary), Benjamin Arendse (Emile de Becque), Ronald Theys (Abner), Lawrence Hosain (Professor), Allie Sydow (Luther Billis), Jimmy Momberg (Stewpot), Trevor Pretorius (McCaffrey), Patricia van Graan (Genevieve Marshall), Martin Johnson (Lt. Joseph Cable), Ernest Janari (William Harbison), Cecil Tobin (George Bracket), Christina Joshua (Ngana), Christopher George (Jerome), Johannes van der Merwe (Henry), and Sherryll Felix (Liat).[48] |

## 1969

The Eight Opera Season.

| | |
|---|---|
| Date | October–November |
| Work | *Il Trovatore* |
| Composer | Giuseppe Verdi |
| Genre | Opera |
| Venue | Cape Town City Hall |
| Conductor | Joseph Manca |

| | |
|---|---|
| Orchestra | Cape Town Symphony Orchestra |
| Producer | Alessandro Rota |
| Cast | Vera Gow (Leonora), Sophia Andrews (Azucena), Vera Neethling (Ines), Jacobus Erasmus (Ferrando), Ronald Theys (Manrico), Charles de Long (Conte di Luna), and Trevor Pretorius (Ruiz).[49] |

| | |
|---|---|
| Date | October–November |
| Work | *Il Barbiere di Siviglia* |
| Composer | Gioacchino Rossini |
| Genre | Opera |
| Venue | Cape Town City Hall |
| Conductor | Joseph Manca |
| Orchestra | Cape Town Symphony Orchestra |
| Producer | Alessandro Rota |
| Cast | Gerald Samaai (Count Almaviva), Martin Johnson (Figaro), Cecil Tobin (Doctor Bartolo), Patricia van Graan (Rosina), Jacobus Erasmus (Don Basilio), James Kalamdien (Fiorelli), and Josephine Liedeman (Berta).[50] |

| | |
|---|---|
| Date | October–November |
| Work | *La Traviata* |
| Composer | Giuseppe Verdi |
| Genre | Opera |
| Venue | Cape Town City Hall |
| Conductor | Joseph Manca |
| Orchestra | Cape Town Symphony Orchestra |
| Producer | Alessandro Rota |
| Cast | Vera Gow (Violetta), Sylvia Lindeboom and Sybille Adams (Flora), Ernest Janari (Marchese D'Obigny), Martin Johnson (Baron Douphol), Jacobus Erasmus (Dottore Grenville), Cecil Tobin (Giorgio Germont), James Momberg (Alfredo Germont), Ronald Bowers (Gastone), and Josephine Liedeman (Annina).[51] |

## 1970

| | |
|---|---|
| Date | August |
| Work | *Carmen Jones* |

| | |
|---|---|
| Composer | George Bizet/Oscar Hammerstein II |
| Genre | Musical |
| Venue | Joseph Stone Auditorium, Athlone |
| Conductor | Joseph Manca |
| Orchestra | The Theatre Orchestra |
| Producer | Stanley Waren |
| Cast | Michael Jass (Corporal Morrel), Patricia van Graan (Cindy Lou), Martin Johnson (Joe), Phillip Swales (Sergeant Brown), Vera Gow (Carmen Jones), Sophia Andrews (Myrt), Freda Koopman (Frankie), Gerald Samaai (Rum), Lawrence Hosain (Dink), and Gerald Arendse (Husky).[52] |

## 1971

| | |
|---|---|
| Date | May (part of celebrations for the Republic Festival) |
| Work | *Rigoletto* |
| Composer | Giuseppe Verdi |
| Genre | Opera |
| Venue | Joseph Stone Auditorium, Athlone |
| Conductor | Joseph Manca |
| Orchestra | Cape Town Symphony Orchestra |
| Producer | Alessandro Rota |
| Cast | Cecil Tobin & Jacobus Erasmus (Rigoletto), Freda Koopman & Juliana Inglis (Gilda), Gerald Samaai and Martin Johnson (Duke of Mantua), Sophia Andrews & Judith Bailey (Maddalene), Phillip Swales (Sparafucile), Benjamin Arendse (Monterone), Michael Jass (Count Ceprano), Ronald Bowers (Matteo Borsa), Ronald Theys (Marullo), Deline Boezak (Countess Ceprano), Josephine Liedeman (Giovanna), and Virginia Damons (Paggio).[53] |

The Ninth Opera Season.

| | |
|---|---|
| Date | October |
| Work | *La Traviata* |
| Composer | Giuseppe Verdi |
| Genre | Opera |
| Venue | Alhambra Theatre |
| Conductor | Joseph Manca |
| Orchestra | Cape Town Symphony Orchestra |

| | |
|---|---|
| Producer | Alessandro Rota |
| Cast | Vera Gow (Violetta), Deline Boezak (Flora), John van der Ross (Marchese D'Obigny), Desmond Desai (Baron Douphol), Phillip Swales (Dottore Grenville), Ronald Bowers (Gastone), Martin Johnson (Alfredo), Cecil Tobin (Giorgio Germont), and Josephine Liedeman (Annina).[54] |
| Date | October |
| Work | *Rigoletto* |
| Composer | Giuseppe Verdi |
| Genre | Opera |
| Venue | Alhambra Theatre |
| Conductor | Joseph Manca |
| Orchestra | Cape Town Symphony Orchestra |
| Producer | Alessandro Rota |
| Cast | Ronald Theys (Rigoletto), Freda Koopman (Gilda), Gerald Samaai (Duke of Mantua), Sophia Andrews (Maddalene), Phillip Swales (Sparafucile), John van der Ross (Monterone), Michael Jass (Count Ceprano), Ronald Bowers (Matteo Borsa), Desmond Desai (Marullo), Deline Boezak (Countess Ceprano), Vera Neethling (Giovanna), and Virginia Damons (Paggio).[55] |
| Date | October |
| Work | *Cavalleria Rusticana* |
| Composer | Pietro Mascagni |
| Genre | Opera |
| Venue | Alhambra Theatre |
| Conductor | Joseph Manca |
| Orchestra | Cape Town Symphony Orchestra |
| Producer | Alessandro Rota |
| Cast | Sophia Andrews (Santuzza), Vera Neethling (Lucia), Benjamin Arendse (Alfio), Lawrence Hosain (Turiddo), and Virginia Damons (Lola).[56] |
| Date | October |
| Work | *I Pagliacci* |
| Composer | Ruggiero Leoncavallo |
| Genre | Opera |

| | |
|---|---|
| Venue | Alhambra Theatre |
| Conductor | Joseph Manca |
| Orchestra | Cape Town Symphony Orchestra |
| Producer | Alessandro Rota |
| Cast | Jacobus Erasmus (Tonio), Charles de Long (Canio), Gerald Samaai (Beppe), May Abrahamse & Patricia van Graan (Nedda), and Ronald Theys (Silvio).[57] |

*Cavalleria Rusticana* and *I Pagliacci* were performed on one evening, with an interval separating the operas.

## 1972

| | |
|---|---|
| Date | March |
| Work | *Cavalleria Rusticana* |
| Composer | Pietro Mascagni |
| Genre | Opera |
| Venue | H. B. Thom Theatre in Stellenbosch |
| Conductor | Joseph Manca |
| Orchestra | The Theatre Orchestra |
| Producer | Alessandro Rota |
| Cast | Sophia Andrews (Santuzza), Vera Neethling (Lucia), Benjamin Arendse (Alfio), Lawrence Hosain (Turiddo), and Virginia Damons (Lola).[58] |

| | |
|---|---|
| Date | March |
| Work | *I Pagliacci* |
| Composer | Ruggiero Leoncavallo |
| Genre | Opera |
| Venue | H. B. Thom Theatre in Stellenbosch |
| Conductor | Joseph Manca |
| Orchestra | The Theatre Orchestra |
| Producer | Alessandro Rota |
| Cast | Jacobus Erasmus (Tonio), Charles de Long (Canio), Gerald Samaai (Beppe), May Abrahamse and Patricia van Graan (Nedda), and Ronald Theys (Silvio).[59] |

*Cavalleria Rusticana* and *I Pagliacci* were performed on one evening, with an interval separating the operas.

## 1974

The Tenth Opera Season.

| | |
|---|---|
| Date | March |
| Work | *Il Barbiere di Siviglia* |
| Composer | Gioacchino Rossini |
| Genre | Opera |
| Venue | Green and Sea Point Civic Centre |
| Conductor | Joseph Manca |
| Orchestra | Eoan Group Theatre Orchestra |
| Producer | Alessandro Rota |
| Cast | Arthur Court (Fiorelli), Gerald Samaai (Count Almaviva), Ronald Theys (Figaro), Martin Johnson (Dr. Bartolo), May Abrahamse (Rosina), Jacobus Erasmus (Don Basilio), Josephine Liedeman (Berta), Isaac Hartzenberg (Officer), and Richard Paulse (Notary).[60] |

| | |
|---|---|
| Date | March |
| Work | Gems from the Operas |
| Composer | Various |
| Genre | Operatic concert |
| Venue | Green and Sea Point Civic Centre |
| Conductor | Joseph Manca |
| Orchestra | Eoan Group Theatre Orchestra |
| Cast | Isaac Hartzenberg, Jennifer Witbooi, Keith Timms, Ronald Bowers, Winifred du Plessis, Jefferine Ludolph, Charles de Long, Arthur Court, Judith Bailey, and the Eoan Group choir.[61] |

## 1975

The Eleventh Opera Season.

| | |
|---|---|
| Date | February–March |
| Work | *La Traviata* |
| Composer | Giuseppe Verdi |
| Genre | Opera |
| Venue | Green and Sea Point Civic Centre |
| Conductor | Joseph Manca |
| Orchestra | Eoan Group Theatre Orchestra |

| | |
|---|---|
| Producer | Alessandro Rota |
| Cast | May Abrahamse (Violetta), Sybille Adams (Flora), Ronald Baatjies (Marchese D'Obigny), John van der Ross (Baron Douphol), Keith Timms (Dottore Grenville), Ronald Bowers (Gastone), Gerald Samaai (Alfredo), Ronald Theys (Giorgio Germont), and Josephine Liedeman and Nellie Solomons (Annina).[62] |

In August 1975 the group went on its first and only tour abroad. A number of fund-raising concerts preceded the tour, some of them historic first performances by coloureds in whites-only venues in Bloemfontein and Johannesburg. During the tour in the United Kingdom, the group gave several operatic concerts in Aberdeen and London, featuring principal singers May Abrahamse, Vera Gow, Gerald Samaai, and Ronald Theys, as well as the choir.

## 1976

| | |
|---|---|
| Date | October |
| Work | Gems from the Operas |
| Composer | Various |
| Genre | Operatic concert |
| Venue | Protea Stage & Cinema Theatre |
| Conductor | Joseph Manca |
| Accompanist | Regina Devereux |
| Cast | May Abrahamse, Sybille Adams, Sidwill Hartman, Isaac Hartzenberg, Jefferine Ludolph, Keith Timms, Ronald Bowers, Charles de Long, Leonie Quickfall, Ronald Baatjies, and Gerald Samaai. Ronald Theys.[63] |

## 1979

| | |
|---|---|
| Date | March 3 |
| Work | *Recital* |
| Composers | Guiseppe Verdi, Vincenzo Bellini, Gaetano Donizetti, Henry Purcell, Michael Balfe, S. Le Roux Marais, Johannes Joubert, Giacomo Puccini, Pietro Mascagni, and Francesco Cilea. |
| Genre | Lieder and opera arias |
| Venue | Nico Malan Opera House |
| Soloist | May Abrahamse |
| Accompanist | Gordon Jephtas[64] |

APPENDIX TWO

# *The Eoan Group Constitution*

The Constitution of the Eoan Group has been in existence since the 1940s, but the oldest full version that has been archived dates from 1959. The constitution has most likely been adjusted fairly regularly over the years; the version included here dates from 1970.[1] It is quoted in full in this appendix because it reflects the values of the "early years" in the first section as well as the extent to which control was exercised over its operations and its members through the formal representation of the Department of Coloured Affairs (DCA) at this time (see clause 6.b). The latter was decided upon by the executive committee on November 25, 1970, and was agreed to at the annual general meeting of December 8, 1970.[2]

## EOAN GROUP
## CONSTITUTION

WHEREAS the EOAN GROUP was founded by Mrs. Helen Southern-Holt as a free Association of voluntary workers banded together in order to carry out certain objects which were set out as follows:-
The aims of the Association shall be "Not for the Self but for the Whole".

(a) To carry on social work amongst, and to promote the well-being culturally, socially, educationally and physically of the Non-European citizens within the Union of South Africa.

(b) To foster, manage and control voluntary associations of groups of Non-European persons throughout the Union of South Africa who accept the Management and control of the Eoan Group, and who have adopted or adopt the ideals of the Eoan Group, which are:

**Brotherhood**
To live a life which shall be free from all bias, and free from prejudice of creed, race or colour.

**Unity**

To live and work always for the good of the whole group, forgetting the personal self, knowing that unity is born out of the unselfish life.

**Purity**

To keep the body pure and clean, knowing that it is the temple of the living spirit. To control the thoughts, to keep the actions pure at, all times.

**Joyous service**

To give service to the Group joyously; such service seeks no special thanks or self-glorification, but serves for the pure joy of service.

**The Group**

To believe in the symbol of service as defined by Eoan, and to take Eoan teaching in order seriously to practice doing all things to become efficient and to give out to others those cultural arts embodied in the work. In order to keep up and advance the standard of Eoan, not to re-teach, show classwork or perform publically without the permission of the Principal in consultation with the head of the particular section concerned and with the concurrence of the Chairman or the Vice-Chairman of the Group.

AND WHEREAS at a Special General Meeting of the Eoan Group it was agreed by a majority of members personally present and entitled to vote thereat to revoke the former Constitution of the Eoan Group and to adopt as its Constitution the following.

NOW THEREFORE THESE PRESENTS WITNESS:

### 1. NAME

The name of the association shall be the EOAN GROUP (hereinafter referred to as "the Group").

### 2. BODY CORPORATE

The Group shall be a body corporate not for gain with perpetual succession and capable of acquiring assets and incurring liabilities for its own account and independently of the members of the Group.

### 3. NON-POLITICAL

The Group shall be non-political.

### 4. OBJECTS

The objects of the Group shall be

(i) Cultural. The establishment, development and conduct of schools of art, ballet, drama, music and opera, the teaching to University level whether to pupils or teachers of the performing arts, the management of theatres and the formation and management of companies for the performance of the performing arts and the performance and public presentation of ballet, drama, music and opera, the holding of art exhibitions and public presentations and performances of every description.

(ii) Play Centres and Creches. The establishment, development, building, conduct and administration of nursery play centres and creches, kindergarten and nursery schools.

(iii) Social and Welfare. The establishment, development, conduct and administration of schools of physical education, men's and boy's clubs for the purposes of training in physical culture or in any other activity, ladies' and girls' clubs for the teaching and practice of sewing and other domestic arts and the teaching of physical education whether to pupils or teachers.

## 5. MEMBERSHIP

(i) The Group shall consist of 4 classes of members

  (a) Ordinary members
  (b) Junior members
  (c) Honorary members
  (d) Life members

(ii) Ordinary Members. Ordinary membership of the Group shall be open to male or female members of the non-white racial groups of the Republic of South Africa with the exception of the Bantu group who shall have attained the age of 18 (eighteen) years and who shall have applied for and been accepted as members of the Group as hereinafter provided.

(iii) Junior Members. Junior membership shall be open to male or female members of the non-white racial groups of the Republic of South Africa with the exception of the Bantu group under the age of 18 (eighteen) years whose parents or guardians shall have applied for membership and whose membership shall have been accepted as hereinafter provided.

(iv) Honorary or Life Members. Honorary or Life membership shall be open to such persons as the Executive Committee of the Group may decide, and may be conferred for special services or assistance to the Group and may be conferred upon such terms and conditions as the Executive Committee shall decide but shall however be subject to confirmation at the Annual General Meeting of the Group.

(v) Application for membership shall be made in such manner and on such forms as the Executive Committee may from time to time prescribe and such applications may be accepted or rejected as the Executive Committee in its discretion shall deem fit. The decision of the Executive Committee shall be final and binding and the Executive Committee shall not be obliged to assign any reason for the refusal of membership.

(vi) The Executive Committee shall cause to be compiled and maintained a register of members which shall indicate the date of granting of membership, the type of membership and whether or not subscriptions as hereinafter fixed have been paid.

(vii) Each member on acceptance of an application for membership shall be entitled to a membership card to be issued in such form as the Executive Committee shall decide which card shall during the validity thereof be conclusive proof of the right of such member to vote at meetings of the Group.

(viii) Membership of the Association shall cease if any member

- (a) Resigns in writing.
- (b) Is expelled from the Group on a decision of the Executive Committee which shall not be obliged to assign reasons therefor.
- (c) Fails to pay within three months of due date the subscriptions as hereinafter defined.

(ix) Subscriptions for membership shall be as under and shall be payable on 1st March in each and every year:

| | |
|---|---|
| Ordinary Members | R2-00 per annum |
| Junior Members | R1-00 per annum |
| Honorary or Life Members | NIL |

## 6. EXECUTIVE COMMITTEE

(i) The affairs of the Group shall be managed by an Executive Committee which shall consist of:

- (a) a Chairman, a Vice-Chairman and seven (7) ordinary members and shall be elected annually by members of the Group entitled to vote at the Annual General Meeting of the Group.
- (b) one member, nominated by the Administration of Coloured Affairs the provisions of clause 6/viii or any other clause of this constitution terminating membership of the Executive Committee for any reason whatsoever, not being applicable to this member.[3]

(ii) The Chairman of the Executive Committee shall be ipso facto the Chairman of the Eoan Group.

(iii) Members of the Executive Committee elected at the Annual General Meeting of the Group shall be members of the Group of not less than one (1) years standing.

(iv) Nominations for appointment to the offices of Chairman, Vice-Chairman or membership of the Executive Committee shall be made in writing and shall be proposed and seconded by members or the Group entitled to vote and shall reach the Secretary of the Group not less than seven (7) days before the holding of the Annual General Meeting.

(v) The Executive Committee shall have power to appoint such other committee or sub-committee as it may deem necessary for the proper administration of the affairs of the Group and shall have power to lay down rules for the establishment and conduct of such committees. The Executive Committee shall also have power in its discretion to terminate the appointment of any committees.

(vi) The quorum at any meeting of the Executive Committee shall be five (5) members or one-half of the total number of members plus one (1) whichever shall be the greater.

(vii) The Executive Committee shall have power to co-opt to the committee such further members as may be necessary to meet the requirements for representation on the Executive Committee of Government, Municipal or local authority bodies, Companies, Trusts and Foundations who render assistance to or are interested in the financing and/or management of the Group. The members so co-opted shall be nominated by the Government, local authority or Municipal bodies, Trust Companies or Foundations concerned which shall also have power to nominate alternates to such members. In addition the Executive Committee shall have power to co-opt to the Committee such further members as it deems fit from persons who have rendered not less than ten years service to the Group. The maximum number of members which may be co-opted in terms of this sub-paragraph shall be five (5). Such members shall have all the rights and powers of ordinary members of the Executive Committee, but their membership thereof shall cease at the Annual General Meeting succeeding their appointment to the committee. Members of the Executive Committee co-opted in terms of this sub-section need not be members of the Group.

(viii) All members of the Executive Committee shall cease to hold office at the Annual General Meeting of the Group but shall be eligible for re-election.

(ix) The Executive Committee shall have power:

- (a) To establish branches of the Group and to lay down rules for the proper management and conduct of such branches.
- (b) To determine such rules and regulations as may be necessary for the proper conduct of the affairs of the Group.
- (c) To take such action as they may deem fit for proper carrying out of the objects of the Group.
- (d) To open Savings or current accounts with banks, building societies or other financial institutions and to operate thereon on such conditions

as they may determine and to invest the funds of the Group from time to time in such manner and on such conditions as they may determine.

(e) For the purposes of the Group to acquire such movable or immovable property as may be necessary and to enter into contracts for the acquisition thereof and to alienate or deal therewith in any manner as they may deem fit.

(f) To appoint employees of the Group upon such terms and conditions as they may determine and to enter into Service Contracts with employees.

(g) To take legal proceedings against any person or persons and to defend any action that may be brought against the Group or against any of its officials and to use the funds of the Group for such purpose. The Executive Committee shall have power by Resolution to appoint one or more of its members to sign Powers of Attorney and other papers necessary to sue and defend actions on behalf of the Group.

## 7. IMMOVABLE PROPERTY OF THE GROUP

The immovable property of the Group shall vest in two Trustees to be appointed by the Group for this purpose from time to time The Group may at any General Meeting of which notice has been given of the Resolution to be taken remove any Trustee and appoint any further Trustee or Trustees. The Trustees shall with the approval of the Executive Committee have power on behalf of the Group to purchase, sell, mortgage, lease or in any other way deal with immovable property or to confirm and adopt any purchase, sale, mortgage, lease or any other dealing with the said property entered into by any person on behalf of the Group. The said Trustees shall have full power, subject to the approval of the Executive Committee, to sign Deeds of Sale, Powers of Attorney and any other documents necessary to give effect to any dealings with the Group's immovable property.

## 8. MEETINGS

### A. *General.*

(i) The Annual General Meeting of the Group shall be held in the month of July in each and every year and notice thereof shall be given to members by the Secretary in writing at least twenty-one (21) days before the date of the meeting and such notice shall advise the time and place of the meeting and the business to be transacted thereat.

(ii) At the Annual General Meeting the following business shall be transacted:

(a) Minutes of the previous Annual General Meeting;

(b) Chairman's annual report;

(c) Financial statement, balance sheets and Auditor's report;

(d) Election of Chairman and Vice-Chairman and members of the Executive Committee;
   (e) Appointment of Auditors;
   (f) Such Resolutions as shall have been proposed and seconded in writing to the Secretary by two members of the Group entitled to vote at the Annual General Meeting which shall have been received by the Secretary not less than seven (7) days before the date of the Annual General Meeting.
   (g) Any other business which may be properly transacted at an Annual General Meeting.

(iii) At the Annual General Meeting twenty-five (25) members of the Group personally present or by proxy shall constitute a quorum. In the event of there being no quorum at the Annual General Meeting the meeting shall stand adjourned to the same time and place one (1) week later and at such adjourned meeting all resolutions taken in accordance with the voting provision hereinafter set forth shall be valid and binding upon the Group notwithstanding the absence of a quorum.

(iv) The Executive Committee may at any time in its discretion summon a Special General Meeting of the Group by fourteen (14) days written notice setting out the time and place of the meeting and the business to be transacted thereat. The provisions relating to a quorum at the Annual General Meeting shall mutatis mutandis apply to Special General Meetings.

(v) An Extraordinary General Meeting of the Group shall be called by the Secretary within twenty-one (21) days after receipt by the Secretary of a requisition in writing to that effect signed by at least twenty-five (25) members of the Group entitled to vote at the Annual General Meeting. Such requisition shall specify the reason for the meeting and the business to be transacted thereat and the provisions relating to notice and quorum at the Annual General Meeting shall mutatis mutandis apply to Extraordinary General Meetings.

(vi) The Chairman of the Annual General Meeting or a Special General Meeting or an Extraordinary General Meeting shall be the Chairman of the Group failing whom the Vice-Chairman failing whom such person as the members of the Group present at the meeting shall appoint from amongst their number.

*B. Executive Committee.*

The Executive Committee shall meet at least once in every calendar month at such place and time as the Committee shall determine. The Chairman of such meeting shall be the Chairman of the Group, failing whom the Vice-Chairman, failing whom such person as the members of the Committee present at the meeting shall appoint from amongst their number.

*C. Other Committees and Special Committees.*

Committees and Special Committees established by the Executive Committee shall meet at such times and on such conditions as the Executive Committee shall determine.

## 9. VOTING

(i) Voting at the Annual General, Special General or Extraordinary meetings of the Group shall be limited to ordinary members of the Group personally present at the meeting and shall be by a show of hands unless the Chairman of the meeting shall direct that voting shall be by ballot. Each member present at the meeting shall be entitled to one (1) vote and the Chairman of the meeting shall have a second or casting vote.

(ii) Voting at meetings of the Executive Committee shall be by a show of hands and each member of the Committee personally present at the meeting shall have one (l) vote save that the Chairman of the meeting shall have a second or casting vote.

## 10. OFFICIALS

The Executive Committee shall appoint a Secretary for the Group and such other officials and employees as it may deem fit and shall determine the terms of any Service Contracts to be entered into with any officials and the remuneration to be paid to such officials. The Executive Committee shall also define the duties to be carried out by officials so appointed.

## 11. LIABILITY OF MEMBERS

Members of the Group shall incur no liability for the obligations of the Group and such members liability shall be limited to the amount of subscriptions unpaid.

## 12. DISSOLUTION OF THE GROUP

The Group shall be dissolved by resolution passed by at least 75% (Seventy-five per cent) of members personally present at a General Meeting of the Group called for the purpose of Dissolution. At such meeting direction shall be given by the meeting on a majority vote of those personally present for the disposal of the assets of the Group and such disposal shall be for the purposes similar or analogous to the purpose of the Group and no disposal of assets amongst members or the Group shall be made.

## 13. AMENDMENT OF CONSTITUTION

This Constitution may be amended by a majority vote taken at any General Meeting of the Group.

# NOTES

## INTRODUCTION

1. Joseph Manca, "Eoan Group," in *South African Music Encyclopedia* (Cape Town: Oxford University Press, 1982), 2:26–29.
2. Joseph Manca to Mr. J. L. Hughes (secretary of NODA in London), February 27, 1956. Eoan Group Archive, box 1, folder 4.
3. "Eoan Sold Out—to C.A.D Apartheid," *Torch*, March 27, 1956.
4. "Eoan Group Has Big Plans to Follow Up Arts Festival," *Sun*, July 27, 1956. Approximately twenty thousand people attended performances at the Arts Festival.
5. Charlie Weich (pseudonym "Emol"), "Kaapse Kleurlinge voer Italiaanse opera met groot welslae uit" [Cape Coloureds perform Italian Opera with great success], *Die Burger*, March 12, 1956.
6. "Eoan Group's *La Traviata* at City Hall Is a Major Artistic Triumph," *Cape Argus*, March 12, 1956.
7. Ibid.
8. "Traviata Success by Eoan Group," *Cape Times*, March 12, 1956.
9. "Eoan Group's Success with *La Traviata*," *Sun*, March 18, 1956.
10. The *Torch*, which had for some time already publicly criticized Eoan for its affiliation with the government, placed no reviews of any of the festival's productions.
11. Joseph Manca to Mr. H. Rosenthal (editor of *Opera*), April 2, 1956. Eoan Group Archive, box 29, folder 200.
12. Joseph Manca, "Historical Overview of Eoan's Activities from 1933–1968," 8. Eoan Group Archive, box 60, folder 494c.
13. Eoan History Project, *Eoan—Our Story* (Johannesburg: Fourthwall Books, 2013), 74.
14. Resistance also came from within the group. Many years later, Ismail Sydow wrote to Gordon Jephtas how the baritone principal, Lionel Fourie, almost sabotaged this very first performance: "I remember that *La Traviata* nearly could not go on stage if it wasn't for me, who spent the whole night pleading with the baritone to

come and sing, because for political reasons he refused to come and sing: so where would the sopranos, Joseph Manca, Alessandro Rota, etc., etc. have been in spite of their hard work, if the Baritone did not come to sing?" Ismail Sydow to Gordon Jephtas, February 16, 1980. Ruth Fourie Scrapbook, Eoan Group Archive.

15. Alex La Guma (Chairman of The South African Coloured People's Organisation) to the Eoan Group, n.d. Eoan Group Archive, box 29, folder 200.

16. Anonymous protest letter distributed on the streets, March 31, 1956. Eoan Group Archive, box 29, folder 200. The way in which this document is filed in the archive illustrates the dismissive approach towards political objections that Manca held throughout his time as director of Eoan: the original copy of the document does not exist in the archive, but Manca copied the wording of the pamphlet on blue typing paper and therefore must have had an original copy. On the side of this copied version, he penciled the following perplexing note by hand: "This I typed to let you know of, though I realise not worth worrying about."

17. Minutes of the General Meeting, June 1, 1980. Eoan Group Archive, box 4, folder 29.

18. See appendix 1 in this book for a listing of the group's music performances.

19. Programme notes for the April/May 2004 production of *La Traviata* by Cape Town Opera, author's private collection.

20. By 1971 the group's repertoire included Verdi's *La Traviata, Rigoletto*, and *Il Trovatore*; Puccini's *La Bohème* and *Madama Butterfly*; Rossini's *Il Babiere di Siviglia*; Mascagni's *Cavalleria Rusticana*; Johan Strauss's *Die Fledermaus*; Donizetti's *L'Elisir D'Amore*; Bizet's *Carmen*; and Leoncavallo's *I Pagliacci*. *La Traviata* remains to this day the most frequently performed opera in the West. Various statistics are available on the World Wide Web; see, for instance, www.operbase.com.

21. The South African Council on Sport (SACOS) was an organization that fought apartheid primarily through sport. It did, however, also direct its energies towards cultural organizations. See, for instance, Noel Goodall, "Opposing Apartheid Through Sport, the Role of SACOS in South African Sport, 1982–1992" (master's thesis, University of Johannesburg, 2004).

22. Amanda Botha, "Oplaas saamsing as gelykes" [Finally singing together as equals], *Rapport Ekstra*, February 10, 1980.

23. Newspaper reporting of the 1940s and 1950s in, for example, the *Cape Standard* and the *Sun*, reflects these attitudes quite clearly.

24. Vernon February, *Mind Your Colour* (London and New York: Kegan Paul International, 1981), vii.

25. During 2009 forty-five interviews were conducted with former members for the Eoan History Project. These interviews were conducted by the committee members who participated in the creation of the oral history book *Eoan—Our Story*, which was edited by Hilde Roos and Wayne Muller.

26. Gerald Samaai (former Eoan principal tenor) in discussion with Wayne Muller, May 12, 2009. Eoan Group Archive.

27. Shortly after the Population Registration Act came into being in 1950, the coloured category included members of the Indian population who were imported

to South Africa in the late nineteenth century as indentured labourers on white-owned farms in the KwaZulu-Natal area. However, by the late 1950s, the apartheid government declared Indians a separate racial grouping, and they remain so today.

28. Mohamed Adhikari, "Hope, Fear, Shame, Frustration: Continuity and Change in the Expression of Coloured Identity in White Supremacist South Africa: 1910–1994," *Journal of Southern African Studies* 32, no. 3 (September 2006): 467–87. It is important to note that to this day, some coloured people reject the term *coloured* and self-identify as black or brown-black.

29. Adhikari, *Hope*, 467.

30. See, for instance, the writings of Goldin (1987), Lewis (1987), Du Pré (1994), Jung (2000), Hammett (2005), Hendricks (2005), Erasmus (2001), Martin (1999, 2013), and Adhikari (2006, 2009, 2010). Full bibliographic details for these publications are listed in the selected bibliography in this book. Ethnomusicologists such as Jorritsma (2011), Bruinders (2011), and Muller (2011) have discussed coloured identity in relation to music in their respective case studies. Erasmus and Martin both focus on the theoretical framework of creolization and Martin applies this to music from the coloured community in the Cape. Creolization, however, is less useful in a discussion of Eoan since its performances of opera clearly aspired towards European ideals and were "in true Italian tradition."

31. Mohamed Adhikari, *Not White Enough, Not Black Enough* (Athens: Ohio University Press, 2006).

32. Adhikari, *Hope*, 468.

33. Mohamed Adhikari, *Burdened by Race: Coloured Identities in Southern Africa* (Cape Town: UCT Press, 2009), 12.

34. Adhikari, *Not White Enough*, 8.

35. Ibid., 10.

36. Ibid., 12.

37. Adhikari, *Burdened by Race*, viii.

38. Adhikari, *Not White Enough*, 13.

39. Leslie Witz, "From Langa Market Hall and Rhodes's Estate to the Grand Parade and the Foreshore: Contesting van Riebeeck's Cape Town," *Kronos Southern African Histories* 25 (1988/1989): 189.

40. Letter from Mrs. R. Smith, March 20, 1965. Eoan Group Archive, box 2, folder 9.

41. "Notes on Carmen." Eoan Group Archive, box 83, folder 646a.

CHAPTER ONE. WE LIVE TO SERVE: A DEMIMONDE BEFORE ART

1. Vivian Bickford-Smith, "The Origins and Early History of District Six to 1910," in *The Struggle for District Six, Past and Present* (Cape Town: Buchu Books, 1990), 35–43.

2. Ibid., 37.

3. Ibid., 43.

4. Ibid., 37.

5. Ibid.

6. Joseph Manca, "Eoan Group," in *South African Music Encyclopedia* (Cape Town: Oxford University Press, 1982), 2:26–29.

7. Regarding Southern-Holt's position with Garlick's, see Alethea Jansen (former Eoan member) in discussion with Ruth Fourie, May 2009; Tillie Ulster (former Eoan member) in discussion with the author, March 2012. Eoan Group Archive. See George Manual, *Kampvegters* (Cape Town: NasouBeperk, n.d.), 69. According to Manual, Southern-Holt came to South Africa in 1930. Regarding Southern-Holt's involvement in helping needy people in the Cape Town area, see "Culture of Coloureds, Fine Work of the Eoan Group," *Province Herald*, August 26, 1947. Eoan Group Archive, box 102, folder 773.

8. Alethea Jansen was ninety-two at the time of this interview in 2009. Tillie Ulster was interviewed twice, the first time in 2009, at age eighty-one, and again in 2012, at age eighty-four.

9. "Culture of Coloureds," *Province Herald*, 1947.

10. "The Eoan Group," *Monitor*, April 12, 1946, 23. Eoan Group Archive, box 102, folder 773. Bishop Lavis's humanitarian efforts were so significant that an entire suburb on the Cape Flats is named after him. He was also a close friend of Helen Southern-Holt and at times helped with fundraising efforts.

11. Speech by Helen Southern-Holt at the National Council of Women in South Africa in 1947, 1. Eoan Group Archive, box 37, folder 300. According to Tillie Ulster, Southern-Holt was in charge of the female coloured workers at Garlick's and therefore came into close contact with them in a professional environment. Ulster interview, 2012.

12. Southern-Holt, 1947 speech, 1.

13. Ibid., 2.

14. "Little School for the Street Children, Eoan Group's First Nursery Centre," *Cape Times*, December 20, 1945. Eoan Group Archive, box 102, folder 773.

15. Jansen interview, 2009.

16. Ibid.

17. Ulster interview, 2012. According to Ulster, the group's first principal, Marie Adams, had such a serious fallout with Southern-Holt that she left the group and afterward avoided Southern-Holt at social events. When, for example, Ulster married in 1952, both Adams and Southern-Holt attended the wedding festivities, but Ulster recalls how she had to walk to the door to greet Adams, who refused to go near the wedding table where Southern-Holt was seated.

18. A number of sources also use the spelling "Maisie," although "Maisy" is used more consistently.

19. Minutes of the Executive Committee Meeting, June 28, 1972. Eoan Group Archive, box 93, folder 757. A memorial service was held for Southern-Holt in the Joseph Stone Auditorium on June 25, 1972.

20. "Your Daughter," *Sun*, October 26, 1945. Eoan Group Archive, box 102, folder 773.

21. "The Eoan Group," *Monitor*, April 12, 1946. Eoan Group Archive, box 102, folder 773.

22. Sylvia Bruinders, "Parading Respectability: An Ethnography of the Christmas Bands Movement in the Cape, South Africa" (PhD diss., University of Illinois at Urbana-Champaign, 2011), 58–60.

23. Ulster interviews, 2009 and 2012; and Jansen interview, 2009.

24. Ibid.

25. Jansen interview, 2009.

26. Ibid.

27. Ibid. See also Jack Stodel, *The Audience Is Waiting* (Cape Town: Howard Timmins, 1962), 173. Stodel reproduced large sections of Southern-Holt's speech verbatim in his book (without acknowledgment).

28. Southern-Holt speech, 1; and Ulster interview, 2009.

29. *Cape Times*, March 16, 1946. Eoan Group Archive, box 102, folder 773. She married Mr. C. Harrison.

30. "The Eoan Group," undated pamphlet published in order to raise funds for its own premises. The pamphlet describes "future plans" for 1939, so it is safe to assume that it originates from early 1939. Eoan Group Archive, box 1, folder 4.

31. Southern-Holt speech, 1.

32. Manca, "Eoan Group," 27.

33. "Eoan Group Gets Opportunity," *Cape Standard*, May 3, 1937.

34. "Eoan Group's Fine Display," *Cape Standard*, December 28, 1937.

35. Ibid.

36. Ulster interview, 2012.

37. "Youths Organisations," *Cape Standard*, October 4, 1946. Eoan Group Archive, box 102, folder 773.

38. "Culture of Coloureds, Fine Work of the Eoan Group," 1947. Eoan Group Archive, box 102, folder 773.

39. Manca, "Eoan Group," 26–27.

40. Regarding Manca's invitation by Southern-Holt, see Jacques P. Malan, "Manca, Joseph Salvatore," in *South African Music Encyclopedia* (Cape Town: Oxford University Press, 1984), 3:192–194. See also Lucy Faktor-Kreitzer, "From Latvia to South Africa," in *The World of South African Music: A Reader* (Cape Town: Oxford University Press, 2005), 149. Regarding Manca becoming Eoan choral director, see Manca, "Eoan Group," 26–29. See also Joseph Manca, "Advance Publicity Material for the 1956 Arts Festival," 2. Eoan Group Archive, box 30, folder 203.

41. John Ulster was born in 1922 and Dan Ulster in 1926. Ulster interview, 2012. Different sets of information exist on the birth of the choir. According to Richard van der Ross, the choir was started by Beatrice Brock, a coloured music teacher. See Richard van der Ross, "A Political and Social History of the Cape Coloured People, 1880–1970" (PhD diss., University of Cape Town, 1973), 605. Van der Ross's

information is, however, sourced from Ismail Sydow. On the basis of many interviews held with former members in the course of 2009 that confirmed that Manca sidelined Dan Ulster, I decided to privilege Tillie Ulster's version of the story.

42. Ulster interview, 2012.

43. Manca's birth and death dates are February 1, 1908–October 10, 1985. Ruth Grevler-Manca (daughter of Joseph Manca), email message to author, October 11, 2011.

44. Brendan Manca (son of Manca's youngest brother Salvatore, also known as Turie), email message to author, October 18, 2011.

45. Malan, "Manca, Joseph Salvatore," 192–94.

46. Ibid.

47. Joseph Manca, "Advance Publicity Material for the 1956 Arts Festival," 3. Eoan Group Archive, box 30, folder 203.

48. "Cape Town Pageant," *Guardian*, May 3, 1945. Eoan Group Archive, box 102, folder 773. On this occasion, £180 was raised for the South African Communist Party.

49. "Eoan Group Play," *Cape Argus*, June 13, 1945. Eoan Group Archive, box 102, folder 773. Regarding coloured dancers in teaching positions, see *Cape Times*, February 27, 1947. Eoan Group Archive, box 102, folder 773.

50. Denis-Constant Martin, *Sounding the Cape: Music, Identity and Politics in South Africa* (Cape Town: African Minds, 2013), 103–72.

51. Ibid., 106; and Carol Ann Muller, *Focus: Music of South Africa* (New York: Routledge, 2008), 75.

52. Valmont Layne, "A History of Dance and Jazz Band Performance in the Western Cape in the Post-1945 Era" (master's thesis, University of Cape Town, 1995).

53. Paula Fourie, "Ghoema vannie Kaap: The Life and Work of Taliep Petersen (1950–2006)" (PhD diss., Stellenbosch University, 2011).

54. "Facing the Music," *Trek*, July 27, 1945. Eoan Group Archive, box 102, folder 773.

55. Ibid.

56. Carol-Ann Muller and Sathima Bea Benjamin, *Musical Echoes: South African Women Thinking in Jazz* (Durham and London: Duke University Press, 2011).

57. For the history presented by Carol-Ann Muller, see Muller and Benjamin, *Musical Echoes*. For the history by Valmont Layne, see Layne, "History of Dance." For the history by Martin, see Denis-Constant Martin, *Coon Carnival: New Year in Cape Town: Past and Present* (Cape Town: David Philip, 1999); and Martin, *Sounding the Cape*.

58. Programme notes. Eoan Group Archive, box 102, folder 773.

59. For mention of Dan Ulster as repetiteur, see Programme notes. Eoan Group Archive, box 102, folder 773. For commentary by Ulster's wife Tillie, see Ulster interview, 2012. The couple married in 1952; her maiden name was Theunissen.

60. "Working Men and Women Who Sing Like Angels," *Cape Argus*, June 15, 1946. Eoan Group Archive, box 102, folder 773.

61. Vincent Kolbe as quoted in Muller and Benjamin, *Musical Echoes*, 57–58.

62. Concert programme, Eoan Group Archive, box 102, folder 773. Southern-Holt's daughter, Maisy, was the director of the dance department, despite living in Grahamstown at the time. "Eoan Group's Tenth Annual Display," *Cape Standard*, March 12, 1946. Eoan Group Archive, box 102, folder 773.

63. "The Tempest a Great Success," *Sun*, April 5, 1946. Eoan Group Archive, box 102, folder 773. The production was not an Eoan initiative, but Eoan members took part.

64. Ibid.

65. "Non-Europeans and Culture," *Torch*, April 1, 1946.

66. Ibid.

67. Ulster interview, 2012.

68. "Eoan Founder Visits P. E.," *Sun*, September 19, 1947. Eoan Group Archive, box 102, folder 773.

69. Programme notes for "Passion Week Concert," April 1, 1947. Eoan Group Archive, box 102, folder 773.

70. For information on the cantata *Sherwood*, see Programme notes. Eoan Group Archive, box 102, folder 773. The text is a poem by Alfred Noyes. Edmunds (1899–1990) lived in Birmingham, England. For further information on the children's choir that performed the cantata, see "500 Coloured Children as Choir with Orchestra," *Sun*, October 17, 1947. Eoan Group Archive, box 102, folder 773. For information on the senior choir's performance of the *Lay of the Bell* cantata, see Programme notes. Eoan Group Archive, box 102, folder 773.

71. "Albert Coates Delighted," *Sun*, October 24, 1947. Eoan Group Archive, box 102, folder 773.

72. Jacques P. Malan, "Cape Town Municipal Orchestra," in *South African Music Encyclopedia* (Cape Town: Oxford University Press, 1979), 1:251–54.

73. Marina Grut, "Ballet in Cape Town," in *South African Music Encyclopedia* (Cape Town: Oxford University Press, 1979), 1:79–81.

74. Ibid., 79.

75. "Royal Academy Successes." Eoan Group Archive, box 102, folder 773 (cutting pasted into folder, name of newspaper and dated of publication omitted).

76. Programme notes, May 17, 1947. Eoan Group Archive, box 102, folder 773.

77. "Nothing But the Truth," *Cape Times*, September 11, 1947. Eoan Group Archive, box 102, folder 773.

78. Peter Voges (former Eoan actor and dancer) in discussion with the author, February 28, 2015.

79. "Dulcie Howes," http://v1.sahistory.org.za/pages/people/bios/howes_d.html, accessed April 30, 2018.

80. *Cape Argus*, May 23, 1945. Eoan Group Archive, box 102, folder 773.

81. "Eoan and Teaching of Illiterates," *Cape Standard*, September 16, 1947. Eoan Group Archive, box 102, folder 773. Many newspaper cuttings in similar vein can be found in this folder.

82. Francois Cleophas, "Physical Education and Physical Culture in the Coloured Community of the Western Cape: 1837–1966" (PhD diss., Stellenbosch University, 2009).

83. Ernst Jokl, "Physical Education, Sport and Recreation," in *Handbook on Race Relations in South Africa* (Cape Town: Oxford, 1949), 443–447.

84. Scrapbook. Eoan Group Archive, box 102, folder 773.

85. "The Eoan Group," *Monitor*, April 12, 1946. Eoan Group Archive, box 102, folder 773.

86. "Constitution of the Eoan Group," revised version of 1959. Eoan Group Archive, box 5, folder 36.

87. The *Cape-Standard* was published from 1936 to 1947; the *Torch* was published from 1946 to 1963; and the *Sun* was published from 1932 to 1956.

88. "Eoan Policy," *Torch*, November 24, 1947. Eoan Group Archive, box 102, folder 773.

89. Scrapbook. Eoan Group Archive, box 102, folder 773. See various newspaper cuttings from the *Torch*, the *Sun*, and the *Standard* in November and December 1947 pasted in this scrapbook.

90. "Eoan Stands Firm," *Sun*, December 5, 1947. Eoan Group Archive, box 102, folder 773.

91. "Letters to the Editor," *Torch*, November 24, 1947. Eoan Group Archive, box 102, folder 773.

92. "Outstanding Eoan Achievements," *Sun*, October 22, 1948. Eoan Group Archive, box 102, folder 773.

93. Marketing brochure. Eoan Group Archive, box 1, folder 4.

94. Ibid.

95. "Founder's Report," *Sun*, July 15, 1949. See also "The Story of Marie Adams," *Cape Argus*, August 16, 1947. Eoan Group Archive, box 102, folder 773. The latter article mentions that she was born from mixed parentage and grew up in England as a European. On returning to South Africa, she chose to be "coloured," because of "her strong desire to throw in her lot with her own people and help them kept her from passing permanently into the European group."

96. "Culture of Coloureds, Fine Work of the Eoan Group," *Province Herald*, August 26, 1947. Eoan Group Archive, box 102, folder 773.

97. "Eoan Centre for City," *Cape Times*, September 1, 1948. Eoan Group Archive, box 102, folder 773.

98. "Eoan Group in Shakespeare," *Cape Argus*, January 26, 1948. Eoan Group Archive, box 102, folder 773.

99. For commentary on *The Rose and the Laurel*, see "New Operetta by Eoan Group," *Cape Times*, November 14, 1948. Eoan Group Archive, box 102, folder 773. Regarding Sheila van Breda, see "Another Eoan Grouper for London," *Sun*, November 26, 1948. Eoan Group Archive, box 102, folder 773.

100. "Costumed Oratorio by Eoan Group," *Cape Times*, March 26, 1949. Eoan Group Archive, box 102, folder 773.

101. "Overview Eoan's Music Productions 1944–1951." Eoan Group Archive, box 1, folder 4.

102. Regarding Eoan's performance of *The Wonderful Inn*, see "Operatic Music and Children's Operetta" held on July 2 and July 9, 1949. Eoan Group Archive, box 102, folder 773. Regarding the choruses performed in that children's operetta, see "Eoan's New Venture, Operatic Musical Concert," *Sun*, July 1, 1949. Eoan Group Archive, box 102, folder 773.

103. Regarding Billie Jones, see Joseph Manca, "Historical Overview of Eoan's Activities from 1933–1968," 17. Eoan Group Archive, box 60, folder 494c. Billie Jones was a white woman who worked with the drama section of Eoan in the 1940s and 1950s. Regarding *A Slave in Araby*, see "A Slave in Araby: A Comic Opera in Two Acts," https://books.google.co.za/books/about/A_Slave_in_Araby_a_Comic_Opera_in_Two_Ac.html?id=Tj9MvgAACAAJ&redir_esc=y, accessed April 30, 2018. Little information is available on the work itself: it is described as a comic opera in two acts that had been composed in 1931, but neither the author of the lyrics nor the composer of the music seems to have gained enough importance to receive any much attention.

104. "Comic Opera in Eastern Setting," *Sun*, August 19, 1949. Eoan Group Archive, box 102, folder 773.

105. Manca, "Historical Overview of Eoan's Activities," 26–29.

106. "A Comic Opera by the Eoan Group," *Cape Argus*, August 8, 1949. Eoan Group Archive, box 102, folder 773.

107. For the *Cape Argus* review, see "Triumph for the Eoan Group," *Cape Argus*, August 15, 1949. Eoan Group Archive, box 102, folder 773. For the *Cape Times* coverage, see "Eoan Group Stage Comic Opera," *Cape Times*, August 15, 1949. Eoan Group Archive, box 102, folder 773. For the *Sun* coverage, see "Comic Opera in Eastern Setting," *Sun*, August 19, 1949. Eoan Group Archive, box 102, folder 773.

108. "Jorda Conducts the Eoan Choir," *Cape Argus*, December 12, 1949. Eoan Group Archive, box 102, folder 773.

109. David Bloomberg, *My Times* (Simons Town: Fernwood Press, 2007), 24–25. Manca, however, received an honorary doctorate from the College of Music at the University of Cape Town in 1963, a clear sign of appreciation of his musical achievements.

110. Jacques P. Malan, "Manca, Joseph Salvatore," in *South African Music Encyclopedia* (Cape Town: Oxford University Press, 1984), 3:192–94.

111. Jacques P. Malan, "Rota, Alessandro," in *South African Music Encyclopedia* (Cape Town: Oxford University Press, 1986), 4:197–98. See also biographical notes on Rota in the 1956 Arts Festival Brochure. Eoan Group Archive, box 40, folder 317.

112. Malan, "Manca," 1984. The source, however, does not mention which of Rota's productions these were.

113. Southern-Holt speech, 1947. See also Bickford-Smith's *Cape Town in the Twentieth Century*, 84; Ulster interview, 2009; Jansen interview, 2009.

114. Southern-Holt speech, 1947; Ulster interview, 2009.

115. "The Eoan Group," undated pamphlet published in order to raise funds for its own premises. The pamphlet describes "future plans" for 1939, so it is safe to assume that it originates from early 1939.

116. Regarding the Eoan group's office on Adderley Street, see "The Eoan Group Needs Office Furniture," *Cape Times*, August 28, 1945. Eoan Group Archive, box 102, folder 773. Regarding its headquarters later being at Zonnenbloem College, see "Concert Programme," March 1946. Eoan Group Archive, box 102, folder 773.

117. Ulster interview, 2012.

118. "Friends of Eoan," *Cape Times*, January 25, 1945. Eoan Group Archive, box 102, folder 773.

119. Regarding government officials being invited to Eoan's concerts in the hope that they might make a contribution, see "Friends of Eoan," *Cape Argus*, March 19, 1945. Eoan Group Archive, box 102, folder 773. Regarding the 1946 contribution from the Department of Social Welfare, see "Letters to the Editor," *Cape Argus*, October 15, 1946. Eoan Group Archive, box 102, folder 773.

120. "Eoan Group Get Hall," *Cape Argus*, August 21, 1949. Eoan Group Archive, box 102, folder 773.

121. "£22,000 Plan for Eoan Centre," *Cape Times*, March 6, 1946. Eoan Group Archive, box 102, folder 773. On December 20, 1937, the *Cape Standard* ran an article titled "A Rich Man's Bequest" discussing Isaac Ochberg's substantial estate that provided donations to local charities such as Jewish orphanages, students, and hospitals; as well as funds for the resettlement of (South African) Jews to Palestine. The *Cape-Standard* article also states: "Colonial-born and coloured children of the Peninsula have been allotted £3,000 for the provision of recreation facilities in the most populated part of Cape Town where Coloured people live. The actual nature of the benefaction is to be in the form of a recreation ground or suitable controlled hall, administered by the trustees in consultation with leaders in the Coloured Community." Exactly how and when these monies were allocated to the Eoan Group is not known.

122. Joseph Manca to Dr. I. D. du Plessis, May 3, 1961. Eoan Archive, box 32, folder 219.

123. The 1927 Act prohibited extramarital sexual relations between whites and blacks; the amendment extended the prohibition to include coloureds and Indians. Interracial relations between blacks, coloureds, and Indians, however, were not prohibited.

124. "The Prohibition of Mixed Marriages Act," http://africanhistory.about.com/library/bl/blsalaws.htm, accessed April 30, 2018.

125. Ibid.

126. "No Apartheid—No Grants—No Culture?," *Sun*, November 2, 1951; and "Eoan Group Founder Retirement," *Sun*, August 3, 1951. Helen Southern-Holt had at this stage just retired, while the group was now headed by Alethea Jansen.

127. Ciraj Rassool and Leslie Witz, "The 1952 Jan Van Riebeeck Tercentenary Festival: Constructing and Contesting Public National History in South Africa," *Journal of African History* 34, no. 3 (1993): 447–468.

128. "Eoan Group to Boycott Tercentenary?," *Torch*, October 9, 1951.

129. See note 28 in the introduction for reference to the literature.

130. Mohamed Adhikari, *Not White Enough, Not Black Enough* (Athens: Ohio University Press, 2006).

131. Richard van der Ross, "A Political and Social History of the Cape Coloured People, 1880–1970"(PhD diss., University of Cape Town, 1973), 607.

132. Ibid., 609.

133. "Battswood Choir in Sacred Cantata," *Sun*, October 1, 1954. Van der Ross supplies a short overview of the Spes Bona Orchestral Society in part 3 of his *A Political and Social History of the Cape Coloured People 1880–1970*; see pages 607–10. He mentions that the orchestra was often dependent on white musicians to augment their numbers or to fill positions for instrumental parts for which no coloured players were available. Apartheid legislation made the functioning and continued existence of this racially mixed set-up very difficult. It is, however, not clear from Van der Ross's research when and under what circumstances the orchestra stopped functioning.

134. "Olivet to Calvary," *Sun*, March 16, 1951.

135. Regarding the dance studio in Ashley Street, see "Ashley Street Studios," *Sun*, February 2, 1951. Regarding activities at the Zonnebloem College, see "Operetta at Zonnebloem Hall," *Sun*, November 22, 1946; and "Outstanding Zonnebloem Art Display," *Sun*, November 1, 1946.

136. "Ambitious Eoan Group Production," *Sun*, October 12, 1951.

137. Joseph Manca, "Advance Publicity Material, 1956 Arts Festival."

138. Regarding the *Magyar Melody* performance, see "Magyar Melody," www.guidetomusicaltheatre.com/shows_m/magyar_melody.htm, accessed April 30, 2018. This musical comedy was adapted by Eric Maschwitz and George Posford from the play by Eric Maschwitz, Fred Thompson, and Guy Bolton. The music was composed by George Posford and Bernard Grun, and the work premiered at the Opera House, Manchester, on November 29, 1938. See Manca, "Advance Publicity Material, 1956 Arts Festival."

139. The *Sun* was a weekly publication. All editions are available on microfilm at the South African National Library in Cape Town.

## CHAPTER TWO. THE *LA TRAVIATA* AFFAIR: FROM COURTESAN TO LOVER

1. "A Comic Opera by the Eoan Group," *Cape Argus*, August 8, 1949. Eoan Group Archive, box 102, folder 793.

2. South African History Online (SAHO), "The African National Congress (ANC)," http://www.sahistory.org.za/organisations/african-national-congress-anc, accessed June 5, 2018.

3. The date of the first draft of the constitution of the Eoan Group is unknown. "Constitution of the Eoan Group," paragraph 1c. Eoan Group Archive, box 37, folder 12.

4. The wording "we live to serve" still features in the group's logo.

5. Patricia van Graan (Eoan principal soprano) in discussion with the author, November 2008.

6. Joseph Manca, "Advance Publicity Material for the 1956 Arts Festival." Eoan Group Archive, box 30, folder 203.

7. "Culture of Coloureds, Fine Work of the Eoan Group," *Province Herald*, August 26, 1947. Eoan Group Archive, box 102, folder 773.

8. Joseph Manca to Andrew Mackrill, July 12, 1955. Eoan Group Archive, box 29, folder 201. Mackrill had liberal political convictions, which he often aired in the newspapers. Despite this he took Eoan's side in a public spat between the group and the *Torch* that was published in July 1951 when the latter accused Eoan's management of segregationist policies. "Eoan Segregation Drama," *Torch*, June 19, 1951. However, in May 1954 he wrote a lengthy letter to the *Sun*, accusing the paper of accepting the political status quo on racial segregation. "Open letter to The Sun," *Sun*, May 28, 1954.

9. Andrew Mackrill to Joseph Manca, July 13, 1955. Eoan Group Archive, box 29, folder 201. It is evident from the remainder of the letter that the relationship between Manca and Mackrill was a particularly warm and appreciative one. Mackrill specifically mentioned the fond memories he had of his time with Eoan and with Manca in particular. See Mackrill's letters in the Eoan Group Archive, box 1, folder 4 and box 29, folder 201.

10. Richard van der Ross, *The Rise and Decline of Apartheid* (Cape Town: Tafelberg, 1986), 170–75.

11. Quoted in ibid.

12. Joseph Manca to Andrew Mackrill, July 27, 1955. Eoan Group Archive, box 1, folder 4.

13. The magazines and newspapers targeted in the marketing campaign included the *Evening Post*, the *Star*, the *Rand Daily Mail*, the *Natal Mercury*, the *Natal Daily News*, *Drum*, the *Golden City Post*, *Life*, the *Sunday Times*, the *Sunday Express*, the *Cape Times*, *Die Landstem*, the *Cape Times*, the *Sun*, *Die Burger*, the *Cape Argus*, the *South African Jewish Times*, and the *SABC*. Eoan Group Archive, box 1, folder 4. The South African, UK, and Italian publications included *Music and Musicians*, *Opera*, and *NODA*, as well as the South African representative of the BBC. Eoan Group Archive, box 1, folder 4.

14. Joseph Manca to Ricordi, November 18, 1955. Eoan Group Archive, box 29, folder 200.

15. Joseph Manca to Mr. A. R. Bell, February 11, 1956. Eoan Group Archive, box 1, folder 4.

16. Joseph Manca to Lewis Hotz of the *South African Jewish Times*, February 8, 1956. Eoan Group Archive, box 1, folder 4.

17. Manca to Bell, February 11, 1956.

18. See full correspondence in Eoan Group Archive, box 1, folder 4.

19. *Talk of the Times*, April 1956, magazine supplement of *Cape Times*. Eoan Group Archive, box 29, folder 200.

20. May Abrahamse (Eoan principal soprano) in discussion with Christine Lucia, July 2009.

21. Ibid.

22. In 1956 Dan Ulster wrote a book, *The Teaching of Music in Primary Schools*, for music education in coloured schools. The book was published by Maskew Miller and reprinted six times, the last time in 1980.

23. Désirée Talbot, *For the Love of Singing: 50 Years of Opera at UCT* (Cape Town: Oxford University Press, 1978), 156–76.

24. Mr. I. L. Cheminais to Joseph Manca, March 17, 1956. Eoan Group Archive, box 29, folder 200.

25. These include Verdi's *La Traviata*, *Rigoletto*, and *Il Trovatore*; Puccini's *La Bohème* and *Madame Butterfly*; Rossini's *Il Babiere di Siviglia*; Mascagni's *Cavalleria Rusticana*; Johan Strauss's *Die Fledermaus*; Donizetti's *L'Elisird'Amore*; Bizet's *Carmen*; and Leoncavallo's *I Pagliacci*.

26. The minutes of this meeting are lost, and the information was gathered from interviews with Tillie Ulster and Alethea Jansen (see note 28). Both interviewees were reluctant to discuss the matter, but nevertheless expressed anger and frustration at the way Southern-Holt was treated by others at the meeting.

27. Alethea Jansen (principal of Eoan) in discussion with the author, May 7, 2009.

28. Jansen interview, 2009; and Tillie Ulster (former Eoan member) in discussion with the author, September 8, 2009.

29. Minutes of the Executive Committee Meeting, June 28, 1972. Eoan Group Archive, box 93, folder 757.

30. Minutes of the 32nd Annual General Meeting, September 29, 1966. Eoan Group Archive, box 1, folder 3. The minutes of the AGM in 1957 when this decision was taken are lost. However, the issue was mentioned in a number of newspaper articles from 1960 and 1961. See, for example, "The Glorious Dawn . . . , *Daily News*, July 15, 1960; *Ilanga Lase*, July 23, 1960; and reviews and newspaper cuttings in Eoan Group Archive, box 30, folder 208. When Eoan reapplied for government funding in 1965, the conditions stated that the group was not allowed to perform before mixed audiences unless it applied for a permit to do so. Eoan Group Archive, box 33, folder 231.

31. See the discussion on the threat of withdrawal of state funds in chapter 1.

32. Information on the net profit is from Manca, "Historical Overview of Eoan's Activities from 1933–1968," 8. Eoan Group Archive, box 60, folder 494c.

33. Jacques P. Malan, "Erik Chisholm," in *South African Music Encyclopedia* (Cape Town: Oxford University Press, 1979), 1:272. See also the list of opera productions held in the Little Theatre, in Donald Inskip, *Forty Little Years* (Cape Town: Timmins, 1972), 119–57.

34. "UCT Musiek Kollege voer Don Giovanni uit in die Little Theatre" [UCT Music College performs Don Giovanni at the Little Theatre], *Die Burger*, May 21, 1956. See also "The Marriage of Figaro," *Die Burger*, June 2, 1956. See also Désirée Talbot, *For the Love of Singing, 50 Years of Opera at UCT* (Cape Town: Oxford University Press, 1978), 162.

## CHAPTER THREE. EOAN'S BEST OPERA SUCCESS: AN AMOROUS FANTASY

1. "Eoan Group, Important Announcement," *Sun*, April 27, 1956.
2. Ibid.
3. Although the Eoan Group Archive is a fairly large one, it also, alas, has many gaps. Just as it lacks records on the early history of the group, the archive holds no letters, personal files, rehearsal schedules, or minutes of meetings on any of the group's activities from 1957 to 1959. The narrative for this section is therefore constructed from newspaper reviews, Programme booklets, and informative articles or referrals to this period in documents of a later date.
4. Hilde Roos, "Opera Production in the Western Cape: Strategies Towards Indigenization" (PhD diss., University of Stellenbosch, 2010). See also chapter 1. Among these were the National Opera Company, the National Opera Society, the National Theatre Organisation, the National Opera Association of South Africa, Die Operavereniging van Suid-Afrika (The Opera Society of South Africa), the South African Opera Federation, and Die Opera-organisasie van Suid-Afrika (The Opera Organisation of South Africa).
5. William Richardson, "Introduction by the Chairman of the Eoan Group," Programme booklet for *Maritza* (1957). University of Cape Town Special Collections, Chisholm Collection, catalog no. BC129.4.19.20.
6. Joseph Manca, "Historical Overview of Eoan's Activities from 1933–1968," 14. Eoan Group Archive, box 60, folder 494c. This play was performed again by the Eoan Group in 1986 at the Nico Malan Theatre. Reviews of the latter performance are archived in the Eoan Group Archive, box 60, folder 494c.
7. "The Music Man," *Alpha* (July 1963): 17. South African National Library.
8. It is important to mention that very little documentation illustrating any kind of resistance from within the coloured community toward the group after 1956 has been archived. This does not mean that there was none or that Eoan's reputation with the political Left has somehow miraculously mended itself. There are two possible explanations for this lack of documents. First, due to Manca's reluctance to the acknowledge such problems, he may have omitted to archive any items that came up. Second, individuals, organizations, and publications that rejected Eoan on political grounds may simply have chosen to ignore the group. The *Torch*, for instance, had always been very critical of Eoan, but reporting on the group almost disappeared from the newspaper after 1956.
9. The *Torch* covered the issue at length in the course of 1958.
10. South African History Online (SAHO), "General South African History Timeline: 1950s," http://www.sahistory.org.za/1900s/1950s, accessed June 6, 2018.
11. "Eoan Group Founder's Retirement," *Sun*, August 3, 1951.
12. Programme booklet for the *Eoan Group 1958 Opera and Ballet Season*. Eoan Group Archive, box 100, folder 770.
13. Désirée Talbot, *For the Love of Singing: 50 Years of Opera at UCT* (Cape Town: Oxford University Press, 1978), 156–76.

14. Ibid., 163.

15. Jacques P. Malan, "Erik Chisholm," in *South African Music Encyclopedia* (Cape Town: Oxford University Press, 1979), 1:272.

16. Talbot, *For the Love of Singing*, 156–76. Examples of lesser-known works staged by the UCT are Gluck's *Ihphigenia in Tauris* and *Orpheus and Euridice*, Berlioz's *Beatrice and Benedict*, Bartok's *Blue Beard Castle*, and Menotti's *The Telephone* and *The Medium*.

17. Talbot, *For the Love of Singing*, 163–68.

18. The University of Cape Town's main campus is in the suburb of Rondebosch outside the city center. The Hiddingh campus is a smaller section situated at the top end of Orange Street, also in the city center.

19. Talbot, *For the Love of Singing*, 163–68. See also Cinema Treasures, "Alhambra Theatre," http://cinematreasures.org/theaters/12772, accessed June 6, 2018.

20. The Society still exists today; see www.gilbertandsullivan.co.za, accessed June 5, 2018.

21. Silver Jubilee Programme booklet of the Gilbert and Sullivan Society, 3. National Library of South African, catalog no A.P.792.0968712.

22. "Non-Europeans Must Boycott Labia," *Torch*, November 6, 1950; and "Successful Boycott of Labia Theatre by Non-Europeans," *Torch*, November 13, 1950.

23. Sheila Patterson, *Colour and Culture in South Africa* (London: Routledge and Paul, 1953), 126. See also Donald Inskip, *Forty Little Years* (Cape Town: Timmins, 1972), 100–103 and 119–157. The group presented a number of plays in the early 1960s at the Little Theatre, linked to the University of Cape Town, which at the time also hosted the Bantu Theatre Company. No evidence exists that casts were racially mixed at that time.

24. Tillie Ulster (former Eoan member) in discussion with the author, March 12, 2012.

25. Ibid.

26. Programme booklet for *Maritza*; "Eoan Group's Success in Rose Marie," *Cape Times*, August 4, 1958; and Programme booklet for *Rio Rita*. University of Cape Town Special Collections, Chisholm Collection, catalog no. BC129.2.12.10.

27. "Eoan Group Offers Opera and Ballet," *Cape Times*, March 11, 1958.

28. "Eoan Group," *Cape Times*, March 22, 1958.

29. Eric Chisholm, "Message from Professor Erik Chisholm," in Programme booklet for the *Eoan Group Opera and Ballet Season*, March 1958. Eoan Group Archive, box 100, folder 770.

30. David Kimbell, *Italian Opera* (Cambridge, UK: Cambridge University Press, 1995), 619.

31. Ibid.

32. Talbot, *For the Love of Singing*, 156–76.

33. "Eoan Group Offers Opera and Ballet," *Cape Times*, March 11, 1958.

34. Sophia Andrews (Eoan mezzo-soprano) in discussion with Lisba Vosloo, October 2012.

35. "Eoan Groep herhaal 'wonderwork' met La Traviata"[Eoan Group Repeats "miracle" with La Traviata], *Die Burger*, March 12, 1958.

36. "Eoan Group in La Traviata," *Cape Times*, March 12, 1958.

37. Ibid.

38. Programme booklet for the *1959 Opera and Ballet Season*. Eoan Group Archive, box 100, folder 770.

39. "Eoan Group Triumphs in Rigoletto at the City Hall," *Cape Argus*, March 9, 1959; "Eoan's Best Opera Success," *Cape Times*, March 9, 1959; and "Eoan Group Presteer met Rigoletto" [Eoan Group excels with Rigoletto], *Die Burger*, March 9, 1959.

40. "Eoan's Best Opera Success"; and "Eoan Group Triumphs in Rigoletto at the City Hall.". Fourie also received many letters from the public, congratulating him on his performances. Ruth Fourie Scrapbook, Eoan Group Archive.

41. "Eoan Group Triumphs Again at City Hall in Traviata," *Cape Argus*, March 13, 1959.

42. Ruth Fourie (widow of former Eoan singer Lionel Fourie) in discussion with the author, April 23, 2013.

43. "Lionel Fourie's Death Is a Loss to South Africa." Ruth Fourie Scrapbook, Eoan Group Archive.

44. Ibid.

45. Lionel Fourie, "Stads-Kleurling is Agterlik—Kultuur is op die Platteland" [City-coloureds Are Backward—Culture Is in the Rural Areas], *Die Burger*, June 13, 1959. Ruth Fourie Scrapbook, Eoan Group Archive.

46. Ibid. Similar to other issues, such as David Poole's "colouredness" or Stanley Glasser's affair as a white man with a coloured jazz singer (Maud Damons), Fourie's alcoholism was one of those things that everybody knew about, but it was never openly discussed, not even during the interviews conducted with approximately forty-five former Eoan members for an aural history project in 2009.

47. Peter Voges (former Eoan actor and dancer) in discussion with the author, February 28, 2012; and Ruth Fourie (widow of former Eoan singer Lionel Fourie) in discussion with the author, October 22, 2008.

48. Ismail Sydow to Mr. Jan Luyt, September 25, 1968. Eoan Group Archive, box 34, folder 233.

49. Patricia van Graan (former Eoan soprano) in discussion with the author, November 19, 2008.

50. "Eoan Group Triumphs in Rigoletto at the City Hall."

51. "Eoan's Best Opera Success."

52. Mabel Kester-Gabriels (widow of Eoan tenor Joseph Gabriels) in discussion with the author, February 7, 2013.

53. Ibid.

54. I have not been able to ascertain when exactly this was and could therefore not determine for how long he sang opera before his first opera performance with Eoan.

55. Kester-Gabriels interview, 2013. See also Eoan History Project, *Eoan—Our Story* (Johannesburg: Fourthwall Books, 2013), 82; and Gregorio Fiasconaro, *I'd Do It Again* (Cape Town: Books of Africa, 1982), 71.

56. "Eoan Group Presteer met Rigoletto."

57. "Eoan's Best Opera Success."

58. Marianne Thamm, "King Kong Lives Again: Iconic 1950s Musical Revival Set to Be Highlight on SA 2017 Cultural Calendar," *Daily Maverick*, January 10, 2017, https://www.dailymaverick.co.za/article/2017-01-10-king-kong-lives-again-iconic-1950s-musical-revival-set-to-be-highlight-on-sa-2017-cultural-calendar/#.WKw-zDt94dV, accessed June 5, 2018.

59. Mona Glasser, *King Kong, a Venture in the Theatre* (Cape Town: Norman Howell Publishers, 1960).

60. Fugard Theatre, "Eric Abraham Presents . . . ," http://www.kingkongstagemusical.com/creative-team, accessed February 21, 2017.

61. David B. Coplan, *In Township Tonight!*, 2nd ed. (Auckland Park: Jacana Media, 2007), 214–17.

62. Thamm, "King Kong Lives Again," 2017.

63. Coplan, *In Township Tonight!*, 215.

64. Stanley Glasser, *Paljas*, http://www.flatinternational.org/template_volume.php?volume_id=204, accessed February 22, 2017.

65. South African History Online (SAHO), "Unlawful Organizations Act, Act No 34 of 1960," http://www.sahistory.org.za/archive/unlawful-organizations-act,-act-no-34-of-1960, accessed June 5, 2018.

66. This is now Gauteng.

67. Ian Goldin, *Making Race: The Politics and Economics of Coloured Identity in South Africa* (London & New York: Longman, 1987), 112–16.

68. South African History Online (SAHO), South African Coloured People's Organisation (SACPO), March 30, 2011, www.sahistory.org.za/topic/south-african-coloured-people-organisation-sacpo, accessed June 29, 2018.

69. Goldin, *Making Race*, 116.

70. The entire cast took three months' unpaid leave from their daytime jobs to go on tour. Although the Eoan Finance Committee paid compensation for loss of wages, no singers or dancers received payment for their performances. For their performances in Durban, Eoan had to apply for special exemption on entertainment duty, which all performers in Natal normally had to pay to provincial authorities. This resulted in an administrative exercise that took many months to play out as Durban officials found it difficult to believe that the company's singers were amateurs. See correspondence in Eoan Group Archive, box 31, folder 210.

71. Joseph Manca, "Advance Publicity Information Fourth Opera and Ballet Season." Eoan Group Archive, box 2, folder 10.

72. "Another Milestone Passed by Eoan Group," *Cape Times*, March 11, 1960; and "Briljante opvoering van La Bohème" [Brilliant performance of La Bohème], *Die Burger*, March 12, 1960.

73. "What a Fund of Talent There Is!," *Cape Argus*, March 11, 1960.

74. "Sensational Success of Rigoletto," *Cape Times*, March 20, 1960; "Confident and Polished Eoan Group Rigoletto," *Cape Argus*, March 19, 1960; and "Eoan Group's Vitality Shines in *La Traviata*," *Cape Argus*, March 15, 1960.

75. "Cavalleria Rusticana at City Hall," *Cape Times*, March 16, 1960.

76. Programme booklets for the *1947 Grand Opera Season*, the *1948 Grand Opera Season*, and the *1950 Season Labia Grand Opera Company*. The South African National Library, catalog no. A.P.792.0968712.

77. Manca, "Advance Publicity Information," 5. Although publicity material could be expected to include statements like this, in this case it was a realistic reflection of the role Manca played in the group.

78. See information on Eoan's 1960 tour to Port Elizabeth, Durban, and Johannesburg. Eoan Group Archive, box 31, folders 209-211.

79. Mohamed Adhikari, *Burdened by Race: Coloured Identities in Southern Africa* (Cape Town: University of Cape Town Press, 2009), viii.

80. Fourie, "Stads-Kleurling is Agterlik—Kultuur is op die Platteland." In this article he discusses what he perceived as the difference between coloureds living in the city and those in rural areas.

81. Joseph Manca, "Eoan Group, 1962 Arts Festival and future Activities," 5. Eoan Group Archive, box 53, folder 436. See also Minutes of the 32nd Annual General Meeting, September 29, 1966. Eoan Group Archive, box 1, folder 3. Total expenditure for the tour came to R58,000.

82. Manca, "Historical Overview," 9.

83. Early in 1960 Manca visited all three cities to investigate the feasibility of a tour and to meet with people who could help with arrangements. He also traveled to Rhodesia and met with several people with the view to extend the tour there, but due to high cost, heavy demands on the group's time, and the lack of a coloured community who could support Eoan with accommodation in that country, the plans were dropped. Eoan Group Archive, box 32, folder 216.

84. The Port Elizabeth Council for Coloured Women to Joseph Manca, March 21, 1960. Eoan Group Archive, box 31, folder 209.

85. "Coloured Boycott Decision," n.d. Eoan Group Archive, box 31, folder 209.

86. Five years later, during Eoan's 1965 tour, the situation in Port Elizabeth was entirely different. Due to apartheid legislation, freedom of movement for coloureds was markedly curtailed, causing many problems for the group.

87. "Press Statement," n.d. Eoan Group Archive, box 31, folder 211.

88. The Provincial Accountant Natal to Joseph Manca, January 11, 1961. Eoan Group Archive, box 40, folder 321.

89. "Eoan Group's 'La Boheme' Takes Durban by Storm," *Natal Mercury*, July 30, 1960. Eoan Group Archive, box 30, folder 208.

90. "Eoan Cast's 'Rigoletto' Delights Audience," *Natal Mercury*, August 2, 1960. Eoan Group Archive, box 30, folder 208.

91. Programme schedule for Eoan's Johannesburg season. Eoan Group Archive, box 31, folder 211.

92. "Press Statement" during Eoan's tour in Johannesburg, n.d. Eoan Group Archive, box 31, folder 211.

93. Christopher Cockburn, "Discomposing Apartheid's Story: Who owns Handel?," in *Composing Apartheid* (Johannesburg: Wits University Press, 2008), 55–78.

94. Sophia Andrews (Eoan mezzo-soprano soloist) in discussion with the author, June 19, 2009. Eoan Group Archive. She worked in the sowing division of Enzyne African Clothing Factory together with hundreds of other unskilled laborers. Her staff number was 1081.

95. Ibid.

96. Ibid.

97. Ruth Goodwin (Eoan soprano soloist) in discussion with Ruth Fourie, May 21, 2009. Eoan Group Archive.

98. Ruth Grevler-Manca (daughter of Joseph Manca) in discussion with the author, May 30, 2009. Eoan Group Archive.

99. "Notes on Carmen." Eoan Group Archive, box 83, folder 646a. This two-page document lists many artistic problems with the production, which was only featured on their countrywide tour in 1965 and was never repeated afterward. It is not clear from the document who the author was.

100. Fiasconaro, *I'd Do It Again*, 69–72.

101. Ibid., 70.

102. Absenteeism and therefore lack of preparation was, for example, one of the reasons the group's 1968 opera season was canceled at the last minute, resulting in major financial difficulties for the group.

103. "Press Release for *The 1965 Eoan Opera Season*," 4. Eoan Group Archive, box 2, folder 9.

104. Fiasconaro, *I'd Do It Again*, 70.

105. "Tribute to the Maestro Gordon Jephtas: 8 March 1943–5 July 1993." Eoan Group Archive, box 55, folder 451; and May Abrahamse (principal soprano) in discussion with Christine Lucia, July 9, 2009.

106. Gerald Samaai (Eoan tenor soloist) in discussion with the author, November 19, 2008. Eoan Group Archive. See also the Jephtas-Abrahamse Correspondence. Eoan Group Archive. In these letters, Jephtas often referred to, for instance, records or books in "his room" at the Sydows' house.

107. Ibid.

108. Gordon Jephtas to May Abrahamse, January 17, 1964. Jephtas-Abrahamse Correspondence, Eoan Group Archive.

109. Ibid.

110. Eoan History Project, *Eoan—Our Story*, 100–106.

111. Abrahamse interview, 2009. Both Gordon Jephtas and May Abrahamse had a high opinion of Fiasconaro.

112. Fiasconaro, *I'd Do It Again*, 71.

113. Amanda Botha, "Oplaas saamsing as gelykes" [Finally singing together as equals], *Rapport Ekstra*, February 10, 1980. It is only by the late 1970s that Eoan dancers started to take part in ballet productions by the UCT Ballet School, and the first Eoan singers found employment with the Cape Provincial Arts Council in 1980.

114. "Didi Sydow, Short Resume of Ballet Career," 2. Eoan Group Archive, box 39, folder 314.

115. "Opera Chorus Rehearsal List," February 1965. Eoan Group Archive, box 3, folder 14.

116. Joseph Manca to Mrs. Bertha Epstein (daughter of Mr. Isaac Ochberg), October 31, 1962. Eoan Group Archive, box 32, folder 221. Eoan continued to use the Ochberg Hall for other activities until the organization was forced out of District Six in the late 1960s.

117. "Permit" issued by the Department of the Interior, April 24, 1961. Eoan Group Archive, box 32, folder 219. Dr I. D. du Plessis was apparently instrumental in having this permit approved. Joseph Manca to Dr. I. D. Du Plessis, May 3, 1961. Eoan Group Archive, box 32, folder 219.

118. Joseph Manca, "Eoan Group, 1962 Arts Festival and Future Activities," 1-2, n.d. Eoan Group Archive, box 53, folder 436. See also "Eoan Group Planning Second S.A. Tour and Visit to Britain," *Cape Argus*, February 16, 1961.

119. Manca, "Eoan Group, 1962 Arts Festival and Future Activities," 6.

120. "Actors and Apartheid," *Cape Times*, March 2, 1961. Eoan Group Archive, box 32, folder 219.

121. "Conflict on Theatre Apartheid," *Cape Times*, March 9, 1961. Eoan Group Archive, box 32, folder 219.

122. See minutes of these meetings in Eoan Group Archive, box 82, folder 634. The directors mentioned are H. G. Ashworth (for Eoan), Joseph Manca (Festival Director), and E. de Klerk (Peninsula Round Table Chairman). The two organizations held weekly meetings during the months preceding the festival.

123. Regarding *Madame Butterfly*, see "Press Release for 1962 Eoan Opera Season." Eoan Group Arichive, box 2, folder 9.

124. "Programme Overview of Eoan Group Peninsula Round Table Arts Festival 1962." Eoan Group Archive, box 2, folder 10.

125. "Eoan Group Opera Season Is Lavishly Planned," *Cape Times*, March 7, 1962.

126. "Eoan Group's Butterfly Is Outstanding Success," *Cape Times*, March 19, 1962. All reviews published in the *Cape Times* were signed with the initials B. M. Guest lists for opera productions revealed that Beatrice Marx was the official critic of the *Cape Times*. See guest lists in the Eoan Group Archive, box 82, folder 636.

127. "Eoan Group's Butterfly Is Outstanding Success."

128. "New Laurels for Eoan Group in La Bohème," *Cape Times*, March 20, 1962.

129. Ibid.

130. "Applause for Debut of New Violetta in La Traviata," *Cape Times*, March 23, 1962.

131. "Young Singer with Great Talent Makes Her Opera Debut," *Cape Argus*, March 23, 1962.

132. Joseph Manca, "Notes on Abeeda Parker." Eoan Group Archive, box 32, folder 221.

133. Ruth Grevler-Manca (daughter of Joseph Manca) in discussion with the author, May 30, 2008.

134. David Bloomberg to Joseph Manca, March 21, 1962. Eoan Group Archive, box 82, folder 633.

135. Minutes of the meetings held by the finance committee on January 19, January 26, February 16, February 23, March 2, and March 16, 1962. Eoan Group Archive, box 83, folder 638.

136. Gregorio Fiasconaro to Joseph Manca, February 14, 1962. Eoan Group Archive, box 82, folder 639.

137. Joseph Manca to Imperial Cold Storage, June 15, 1962. Eoan Group Archive, box 82, folder 643.

138. The first quote is from "Verdi at City Hall," *Cape Times*, August 6, 1962. The two others are from "Another Major Success for the Eoan Group," *Cape Argus*, August 6, 1962.

139. Manca, "Eoan Group, 1962," 26–29.

140. Manca, "Historical Overview," 12.

141. Eduard Greyling (former principal dancer at CAPAB and current teacher at the UCT Ballet School), email message to the author, March 12, 2013. Greyling attached copies of Programme notes on these works in the email.

142. See interviews with Peter Voges (September 11, 2009), Emma Renzi (July 15, 2009), Lydia Johnson (September 26, 2009), and Tillie Ulster (September 15, 2009) in the Eoan Group Archive.

143. "Dawid Poole had die gawe van menswees" [Dawid Poole had the gift of humanity], *Die Burger*, August 31, 1991.

144. This fact has for many years not been documented, and neither the reporting on Poole during his life nor the obituaries published after his death in August 1991 mention his racial status. The issue has, however, been commented on extensively in interviews for the Eoan History Project's oral history book *Eoan–Our Story*, published in 2013. During the interview process it became clear that Poole's racial status was one of those things that everybody knew of but nobody talked about. See, for instance, Voges interview, 2009; Renzi interview, 2009; Johnson interview, 2009; and Ulster interview, 2009.

145. Minutes of the General Meeting, June 1, 1980, Eoan Group Archive, box 4, folder 29.

146. "First All-South African Full-length Ballet," *Cape Times*, August 16, 1962.

147. Ibid.

148. "Fine Staging, Fine Dancing in New Jazz Ballet," *Cape Times*, August 30, 1962; and "The Square Is Artistic, Vital," *Cape Argus*, August 30, 1962.

149. Marina Grut, *The History of Ballet in South Africa* (Cape Town: Human & Rousseau, 1981), 35.

150. Stanley Glasser, "The Square," score 1962. Stanley Glasser Collection.

151. Grut, *History of Ballet in South Africa*, 35.

152. "Chance of a Lifetime, Auditions for Eoan Arts Festival," *Cape Times*, April 21, 1962.

153. Glasser, *Paljas*.

154. Peter Voges (former Eoan ballet dancer and actor) in discussion with the author, October 22, 2008.

155. The Immorality Act of 1950 forbade sexual relations between members of the white and nonwhite races.

156. Although the information on this incident existed in the realm of "hearsay" for many years, the incident was confirmed by the journalist Michael Green, who related it in his book *Around and About* (Claremont: David Philip, 2004), 52. Green, however, connected the incident to the production of the musical *King Kong*. See also Voges interview, 2008.

157. Maud Damons adopted the stage name Maxine Day in 1965, and her style is said to have emulated the singing of Doris Day.

158. Programme booklet for *Die Fledermaus*. Eoan Group Archive, box 32, folder 221.

159. Richard Taruskin, *The Oxford History of Western Music* (Oxford: Oxford University Press, 2010), 3:648.

160. "Die Fledermaus," in *The Guide to Light Opera & Operetta*, n.d., http://www.musicaltheatreguide.com/composers/straussjnr/fledermaus.htm, accessed June 6, 2018.

161. "Brilliant Production of Operetta by the Eoan Group," *Cape Argus*, October 23, 1962.

162. "Die Mimi Coertse-beurs" [The Mimi Coertse bursary], *Eikestad Nuus*, September 14, 1962.

163. Mimi Coertse, *'n Stem vir Suid-Afrika: My storie, soos vertel aan Ian Raper* (Pretoria: Litera, 2007), 78–79. See also Kester-Gabriels interview, 2013. She recalled that auditions were held at UCT in Cape Town and not in Pretoria. The *Eikestad Nuus* also reported that previous winners of the competition included Gert Potgieter, Wolfgang Anheisser, Maria Navarro, and Hans van Heerden. "Die Mimi Coertse-beurs," *Eikestad Nuus*, September 14, 1962.

164. "Coertse beurs" [Coertse bursary], *Die Burger*, October 10, 1962.

165. Regarding Manca's honorary doctorate, see Jacques P. Malan, "Manca, Joseph Salvatore," in *South African Music Encyclopedia* (Cape Town: Oxford University Press, 1984), 3:192–194. The quote is from "Press Release for 1965 Eoan Opera Season." Eoan Group Arichive, box 2, folder 9.

166. "The Music Man," 16–21.

167. The only documentation regarding the award found in UCT's archives is the recommendation that was read during the ceremony.

168. "Little Theatre to Present Play by Cape Town Author," *Cape Times*, September 18, 1963. Flora Stohr was the daughter-in-law of a well-known Cape Town pianist, Elsie Hall.

169. Manca, "Historical Overview," 14.

170. "Play Is Excellent Entertainment," *Cape Times*, September 23, 1963.

171. Ruth Fourie (widow of Lionel Fourie) in discussion with the author, May 8, 2013.

172. Fourie interview, 2008.

173. Ismail Sydow to Gordon Jephtas, February 16, 1980. Ruth Fourie Scrapbook, Eoan Group Archive.

174. "Lionel Fourie's Death Is a Loss to South Africa." Ruth Fourie Scrapbook, Eoan Group Archive. (The date and name of the newspaper are not visible.)

## CHAPTER FOUR. SCALA IS SCALA AND EOAN IS EOAN: THE STRUGGLE TO BREATHE

1. Minutes of the 32nd Annual General Meeting, September 29, 1966. Eoan Group Archive, box 1, folder 3.
2. Ismail Sydow, "Foreword to the 1969 Opera Season Programme." Eoan Group Archive, box 36, folder 279.
3. Ibid.
4. Eoan Group Trust to Joseph Manca, May 6, 1966. Eoan Group Archive, box 33, folder 231. The Eoan Group Trust members were C. S. Corder, David Bloomberg, D. R. D'Ewes, W. Gradner, G. K. Lindsay, P. Morkel, Mrs. J. Newton Thompson, J. J. Piek, F. C. Robb, R. Sonnenberg, Prof. W. H. van der Merwe, Louis Charles Vivian Walker and Dr. I. D. du Plessis. The minutes of the Eoan Group Trust meeting held on January 22, 1965, however, also mention William Murray Bisset (secretary), Harold Lister Kennedy, and Eric Richard Liefeldt. Eoan Group Archive, box 33, folder 231.
5. The trust also functioned as a guarantor for the group's bank overdraft, with the result that whenever its cash flow trailed into the overdraft, money from the trust was temporarily deposited into the group's account until new income was generated. The funds in the trust, however, never generated much interest. This was also partly due to the group's frequent use of its overdraft. See correspondence from the trust to the group in the Eoan Group Archive, box 11, folder 75.
6. Ismail Sydow, "Statement by the Chairman: Mr I. Sydow on Establishment and Acceptance of Eoan Group Trust," 1. Eoan Group Archive, box 53, folder 439.
7. Ibid., 2.
8. Ibid., 4.
9. Ibid., 6.
10. Forty-five interviews were conducted in 2009 with former members for the oral history book *Eoan—Our Story*, published in 2013. Copies of all interviews were held in the Eoan Group Archive at Domus.
11. See interviews with Peter Voges (September 11, 2009), May Abrahamse (July 9, 2009), and Tillie Ulster (September, 15 2009), Eoan Group Archive.
12. Jacques P. Malan, "Cape Town Municipal Orchestra," in *South African Music Encyclopedia* (Cape Town: Oxford University Press, 1979), 1:252–53. Jorda was conductor of the Cape Town Municipal Orchestra from 1947 to 1954.
13. Tillie Ulster (former Eoan member) in discussion with the author, March 2012; and Peter Voges (former Eoan ballet dancer and actor) in discussion with the author, October 22, 2008.
14. Gordon Jephtas to May Abrahamse, December 11, 1966. Jephtas-Abrahamse Correspondence, Eoan Group Archive.

15. On preparing for the 1965 season, see Joseph Manca to David Tidboald, January 24, 1963. Eoan Group Archive, box 3, folder 23. On the production of *Showboat*, see "Showboat het waarlik iets vir almal" [Showboat truly offers something for everybody], *Die Burger*, March 13, 1964.

16. J. Brooks Spector, "The Johannesburg Civic Theatre, 1962 to 2007—the First 45 Years," 10, http://www.joburgtheatreptyltd.co.za/The%20First%2045%20Years.pdf, accessed March 16, 2017.

17. Ibid, 10.

18. Joseph Manca to David Tidboald, January 24, 1963. Eoan Group Archive, box 3, folder 23.

19. Ibid.

20. Inia Te Wiata to Joseph Manca, February 12, 1964, Eoan Group Archive, box 3, folder 23.

21. The group consisted of Nelson Mandela, Walter Sisulu, Govan Mbeki, Ahmed Kathrada, Rusty Bernstein, Dennis Goldberg, James Kantor, Andrew Mlangeni, Elias Motsoaledi, and Raymond Mhlaba.

22. South African History Online, "Forced Removals in South Africa," May 25, 2016, www.sahistory.org.za/article/forced-removals-south-africa, accessed June 29, 2018.

23. Ian Goldin, *Making Race: The Politics and Economics of Coloured Identity in South Africa* (London & New York: Longman, 1987), 151.

24. Cited in ibid.

25. Joseph Manca to David Tidboald, January 24, 1963. Eoan Group Archive, box 3, folder 23.

26. These include Giuseppe Verdi's *La Traviata*, *Rigoletto* and *Il Trovatore*, Giacomo Puccini's *La Bohème* and *Madama Butterfly*, Pietro Mascagni's *Cavalliera Rusticana*, Gaetano Donizetti's *L'Elisire D'Amore*, George Bizet's *Carmen*, and Johann Strauss's *Die Fledermaus*.

27. Minutes of the 32nd Annual General Meeting, 3–4.

28. "Cape Town Municipal Orchestra Call Sheet March 1965." Eoan Group Archive, box 33, folder 228.

29. "Press Release for the 1965 Eoan Opera Season," 4. Eoan Group Archive, box 2, folder 9.

30. Ibid.

31. "Eoan Group in a Triumphant Presentation of Trovatore," *Cape Times*, March 19, 1965; and "Jong Tenoor Sing Uitnemend in Il Trovatore" [Young tenor sings exquisitely in Il Trovatore], *Die Burger*, March 20, 1965.

32. "Eoan Group Season's Fine Beginning," *Cape Argus*, March 19, 1965.

33. "Jong Tenoor Sing Uitnemend in Il Trovatore."

34. "Eoan Group Strikes a Lighter Note," *Cape Times*, March 26, 1965.

35. "Eoan Group's Light Opera Is Good Entertainment," *Cape Argus*, March 26, 1965.

36. Erik Chisholm to Joseph Manca, May 19, 1965. Eoan Group Archive, box 3, folder 23. The tone of the letter is indicative of Chisholm's socialist convictions and

that he admired Manca for bringing opera by the working class to the working class. Although the admiration he speaks of might have been on a political rather than a musical level, it is also clear that there was little professional rivalry between the two men. Chisholm died on June 8, 1965.

37. Mrs. R. Smith to Joseph Manca, March 20, 1965. Eoan Group Archive, box 2, folder 9.

38. "Rehearsal Schedules for the 1965 Opera Season." Eoan Group Archive, box 3, folder 17.

39. Joseph Manca, "Advance Publicity 1965 Opera Tour, Johannesburg Season," n.d., 6. Eoan Group Archive, box 83, folder 646a.

40. "Uitdaging het Jephtas gelok" [Challenge attracted Jephtas], *Die Burger*, April 2, 1986. See also Joseph Manca, "Historical Overview of Eoan's Activities from 1933–1968," 24. Eoan Group Archive, box 60, folder 494c.

41. Désirée Talbot, *For the Love of Singing: 50 Years of Opera at UCT* (Cape Town: Oxford University Press, 1978), 168–69.

42. Ibid.

43. Regarding *The Bartered Bride*, see Elizabeth Blanckenberg, "The Music Activities of the Cape Performing Arts Board (CAPAB): A Historical Survey" (master's diss., Stellenbosch University, 2009), 18. Regarding singers of the roles, see Gunter Pulvermacher, "Briljante en Kleurryke Voorstelling van die Verkoopte Bruid" [Brilliant and colourful presentation of the Bartered Bride"], *Die Burger*, February 10, 1965.

44. Noel Storr, "Tremendously Colourful Opera Presentation," *Cape Times*, February 9, 1965.

45. Manca, "Historical Overview," 24.

46. Joseph Manca, "Advance Publicity for the 1965 Opera Tour." Eoan Group Archive, box 53, folder 437.

47. See correspondence in Eoan Group Archive, box 83, folder 646a.

48. The Department of Community Development to the Eoan Group, June 1, 1965. Eoan Group Archive, box 83, folder 646a.

49. "1965 Eoan Tour Performance Schedule." Eoan Group Archive, box 83, folder 646a.

50. Minutes of the 32nd Annual General Meeting; "Financial Planning Documentation." Eoan Group Archive, box 3, folder 23; and Manca, "Historical Overview," 24.

51. The Department of Home Affairs to the Eoan Group, July 22, 1965. Eoan Group Archive, box 83, folder 646b.

52. Ismail Sydow to the Secretary of the Interior, July 23, 1965. Eoan Group Archive, box 83, folder 646b.

53. The Department of Community Development to the Eoan Group, July 20, 1965. Eoan Group Archive, box 83, folder 646b.

54. Ibid.

55. Ismail Sydow to the Secretary of Coloured Affairs, July 23, 1965. Eoan Group Archive, box 83, folder 646b.

56. Joseph Manca to Murray Bisset, July 8, 1965. Eoan Group Archive, box 83, folder 646a.

57. Hymie Udwin to Murray Bisset, September 15, 1965. Eoan Group Archive, box 83, folder 646a.

58. Daily News reporter, "Coloureds Snub Eoan Group," *Daily News*, n.d. Eoan Group Archive, box 60, folder 494a.

59. Oliver Walker, "Triumph for Cape Town Violetta," name of newspaper unknown, n.d. Eoan Group Archive, box 93, folder 765.

60. Pieter Serfontein, "Eoan-groep se La Traviata 'n belewenis" [Eoan Group's La Traviata an experience], name of newspaper unknown, n.d. Eoan Group Archive, box 93, folder 765.

61. See newspaper reviews in the Eoan Group Archive, box 93, folder 765. Reviews were cut and pasted into a scrapbook without referencing the newspapers in which they were published or the dates of publication.

62. "Thank You for Coming and for Traviata," name of newspaper unknown, n.d. Eoan Group Archive, box 93, folder 765.

63. "Notes on Carmen." Eoan Group Archive, box 83, folder 646a. This document is the only evidence retained in the Eoan Group Archive of an internal critical approach toward the group's artistic endeavors.

64. The Eoan Group Trust to the Department of Coloured Affairs, December 10, 1965. Eoan Group Archive, box 33, folder 231.

65. Manca, "Historical Overview," 24.

66. Ibid., 21.

67. Minutes of the 32nd Annual General Meeting, 4–5. The minutes of the meeting in 1957 at which the group decided to renounce state funding did not survive. However, the fact is mentioned in various newspaper articles and was discussed at meetings. See also Minutes of the 33rd Annual General Meeting, December 8, 1970, 6. Eoan Group Archive, box 2, folder 8.

68. Permit issued to Eoan for its 1968 Opera Season, May 27, 1968. Eoan Group Archive, box 34, folder 233.

69. Joseph Manca, "Eoan Group," in *South African Music Encyclopedia* (Cape Town: Oxford University Press, 1982), 2:26–29.

70. Manca, "Historical Overview," 24.

71. Minutes of the 32nd Annual General Meeting, 8.

72. Gordon Jephtas to May Abrahamse, August 24, 1966. Gordon Jephtas–May Abrahamse Correspondence, Eoan Group Archive.

73. Ibid., 9.

74. Ibid., 12.

75. The implication is that the minutes of all thirty-one preceding annual general meetings are lost.

76. Minutes of the 32nd Annual General Meeting, 7.

77. Ibid.

78. Ibid., 3.

79. Ibid., 2–3.

80. Ibid., 3–4.

81. Ibid., 5.

82. Gerald Samaai (Eoan tenor soloist) in discussion with Wayne Muller, May 12, 2009. Eoan Group Archive.

83. Ibid.

84. Ibid.

85. Tsafendas was known to have schizophrenia, as a result of which he was spared the death penalty for the murder.

86. "White Officials Barred from Non-White Cycling Event," *Cape Argus*, March 23, 1965.

87. "Non-Whites Will Attend Boxing," *Cape Argus*, March 26, 1965.

88. "Not Yet Possible to Pay Coloured Same as White Teachers," *Cape Argus*, March 26, 1965.

89. Tillie Ulster (former Eoan member) in discussion with the author, October 22, 2008. According to her, Ismail and Carmen Sydow had no children of their own, and Didi was an adopted daughter. They also had an adopted son, Allie, who took part in Eoan's productions as a singer for a short while. Allie Sydow died on October 7, 1972. See "Members of Executive Committee." Eoan Group Archive, box 9, folder 63.

90. Ismail Sydow to Joseph Manca, June 5, 1967. Eoan Group Archive, box 86, folder 686.

91. Sydow was Muslim, hence the translation of "Joseph" to "Yusuf." Manca was Roman Catholic.

92. Ismail Sydow and Joseph Manca, June 29, 1967. Eoan Group Archive, box 86, folder 686.

93. May Abrahamse (Eoan soprano soloist) in discussion with the author, October 1, 2008. She explained why Jephtas was unwilling to come back to South Africa: "Look, Dr. Manca was a bit of a dictator. He wanted to control everything. Gordon did not want to come because he had many more opportunities in Europe. He also had developed musically much further than Dr. Manca and he knew that if he came, he would just have to play the piano and do what Dr. Manca tells him to."

94. Virginia Davids (Eoan soprano soloist) in discussion with Phillip Swales, July 6, 2009. Eoan Group Archive.

95. D. de Villiers, "His Pupils Want Presley—Not Verdi," *Cape Argus*, February 28, 1958.

96. Eoan History Project, *Eoan—Our Story* (Johannesburg: Fourthwall Books, 2013), 55.

97. It is not clear from the archive how and why the Bernard van Leer Foundation became involved with Eoan. This organization is still active in The Netherlands today, and inquiries by this author about their donation to the building of the Joseph Stone Auditorium in 1969 remained unanswered.

98. Manca, "Eoan Group," 26–29.

99. Hans Kramer, "Soprano Rose to Great Heights in Her Tragic Roles," *Cape Times*, September 18, 1967. See also Pieter Kooij, "Vera Gow skitter as Violetta" [Vera Gow shines as Violetta], *Die Burger*, September 18, 1967.

100. The first quotation is from Hans Kramer, "Eoan Group Again Score Success in Sparkling Opera," *Cape Times*, September 21, 1967. The second is from Hans Kramer, "Glowing Performance of a Favourite Opera," *Cape Times*, September 15, 1967.

101. Rita Scholtz, "Operaseisoen van Eoan Group begin op hoënoot" [Eoan Opera Season Starts on High Note], *Die Burger*, September 16, 1967.

102. "Opera seisoen verleng" [Opera season extended], *Die Burger*, September 28, 1967.

103. David Bloomberg, *My Times* (Cape Town: Fernwood Press, 2007). Bloomberg was an attorney and became famous when he defended Demitrio Tsafendas, who had assassinated then prime minister Hendrik Verwoerd in 1966. Bloomberg had a great interest in the arts and spent much of his spare time and energy in the theater. He managed to bring a number of internationally acclaimed performers to Cape Town and was responsible for many theater productions between 1956 and 1967. He was on the board of the Cape Performing Arts Board and closely involved with the Cape Town Municipal Orchestra. Bloomberg was mayor of Cape Town from 1973 until 1975. He and his wife emigrated to England in 1988.

104. Bloomberg, *My Times*, 25.

105. See notes 108–10.

106. David Bloomberg to Joseph Manca, November 25, 1966. Eoan Group Archive, box 85, folder 684.

107. It is not clear from documents in the archive how the group reacted to this news.

108. "Eoan-Groep Het met Hart en Siel aan Oklahoma Gewerk" [Eoan Group worked with heart and soul on Oklahoma], *Die Burger*, January 21, 1967.

109. Owen Williams, "Eoan Group's Natural Charm in Pleasant Oklahoma," *Cape Argus*, January 20, 1967.

110. Stanley A. Waren, "Theatre in South Africa," *Educational Theatre Journal* 20, no. 3 (October 1968): 411.

111. Ibid., 413.

112. Minutes of the Financial Committee Meeting, October 11, 1969. Eoan Group Archive, box 93, folder 758.

113. Bloomberg, *My Times*, 24–31.

114. Ibid., 29.

115. Ibid., 28–29.

116. Ibid., 29.

117. Terry Herbst, "Eoan Group Players Can Be Proud of Imaginative South Pacific," *Cape Times*, February 29, 1968.

118. Ben de Kock, "South Pacific 'n Triomf vir Eoan Groep" [South Pacific a triumph for Eoan Group], *Die Burger*, March 1, 1968.

119. "South Pacific Rehearsal Schedule." Eoan Group Archive, box 53, folder 433.

120. Bloomberg, *My Times*, 26.

121. Dr. Archie Mafeje completed his PhD in anthropology from Cambridge University in England in 1966. Martin Plaut, "How the 1968 Revolution Reached

Cape Town," January 9, 2011, https://martinplaut.wordpress.com/2011/09/01/the-1968-revolution-reaches-cape-town/, accessed June 9, 2018.

122. "Rehearsal Schedules." Eoan Group Archive, box 34, folder 233.

123. Various such letters between cast members and Joseph Manca are stored in the archive. Eoan Group Archive, box 34, folder 233.

124. Ismail Sydow to the Town Clerk, Mr. Jan Luyt, September 25, 1968. Eoan Group Archive, box 34, folder 233.

125. Trevor Oosterwyk, "It's Eoan vs Eoan in Auditorium Tussle," *Cape Argus*, May 21, 2001. The relationship between the Eoan Group and the Eoan Group Trust continues to be problematic to this day. In May 2001 the trust was on the verge of evicting the group from the premises. Similarly, Shafiek Rajap, the current chairman of the Eoan Board, conceded that a relationship with the trust was almost nonexistent. Shafiek Rajap in discussion with the author, June 4, 2008.

126. The Eoan Group Trust to Ismail Sydow, January 7, 1969. Eoan Group Archive, box 53, folder 437.

127. Minutes of the Special General Meeting, August 26, 1969, 9. Eoan Group Archive, box 25, folder 178.

128. Elsa Winckley, "Eoan Group Shines Brightly as Ever," *Sunday Express*, March 30, 1969.

129. "Mayor to Hear Top Soprano," name of newspaper unknown, June 1969. Eoan Group Archive, box 36, folder 270.

130. "Rehearsal Schedules." Eoan Group Archive, box 36, folder 286.

131. Ibid.

132. Other efforts include operas by lesser-known composers such as Alexander Reinagle (1794), Samuel Arnold (1974), Nicolas Isouard (1796), and Francesco Morlacchi (1816).

133. David Kimbell, *Italian Opera* (Cambridge, UK: Cambridge University Press, 1995), 363.

134. Leonard D. Lourens, "The Barber Was Magnificent," *Cape Argus*, October 27, 1969.

135. Hans Kramer, "Eoan Group Premiere of Rossini's Barber Sparkles and Delights," *Cape Times*, October 27, 1969; and Pieter Kooij, "Aan die Barbier had mens tog veel genot" [Barber provided much enjoyment], *Die Burger*, October 27, 1969.

136. Antoinette Silverstri, "Vera Gow Excels in an Enjoyable Trovatore," *Cape Argus*, October 24, 1969.

137. Hans Kramer, "Triumphant Opening of Eoan Group's Eighth Opera Season," *Cape Times*, October 24, 1969; and Pieter Kooij, "Opera reeks begin met klinkende sukses" [Opera season starts with resounding success], *Die Burger*, October 25, 1969.

138. Silvestri, "Vera Gow Excels."

139. "Financial Brain behind the Baton," *Cape Argus*, November 19, 1969.

140. Ibid.

141. "Chairman's Report," Minutes of the Special General Meeting, August 26, 1969, 12. Eoan Group Archive, box 25, folder 178.

142. Ismail Sydow, "Foreword to the 1969 Opera Season Programme." Eoan Group Archive, box 36, folder 279.

143. Kolbe as quoted in Denis-Constant Martin, *Sounding the Cape: Music, Identity and Politics in South Africa* (Cape Town: African Minds, 2013), 196–97.

144. Martin, *Sounding the Cape*, 244 (*langarm*, *vastrap* and *sopvleis*), 245 (*ghoema* beat).

145. Eoan Group Trust to Joseph Manca, October 20, 1969. Eoan Group Archive, box 53, folder 439.

146. Minutes of the Special General Meeting, 3. Eoan Group Archive, box 25, folder 178. This amount consisted of ZAR8,000 profit earned from the sale of the Ochberg Hall and ZAR25,000 profit earned from the performances of the musicals *Oklahoma* and *South Pacific* in 1967 and 1968.

147. Minutes of the Special General Meeting, 11.

148. The Eoan Group Trust to Ismail Sydow, January 7, 1969. Eoan Group Archive, box 53, folder 437. The letter does not indicate where this idea originated from, although it is possible that in the light of the government's policy of separate universities, it could have been suggested by the government.

149. David Bloomberg in discussion with the author, February 14, 2013. Bloomberg's legal firm handled the divorce procedure for Stone. Stone's only son, who apparently had no children, had passed away some years before the Eoan Group Archive came to Stellenbosch University.

150. Bernard van Leer Foundation, www.bernardvanleer.org, accessed June 9, 2018. See also various the letters from Sydow to Manca in the Eoan Group Archive, box 86, folder 686.

151. "Bernard van Leer Foundation Policy Document." Eoan Group Archive, box 1, folder 3.

152. Ismail Sydow to the Eoan Group Trust, February 24, 1975. Eoan Group Archive, box 1, folder 3.

153. Minutes of the 32nd Annual General Meeting, 6–7. According to Lorna Hansen of Revel Fox Architects, the complex won the Cape Provincial Institute of Architects medal for the best example of architecture in the Cape Province in 1969. Lorna Hansen, email correspondence with the author, February 5, 2018.

154. Blanckenberg, "Music Activities of the Cape Performing Arts Board," 39.

155. Manca, "Eoan Group", 26–29. Today the center is known as the Joseph Stone Auditorium. It is not clear when the name was officially changed.

156. Minutes of the 33rd Annual General Meeting, 6.

157. Minutes of the 32nd Annual General Meeting, 7.

158. Minutes of the 33rd Annual General Meeting, 10.

159. Programme booklet for *Carmen Jones*. Eoan Group Archive, box 100, folder 773.

160. "Advance Publicity Material," 1. Eoan Group Archive, box 10, folder 68.

161. Melinda Boyd, "The Politics of Color in Oscar Hammerstein's *Carmen Jones*." in *Blackness in Opera* (Urbana, Chicago, and Springfield: University of Illinois Press, 2012), 212.

162. Ibid.
163. "Advance Publicity Material," 1.
164. Boyd, "Politics of Color," 212–35.
165. Joseph Manca, "Invitation Letter to Newspaper Critics," July 10, 1970. Eoan Group Archive, box 10, folder 68.

## CHAPTER FIVE. SLOW DEATH: ON TWILIGHT AND LOSS

1. Raymond Ericson, "Joseph Gabriels of South Africa Makes Debut in Pagliacci," *New York Times*, February 7, 1971.
2. Mabel Kester-Gabriels (widow of tenor Joseph Gabriels) in discussion with the author, February 7, 2013.
3. Mabel Kester-Gabriels, email message to the author, March 23, 2010.
4. The couple had two children, Vanessa (born September 3, 1966) and Marcello (born November 30, 1969).
5. Kester-Gabriels interview, 2013.
6. Ibid.
7. Ibid.
8. Kester-Gabriels email, 2010.
9. Kester-Gabriels interview, 2013.
10. Emma Renzi (South African soprano) in discussion with Christine Lucia, July 12, 2009.
11. The Joseph Gabriels Scrapbook. Eoan Group Archive.
12. Ibid.
13. Ericson, "Joseph Gabriels of South Africa Makes Debut in Pagliacci."
14. "Profile: He Turned Italian to Sing," *Alpha* (April 1986): 1–3. This article erroneously states that he sang with La Scala for several years.
15. The first quotation is from Susie Gilbert, *Opera for Everybody: The Story of English National Opera* (London: Faber & Faber, 2008), 270. the second is from Rodney Milnes, "Crossroads," *Spectator*, August 31, 1974, http://archive.spectator.co.uk/article/31st-august-1974/24/opera, accessed March 16, 2017.
16. Ibid.
17. Kester-Gabriels interview, 2013.
18. Jan Badenhorst, "Fresh Distinction for S.A. Tenor," *Star*, February 3, 1971; and Jan Badenhorst, "S.A. tenoor kry sy vuurdoop" [S.A. tenor's baptism of fire], *Die Burger*, July 6, 1972.
19. Gordon Jephtas to May Abrahamse, February 23, 1976. Jephtas-Abrahamse Correspondence, Eoan Group Archive.
20. Kester-Gabriels interview, 2013.
21. The Administration of Coloured Affairs to the Eoan Group, September 8, 1970. Eoan Group Archive, box 53, folder 436.
22. The Administration of Coloured Affairs to the Eoan Group, September 11, 1970. Eoan Group Archive, box 53, folder 436.

23. Eoan Group to the Commissioner of Coloured Affairs, April 19, 1971. Eoan Group Archive, box 71, folder 548. The exact wording of the adjustment to Eoan's constitution can be found in the Minutes of the Executive Committee Meeting, November 25, 1970. Eoan Group Archive, box 93, folder 757.

24. Joseph Manca, "Financial Estimate," n.d. Eoan Archive, box 7, folder 51. See also Manca to the Town Clerk regarding Eoan's 1971 activities, November 26, 1970. Eoan Archive, box 12, folder 84.

25. Manca, "Financial Estimate."

26. Programme booklet for Eoan's Republic Festival celebrations. Eoan Group Archive, box 100, folder 770.

27. "Commission of Inquiry into Matters Relating to the Coloured Population Group: Group 5: Culture. Questionnaire to Organizations Practising the Performing Arts," 7. Eoan Group Archive, box 9, folder 59.

28. Regarding students from UCT handing out protest pamphlets, see "Storm Scatters Opera Protesters," *Cape Times*, May 20, 1971. Regarding the campaign against the color bar, see "More against Opera Ban on Non-whites," *Cape Times*, May 20, 1971.

29. Ibid.

30. "Glitter and dissent at Nico Opening," *Argus*, May 20, 1971.

31. "An Operatic Tragedy," *Cape Times*, May 19, 1971.

32. Ibid.

33. Ibid.

34. "Rotten Sentiments on Opera House," *Cape Times*, May 28, 1971.

35. Ibid.

36. "Coloured People No Longer Submissive," *Cape Times*, May 6, 1971.

37. Sophia Andrews (Eoan principal mezzo-soprano) in discussion with the author, June 19, 2009. Eoan Group Archive.

38. "Nico Malan Theatre Centre," *Scenaria*, December 1977/January 1978, 14.

39. "John Orr in Conversation with David Poole, 'CAPAB—25th Anniversary'," broadcast on Radio South Africa on April 19, 1988. Sound Archives of the South African Broadcasting Co-operation, catalog no. T88/418.

40. Joseph Manca, "Budget Application to the Commissioner of Coloured Affairs," July 1, 1971. Eoan Group Archive, box 10, folder 70.

41. "Voice Production School Contracts and Conditions of Enrolment." Eoan Group Archive, box 7, folder 48.

42. "List of Performances for the 1971 Opera Season." Eoan Group Archive, box 11, folder 79.

43. Burkholder, Grout &Palisca, *A History of Western Music*, 7th ed. (New York: Norton & Company, 2006), 688.

44. Roy Pheiffer, "Eoan Group's Opera Season—Auspicious Opening Night," *Cape Times*, October 19, 1971.

45. Mariénne Uys, "May Abrahamse, a Dream Come True," *Musicus* 33, no. 2 (2005): 103–8.

46. Abrahamse preserved all the letters Jephtas sent her from 1962 until 1990. These have been made available to the Eoan Group Archive by her daughters, Trudy Rushin and Wendy Abrahams. Abrahamse's letters to Jephtas have not survived.

47. Gordon Jephtas to May Abrahamse, September 15, 1971. Jephtas-Abrahamse Correspondence, Eoan Group Archive.

48. Gordon Jephtas to May Abrahamse, October 1, 1967. Jephtas-Abrahamse Correspondence, Eoan Group Archive.

49. Virginia Damons, today known by her married surname Davids, became one of Eoan's most prominent singers to have a career in South African opera houses after the collapse of Eoan's opera section.

50. Andrews interview, 2009.

51. John van der Ross in discussion with the author, September 26, 2009. The issue is also discussed at length in the KykNet documentary by Lisba Vosloo, *Eoan—Ode aan die opera era* [Eoan—ode to the opera era]. A copy of this film is available at the Documentation Centre for Music (DOMUS) at Stellenbosch University (see www.domus.ac.za).

52. Arlina Parsons, "Excellent Production of Eoan's Rigoletto," *Cape Times*, October 21, 1971.

53. Pieter Kooij, "Sangers skitter in Rigoletto" [Singers shine in Rigoletto], *Die Burger*, October 21, 1971.

54. Pieter Kooij, "Vera Gow heel bo in La Traviata" [Vera Gow at the top in La Traviata], *Die Burger*, October 23, 1971.

55. "Eoan Group Opera Budget—October 1971." Eoan Group Archive, box 1, folder 1.

56. Minutes of the Executive Committee Meeting, March 29, 1972. Eoan Group Archive, box 93, folder 757.

57. Correspondence. Eoan Group Archive, box 40, folder 318.

58. Regarding the purchase of the car, see Minutes of the Finance Committee Meeting, June 9, 1971. Eoan Group Archive, box 93, folder 758. Regarding the use of the car, see Gerald Samaai (Eoan principal tenor) in discussion with the author, November 19, 2008. Manca apparently stopped driving after a car accident in 1952.

59. See budgets for 1970/1971. Eoan Group Archive, box 1, folder 1.

60. "Auditor's Report 1969 Opera Season." Eoan Group Archive, box 1, folder 3.

61. "Hier kom gelyke geld vir gelyke werk, dis ongeage jou velkleur" [Equal pay for equal work on its way, regardless of your skin color], *Die Rapport Ekstra*, January 9, 1977.

62. "Gelyke lone kom vir bruinmense" [Equal pay on its way for coloured people], *Die Rapport Ekstra*, 1970. Amanda Botha Scrapbook, Eoan Group Archive.

63. "Groter voordele kom vir werkers" [Bigger benefits on way for workers], *Die Rapport Ekstra*, December 31, 1972. Amanda Botha Scrapbooks, Eoan Group Archive.

64. Ismail Sydow to the Commissioner for Coloured Affairs, November 16, 1971. Eoan Group Archive, box 39, folder 314.

65. Didi Sydow to the Eoan Group, September 10, 1971. This letter was appended to the letter by Ismail Sydow to the Commissioner for Coloured Affairs, November 16, 1971. Eoan Group Archive, box 39, folder 314.

66. Sydow to the Commissioner for Coloured Affairs, November 16, 1971.

67. Department of Community Development to the Eoan Group, October 15, 1973. Eoan Group Archive, box 37, folder 300.

68. Gordon Jephtas to May Abrahamse, February 11, 1974. Jephtas-Abrahamse Correspondence, Eoan Group Archive.

69. Amanda Botha, "Kaartjies is in 'n japtrap verkoop" [Tickets sold in a jiffy], *Die Rapport Ekstra*, n.d. Amanda Botha Scrapbooks, Eoan Group Archive.

70. There is, for example, a paper trail of bitter exchanges between Manca and David Poole, head of the UCT Ballet School and CAPAB Ballet, regarding Eoan dancers whom Manca did not want to take part in UCT or CAPAB productions without his permission.

71. In South Africa the financial year runs from March to February.

72. The Eoan Group to the Commissioner of Coloured Affairs, January 1971. Eoan Group Archive, box 1, folder 1.

73. Joseph Manca, "Financial Report," November 6, 1973. Eoan Group Archive, box 21, folder 144.

74. The Administration of Coloured Affairs to the Eoan Group, March 23, 1972. Eoan Group Archive, box 53, folder 436.

75. The Eoan Group to the Administration of Coloured Affairs, April 10, 1972. Eoan Group Archive, box 53, folder 436.

76. The Eoan Group held their AGMs as well as many choir rehearsals in the banqueting hall on the second floor of the City Hall for many years.

77. Eoan Group to the Administration of Coloured Affairs, 10 April 10, 1972.

78. Ibid.

79. Ibid., 4.

80. Minutes of the 36th Annual General Meeting, November 6, 1973. Eoan Group Archive, box 72, folder 553.

81. Erika Theron and J. B. du Toit, *Kortbegrip van die Theron-verslag* [Summary of the Theron-report] (Cape Town: Tafelberg, 1977), 1.

82. "Commission of Inquiry into Matters Relating to the Coloured Population Group," p. 2.

83. Ibid., 9.

84. Ibid., 10.

85. Ibid., 6.

86. Ibid., 4–5.

87. The Eoan Group to Prof. J. B. du Toit of the Commission of Inquiry into Matters Relating to the Coloured Population Group, March 7, 1974. Eoan Group Archive, box 9, folder 59.

88. "1974 Season Schedule." Eoan Group Archive, box 6, folder 46. See also the increased newspaper reporting on the activities of Eoan's ballet section in the Amanda Botha Scrapbooks, Eoan Group Archive.

89. Letter to the Department of Community Development, February 14, 1973. Eoan Group Archive, box 6, folder 46.

90. Ibid.

91. "Permit Issued to the Eoan Group", April 25, 1973. Eoan Group Archive, box 16, folder 114.

92. The three quotes are from, respectively, "Eoan Opera of High Standard," *Argus*, March 15, 1974; "Spirited Rossini by Eoan," *Cape Times*, March 14, 1974; and "Eoan Ballet's Hard Work," *Cape Times*, March 16, 1974.

93. "Spirited Rossini by Eoan," *Cape Times*, March 14, 1974.

94. Ibid.

95. "Eoan Opera of High Standard," *Argus*, March 15, 1974. See also "Eoan Group slaag" [Eoan Group succeeds], *Die Burger*, March 16, 1974.

96. "Some Gems Lovely," *Cape Times*, March 19, 1974.

97. "Eoan Ballet's Hard Work," *Cape Times*, March 16, 1974. See also "Dansers blink uit" [Dancers shine], *Die Burger*, March 16, 1974.

98. J. C. Moll, *Akademie 75*. (Goodwood: Nasionale Boekdrukkery, 1984), 126.

99. Ibid., 1.

100. Acknowledgment of influence on the formation of the language by other population groups that also spoke Afrikaans has long been suppressed.

101. Moll, *Akademie 75*, 126.

102. John van der Ross interview, 2009.

103. Ismail Sydow to Joyce Bryer, March 20, 1974. Eoan Group Archive, box 53, folder 436.

104. Elizabeth Blanckenberg, "The Music Activities of the Cape Performing Arts Board (CAPAB): A Historical Survey" (master's diss., Stellenbosch University, 2009), 42.

105. "Rehearsal and Performance Schedule for the 1975 Opera Season." Eoan Group Archive, box 9, folder 64.

106. "An Operatic Curate's Egg," *Cape Times*, February 27, 1975.

107. Ibid.

108. "La Traviata puik" [La Traviata outstanding], *Die Burger*, February 28, 1975.

109. "Dansers vaar goed" [Dancers excel], *Die Burger*, March 10, 1975.

110. Lydia Johnson (Eoan ballet dancer and teacher) in discussion with the author, September 26, 2009.

111. The seasons were in 1956, 1958, 1959, 1960, 1962, 1965, 1967, 1969, 1971, and 1975. An additional special performance was held during the Republic Festival in 1966. The artists in these performances included May Abrahamse, Ruth Goodwin, Abeeda Parker, Winifred du Plessis, and Vera Gow. See appendix 1.

112. "An Operatic Curate's Egg."

113. "Nico Malan Theatre Centre," *Scenaria*, December 1977/January 1978, 14.

114. This campaign was referred to as the "3B campaign": the Brian Bamford Boycott. "Three Bs help Opera House," *Argus*, May 14, 1971.

115. "Nico Malan Debacle: The Facts," *Argus*, February 22, 1973.

116. Ibid.

117. Hilde Roos, "Indigenization and History: How Opera in South Africa Became South African Opera," *Acta Academica*, supp. 1 (2012): 132–33.

118. "Lift the Nico Malan Ban," *Argus*, February 21, 1973.

119. Ibid.

120. Blanckenberg, "Music Activities of the Cape Performing Arts Board," 41.

121. Ibid., 41–43. See also Ronnie Samaai (violinist and brother of Eoan tenor Gerald Samaai), in discussion with Wayne Muller, October 6, 2009.

122. "Musicians Welcome City Hall Decision," *Cape Times*, February 28, 1975.

123. Ibid.

124. Pinkard's company, London Associates, handled the bulk of the arrangements in the United Kingdom. Correspondence to that effect is stored in the Eoan Group Archive, box 24, folder 174. Regarding Didi Sydow, see "Pa se dogter sit agter Eoan Group se triomf" [Father's daughter behind Eoan Group triumph], *Die Rapport Ekstra*, September 21, 1975.

125. Ismail Sydow to South African Airways, October 7, 1974. Eoan Group Archive, box 24, folder 172.

126. Joyce Bryer to Ismail Sydow, February 11, 1974. Eoan Group Archive, box 24, folder 172.

127. Ibid., 2.

128. The Eoan Group to the Municipality of the City of Cape Town, June 9, 1975. Eoan Group Archive, box 24, folder 174.

129. The Eoan Group to Mr. L. C. Walker, April 28, 1974. Eoan Group Archive, box 24, folder 174.

130. Permit issued to the Eoan Group, April 25, 1973. Eoan Group Archive, box 16, folder 114.

131. The Eoan Group to the Municipality of theCity of Cape Town, June 9, 1975.

132. The South African tenor Sidwill Hartman and his three sisters, Avril, Jennifer, and Veida, were all part of the choir. A list of participants can be found in the Eoan Group Archive, box 24, folder 174. Ismail Sydow to Joyce Bryer, April 1, 1975. Eoan Group Archive, box 24, folder 174.

133. Joseph Manca to the Commissioner of Coloured Affairs, "Full Report," December 2, 1975. Eoan Group Archive, box 93, folder 759. The Nico Malan Theatre became accessible to all races in 1975.

134. This concert was organized by Die Vryburgers van Bloemfontein. The Eoan Group to the Municipality of the City of Cape Town, June 9, 1975.

135. Ibid.

136. According to Winfried Lüdemann, it was clear that Manca was not a good conductor. Apparently the orchestra followed the concertmaster instead of the conductor. Winfried Lüdemann (musicologist and professor at Stellenbosch University) in discussion with the author, January 14, 2009.

137. "Pa se dogter sit agter Eoan Group se triomf."

138. "Outline Itinerary U.K. Visit Eoan Group 1975." Eoan Group Archive, box 24, folder 174.

139. Apparently the South African team consisting of Eoan members and South Africa Youth Orchestra players lost 6–0 against Poland. Lüdemann interview, 2009.

140. "Eoan-dansers vol vuur terug in S.A." [Eoan dancers return motivated to S.A.], *Die Rapport Ekstra*, September 28, 1975.

141. Judith Bailey (Eoan principal mezzo-soprano) in discussion with the author, September 14, 2009.

142. "Eoan Group kry moontlik kragtige bystand" [Eoan may get strong assistance], *Die Rapport Ekstra*, February 8, 1976.

143. "Ismail Sydow vereer" [Ismail Sydow honoured], *Die Rapport Ekstra*, February 29, 1976.

144. The Eoan Group to the Commissioner of Coloured Affairs, July 8, 1976. Eoan Group Archive, box 7, folder 55.

145. South African History Online (SAHO), Cape Town timeline 1300–1997, http://www.sahistory.org.za/topic/cape-town-timeline-1300-1997?page=6, accessed June 10, 2018.

146. Ibid.

147. Programme booklet for a Gems of the Opera concert in October 1976. Eoan Group Archive, box 100, folder 771.

148. "Eoan presteer pragtig" [Eoan excells well], *Die Rapport Ekstra*, October 24, 1976, 3.

149. See reporting in the Amanda Botha Scrapbooks, specifically 1976–1978, in the Eoan Group Archive.

150. Bruce Heilbuth, "The Eoan Group, Is This the End?," *Scenaria*, June/July 1978, 16–17.

151. May Abrahamse (principal soprano) in discussion with Christine Lucia, July 9, 2009.

152. Eoan History Project, *Eoan—Our Story* (Johannesburg: Fourthwall Books, 2013), 65.

153. Ibid., 56.

154. Heilbuth, "The Eoan Group, Is This the End?"

155. Minutes of the Executive Committee Meeting, May 3, 1978. Eoan Group Archive, box 37, folder 300.

156. Ibid., 2.

157. Amanda Botha, "Stories oor Eoan Groep" [Gossip about Eoan Group], *Die Rapport Ekstra*, February 19, 1978.

158. Minutes of the Executive Committee Meeting, May 3, 1978.

159. Ibid., 3.

160. Ibid.

161. Minutes of the Executive Committee Meeting, March 29, 1978. Eoan Group Archive, box 37, folder 300.

162. Minutes of the Executive Committee Meeting, May 3, 1978.

163. Jephtas-Abrahamse Correspondence, Eoan Group Archive. See also Hilde Roos, "Briewe aan 'n diva: Die verswyging van gay-identiteit in Gordon Jephtas se briewe aan May Abrahamse" [Letters to a diva: The concealment of gay identity in

the letters of Gordon Jephtas to May Abrahamse], *Litnet Akademies* 13, no. 1 (March 2016): 31–55. One of the highlights of his early career occurred in September 1973, when he was contracted by the soprano Renata Tebaldi to perform in two concerts, on October 9 and 14, respectively. For these occasions, he accompanied her and Franco Corelli in recitals in the Royal Albert Hall in London and the Grosse Saal des Musikvereins in Vienna. These concerts are the only commercial recordings available of Jephtas in performance. See *Renata Tebaldi and Franco Corelli in Vienna* (Vienna 1973, Myto Records Italy, ASIN: B00005090M).

164. Gordon Jephtas to May Abrahamse, January 17, 1964. Jephtas-Abrahamse Correspondence, Eoan Group Archive. His disquiet over Eoan soloists and Manca in this regard remains a concern throughout the correspondence.

165. Gordon Jephtas to May Abrahamse, February 23, 1970. Jephtas-Abrahamse Correspondence, Eoan Group Archive.

166. Jephtas-Abrahamse Correspondence, Eoan Group Archive.

167. There is a widespread assumption that Abrahamse was the first coloured person to sing a solo performance in the Nico Malan Theatre; see, for example, Eoan History Project, *Eoan—Our Story*, 104. This is only partly true; Abrahamse was indeed the first coloured female singer to do so, but according to Elizabeth Blanckenberg's work on the history of CAPAB, a singer from Stellenbosch, Pieter Abel, presented a recital there in November 1977. Blanckenberg, "Music Activities of the Cape Performing Arts Board," 42–43.

168. Abrahamse moved to and lived in Durban between June 1968 and February 1972, where her husband Jonathan worked. During this time she was contracted for the 1971 Eoan Opera Season. See Jephtas's letters to Abrahamse in the Eoan Group Archive.

169. Gordon Jephtas to the Eoan Group, July 15, 1973. See Jephtas-Abrahamse Correspondence, Eoan Group Archive. Many of Jephtas's letters to Abrahamse after this date lament Eoan's refusal to stage the recital.

170. Eoan History Project, *Eoan—Our Story*, 104.

171. "The Eoan Group Presents a Recital." Eoan Group Archive, box 100, folder 773.

172. Antoinette Silvestri, "Most Dramatic Recital at Nico," in the "Tonight" supplement, *Cape Argus*, March 5, 1979.

173. Ibid.

174. Jephtas to Eoan management, telegram, August 27, 1979. Eoan Group Archive, box 67, folder 511.

175. Gordon Jephtas, "Plans for 1980," n.d. Eoan Group Archive box 67, folder 511.

176. Minutes of the Annual General Meeting, October 25, 1979. Eoan Group Archive, box 4, folder 29. The alleged report was not filed with the minutes of this meeting and has not been found.

177. Aneez Salie, "'Coloured' Shock in Secret Eoan Report," *Cape Herald*, n.d. Eoan Group Archive, box 67, folder 511.

178. "Eoan Group Rejects Racial Report," name of newspaper unknown, n.d. Eoan Group Archive, box 67, folder 511.

179. Ibid.

180. Gordon Jephtas to May Abrahamse, May 26, 1987, and February 8, 1988. Jephtas-Abrahamse Correspondence, Eoan Group Archive.

181. Conrad Sidego, "Julle is sommer vrek lui" [You are just very lazy], *Rapport Extra*, November 11, 1979. Eoan Group Archive, box 67, folder 511.

182. Ibid.

183. Peter Voges, "Artistic Report," November 1980. Eoan Group Archive, box 45, folder 352.

184. See, for example, Eoan History Project, *Eoan—Our Story*, 102; and Jephtas's letters to Abrahamse from this period.

185. Aubrey Hardine, "Klaviermeester van SA sterf aan vigs in Amerika" [Piano master from SA dies of AIDS in America], *Die Burger*, July 6, 1992.

186. Voges, "Artistic Report."

187. "Minutes of the Artistic Committee Meeting, November 5, 1980. Eoan Group Archive, box 45, folder 352.

188. Peter Voges (former Eoan dancer and actor) in discussion with the author, February 24, 2015.

189. Voges, "Artistic Report," 1980.

190. See, for example, minutes from 1979 and 1980 filed in the Eoan Group Archive, box 67, folder 511.

191. Roy Stoffels, "Reasons Why the Eoan Group Is No Longer a Viable Arts Project," n.d. Eoan Group Archive, box 4, folder 30. See also Minutes of the Annual General Meeting, June 1, 1980. Eoan Group Archive, box 4, folder 29.

192. Stoffels, "Reasons Why the Eoan Group Is No Longer a Viable Arts Project."

193. Minutes of the Annual General Meeting, June 1, 1980. Eoan Group Archive, box 4, folder 29.

194. Ibid.

195. Minutes of the Executive Committee Meeting, October 30, 1980. Eoan Group Archive, box 45, folder 352.

196. Ibid., 4.

197. Amanda Botha, "Oplaas saamsing as gelykes" [Finally singing together as equals], *Rapport Ekstra*, February 10, 1980.

198. Sidwell Hartman studied singing at the Julliard School in New York in 1984 and 1985 and won the Standard Bank Young Artist of the Year award in 1985. This occasion was celebrated with a recital at the National Arts Festival in Grahamstown, where Gordon Jephtas accompanied Hartman on the piano. Sidwell Hartmann (tenor) in discussion with the author, May 21, 2015.

199. May Abrahamse curriculum vitae, January 2007. Eoan Group Archive, box 60, folder 494e.

200. Trevor Oosterwyks, "It's Eoan versus Eoan in Auditorium Tussle," *Cape Argus*, May 17, 2001.

201. "The Eoan Group Will No Longer Accept Finance from the State," *Cape Argus*, March 17, 1989.

202. Interviews with members of the Eoan Board, including the chair, Shafiek Rajab, on October 1, 2008, revealed that post-1994 state institutions continue to be unwilling to fund the group due to its politically tainted past.

## POSTSCRIPT

1. These publications are listed in the selected bibliography. Pistorius's research includes her article "Coloured opera as subversive forgetting" in the journal *Social Dynamics*, published in 2017, as well as her soon to be awarded PhD at Oxford University titled "The Eoan Group and the Politics of Coloured Opera in Apartheid South Africa" and forthcoming publications in the journals *South African Music Studies (SAMUS)* and the *Cambridge Opera Journal*.
2. Hilde Roos, "Remembering to Forget the Eoan Group—the Legacy of an Opera Company from the Apartheid Era," *South African Theatre Journal* 27, no. 1 (March 2014): 1–18.
3. Aryan Kaganof, *An Inconsolable Memory*, 103 minutes (South Africa, African Noise Foundation, 2013). Eoan Group Archive.
4. Aryan Kaganof (filmmaker) in discussion with Kgomotso Moncho, October 18, 2013, http://kaganof.com/kagablog/2013/10/18/kgomotso-moncho-interviews-aryan-kaganof-2/, accessed March 15, 2017.

## APPENDIX ONE. EOAN'S MUSIC PRODUCTIONS

1. Programme notes for *The Redeemer*. Eoan Group Archive, box 102, folder 773.
2. Programme notes. Eoan Group Archive, box 102, folder 773.
3. Ibid.
4. Ibid.
5. "New Operetta by Eoan Group," *Cape Times*, November 14, 1948. Eoan Group Archive, box 102, folder 773.
6. "Costumed Oratorio by Eoan Group," *Cape Times*, March 26, 1949. Eoan Group Archive, box 102, folder 773.
7. Programme booklet for *A Slave in Araby*. Eoan Group Archive, box 102, folder 773.
8. "Eoan Presents Hong Kong," *Torch*, October 30, 1950; and "Comic Operetta," *Sun*, October 13, 1950.
9. "Ambitious Eoan Group Production," *Sun*, October 12, 1951; and "Eoan Group Score Great Success," *Sun*, November 2, 1951.
10. Joseph Manca, "Eoan Group Choir's Activities—1953," *Sun*, February 19, 1954.
11. Programme booklet for *The Gypsy Princess*. University of Cape Town Special Collections, BC 129 4.19.18.
12. Manca, "Eoan Group Choir's Activities—1953."
13. "Eoan Group Scores Again," *Sun*, September 17, 1954.

14. *Eoan Group 1956 Arts Festival Programme.* Eoan Group Archive, box 40, folder 317.
15. Ibid.
16. Ibid.
17. Ibid.
18. Ibid.
19. Programme booklet for *Martiza.* Chisholm Collection, UCT Special Collections, BC129.4.19.20.
20. Programme booklet for *Eoan Group 1958 Opera and Ballet Season.* Eoan Group Archive, box 100, folder 770.
21. Ibid.
22. "Eoan Group's Success in Rose Marie," *Cape Times,* August 4, 1958, 4.
23. Programme booklet for *Eoan Group 1959 Opera and Ballet Season.* Eoan Group Archive, box 100, folder 770.
24. Ibid.
25. Ibid.
26. Programme booklet for *Rio Rita.* Chisholm Collection, UCT Special Collections, BC129.2.12.10.
27. Programme booklet for *Eoan Group 1960 Opera and Ballet Season.* Chisholm Collection, UCT Special Collections, BC129.4.19.21.
28. Ibid.
29. Ibid.
30. Ibid.
31. Programme booklet for *Eoan Group Peninsula Round Table Arts Festival 1962.* Eoan Group Archive, box 2, folder 10.
32. Ibid.
33. Ibid.
34. Programme booklet for *Eoan Group Peninsula Round Table Arts Festival 1962, Verdi Requiem.* Eoan Group Archive, box 32, folder 221.
35. Programme booklet for *Die Fledermaus.* Eoan Group Archive, box 32, folder 221.
36. Programme booklet for the Stellenbosch performance of *La Traviata.* Eoan Group Archive, box 32, folder 221.
37. Programme booklet for *Eoan Group Sixth Opera Season.* Eoan Group Archive, box 100, folder 770.
38. Ibid.
39. Ibid.
40. Ibid.
41. Programme booklet for *Eoan Group Sixth Opera Season Tour.* Eoan Group Archive, box 100, folder 770.
42. Joseph Manca, "Historical Overview of Eoan's Activities from 1933–1968." Eoan Archive, box 60, folder 494c.
43. Programme booklet for *Oklahoma!* Eoan Group Archive, box 100, folder 770.
44. Programme booklet for *La Traviata.* Eoan Group Archive, box 100, folder 770.

45. Programme booklet for *Eoan Group Seventh Opera Season*. Eoan Group Archive, box 100, folder 770.
46. Ibid.
47. Ibid.
48. Programme booklet for *South Pacific*. Eoan Group Archive, box 100, folder 770.
49. Programme booklet for *Eoan Group Eighth Opera Season*. Eoan Group Archive, box 100, folder 770.
50. Ibid.
51. Ibid.
52. Programme booklet for *Carmen Jones*. Eoan Group Archive, box 100, folder 770.
53. Programme booklet for *Eoan Group 1971 Republic Festival Souvenir Programme*. Eoan Group Archive, box 100, folder 770.
54. Programme booklet for Eoan's 1971 production of *La Traviata*. Eoan Group Archive, box 100, folder 770.
55. Programme booklet for Eoan's 1971 production of *Rigoletto*. Eoan Group Archive, box 100, folder 770.
56. Programme booklet for Eoan's 1971 production of *Cavalleria Rusticana & I Pagliacci*. Eoan Group Archive, box 100, folder 770.
57. Ibid.
58. Programme booklet for Eoan's 1972 production of *Cavalleria Rusticana & I Pagliacci*. Eoan Group Archive, box 100, folder 770.
59. Ibid.
60. Programme booklet for Eoan's 1974 production of *Il Barbiere di Siviglia*. Eoan Group Archive, box 100, folder 770.
61. Programme booklet for Eoan's 1974 production of Gems from the Opera. Eoan Group Archive, box 100, folder 770.
62. Programme booklet for Eoan's 1975 production of *La Traviata*. Eoan Group Archive, box 100, folder 770.
63. Programme booklet for Eoan's 1976 production of Gems from the Opera. Eoan Group Archive, box 100, folder 770.
64. Programme booklet for *Nico Malan Lieder Recital*. Eoan Group Archive, box 100, folder 770.

### APPENDIX TWO. THE EOAN GROUP CONSTITUTION

1. The Eoan Group Constitution. Eoan Group Archive, box 93, folder 757.
2. The minutes of this meeting have not been stored in the archive and are considered lost.
3. Minutes of the Executive Committee Meeting, November 25, 1970. Eoan Group Archive, box 93, folder 757.

SELECTED BIBLIOGRAPHY

The research presented in this book is for the most part based on primary sources from the Eoan Group Archive housed at the Documentation Centre for Music (DOMUS) at Stellenbosch University. The archive, consisting of 102 boxes and 773 folders as well as a number of oversized items, has been presorted but not yet cataloged or digitized. The primary materials include, among others, interviews, programs, letters, notes, minutes, reports, memoranda, budgets, financial documents, pencil sketches, leaflets, newspaper cuttings, photographs, posters, scrapbooks, periodicals, and sound recordings. All references to primary material can be found in the endnotes and are not repeated here. The many newspaper clippings that have been sourced from newspapers housed at the South African National Library in Cape Town are also cited in the endnotes. This selected bibliography lists secondary sources consulted for the writing of this book.

Adhikari, Mohamed. *Burdened by Race: Coloured Identities in Southern Africa*. Cape Town: University of Cape Town Press, 2009.

———. "Hope, Fear, Shame, Frustration: Continuity and Change in the Expression of Coloured Identity in White Supremacist South Africa, 1910–1994." *Journal of Southern African Studies*, 32, no. 3, (September 2006): 467–87.

———. *Not White Enough, Not Black Enough*. Athens: Ohio University Press, 2005.

Bickford-Smith, Vivian. "The Origins and Early History of District Six to 1910." In *The Struggle for District Six, Past and Present*, edited by Shamil Jeppie and Crain Soudien, 35–43. Cape Town: Buchu Books, 1990.

Blanckenberg, Elizabeth. "The Music Activities of the Cape Performing Arts Board (CAPAB): A Historical Survey." Master's diss., Stellenbosch University, 2009.

Bloom, Harry. *King Kong: An African Jazz Opera*. London: Collins, 1961.

Bloomberg, David. *My Times*. Cape Town: Fernwood Press, 2007.

Boyd, Melinda. "The Politics of Color in Oscar Hammerstein's Carmen Jones." In *Blackness in Opera*, edited by Naomi Adele André; Karen M. Bryan (Karen

McGaha), and Eric Saylor, 212–35. Urbana, Chicago and Springfield: University of Illinois Press, 2012.

Brooks Spector, J. "The Johannesburg Civic Theatre, 1962 to 2007—the First 45 Years." Accessed March 16, 2017. http://www.joburgtheatreptyltd.co.za/The%20First%2045%20Years.pdf.

Bruinders, Sylvia. "Parading Respectability: An Ethnography of the Christmas Bands Movement in the Cape, South Africa." PhD diss., University of Illinois at Urbana-Champaign, 2011.

Budden, Julian. *The Master Musicians: Verdi*. London & Melbourne: J.M. Dent &Sons Ltd., 1985.

Burkholder, J. Peter, Donald Jay Grout, and Claude V. Palisca. *A History of Western Music*. 7th ed. New York: Norton & Company, 2006.

Clément, Catherine. *Opera, or the Undoing of Women*. Translated by Betsy Wing. Minneapolis: University of Minnesota Press, 1988.

Cleophas, Francois. "Physical Education and Physical Culture in the Coloured Community of the Western Cape: 1837–1966." PhD diss., Stellenbosch University, 2009.

Cockburn, Christopher. "Discomposing Apartheid's Story: Who Owns Handel?" In *Composing Apartheid*, edited by Grant Olwage, 55–78. Johannesburg: Wits University Press, 2008.

Coertse, Mimi. *'n Stem vir Suid-Afrika: my storie, soos vertel aan Ian Raper* [A Voice for South Africa: My story, as told to Ian Raper]. Pretoria: Litera, 2007.

Coplan, David B. *In Township Tonight!* 2nd ed. Auckland Park: Jacana Media, 2007.

Du Pre, Roy Howard. *Separate but Unequal: The "Coloured" People of South Africa—a Political History*. Johannesburg: Jonathan Ball, 1994.

Eoan History Project. *Eoan—Our Story*. Johannesburg: Fourthwall Books, 2013.

Erasmus, Zimitri. *Coloured by History, Shaped by Place: Perspectives on Coloured Identities in Cape Town*. Cape Town: Kwela Books, 2001.

Faktor-Kreitzer, Lucy. "From Latvia to South Africa." In *The World of South African Music: A Reader*, edited by Christine Lucia, 149–53. Cape Town: Oxford University Press, 2005.

February, Vernon. *Mind Your Colour*. London and New York: Kegan Paul International, 1981.

Fiasconaro, Gregorio. *I'd Do It Again*. Cape Town: Books of Africa,1982.

Fourie, Paula. "Ghoema vannie Kaap: The Life and Work of Taliep Petersen (1950–2006)." PhD diss., Stellenbosch University, 2011.

Gilbert, Susie. *Opera for Everybody: The Story of English National Opera*. London: Faber & Faber, 2008.

Glasser, Mona. *King Kong, a Venture in the Theatre*. Cape Town: Norman Howell Publishers, 1960.

Green, Michael. *Around and About: Memoirs of a South African Newspaperman*. Claremont: David Philip, 2004.

Goldin, Ian. *Making Race: The Politics and Economics of Coloured Identity in South Africa*. London: Longman, 1987.

Goodall, Noel. "Opposing Apartheid Through Sport, the role of SACOS in South African sport, 1982–1992." Master's diss., University of Johannesburg, 2004.

Groos, Arthur, and Rodger Parker. *Giacomo Puccini: La Bohème*. Cambridge, UK: Cambridge Opera Handbooks, 1986.

Grut, Marina. 1979. "Ballet in Cape Town." In *South African Music Encyclopedia*, edited by Jacques P. Malan, 1:79–81. Cape Town: Oxford University Press, 1979.

———. *The History of Ballet in South Africa*. Cape Town: Human & Rousseau, 1981.

Hammett, Daniel. "Ongoing Contestations: The Use of Racial Signifiers in Post-apartheid South Africa." *Social Identities* 16, no. 2 (March 2010): 247–60.

Hendricks, Cheryl. "Debating Coloured Identity in the Western Cape: Commentary." *African Security Review* 14, no. 4 (2005): 117–19.

Inskip, Donald. *Forty Little Years*. Cape Town: Timmins, 1972.

Jensen, Sune Q. "Othering, Identity Formation and Agency." *Qualitative Studies* 2, no. 2 (2011): 63–78.

Jokl, Ernst. "Physical Education, Sport and Recreation." In *Handbook on Race Relations in South Africa*, edited by Ellen Hellmann and Leah Abrahams, 443–47. Cape Town: Oxford, 1949.

Jorritsma, Marie. *Sonic Spaces of the Karoo*. Philadelphia: Temple University Press, 2011.

Jung, Courtney. *Then I Was Black: South African Political Identities in Transition*. New Haven, CT: Yale University Press, 2000

Kimbell, David. *Italian Opera*. Cambridge, UK: Cambridge University Press, 1995.

Layne, Valmont. "A History of Dance and Jazz Band Performance in the Western Cape in the Post-1945 era." Master's diss., University of Cape Town, 1995.

Lewis, Gavin. *Between the Wire and the Wall: A History of South African "Coloured" Politics*. Cape Town: David Philip, 1987.

Lindenberger, Herbert. *Opera in History, from Monteverdi to Cage*. Stanford, CA: Stanford University Press, 1998.

Malan, Jacques P. "Cape Town Municipal Orchestra." In *South African Music Encyclopedia*, edited by Jacques P. Malan, 1:251–54.Cape Town: Oxford University Press, 1979.

———. "Erik Chisholm." In *South African Music Encyclopedia*, edited by Jacques P. Malan, 1:271–75 Cape Town: Oxford University Press, 1979.

———. "Manca, Joseph Salvatore." In *South African Music Encyclopedia*, edited by Jacques P. Malan, 3:192–94.Cape Town: Oxford University Press, 1984.

———. "Rota, Alessandro." In *South African Music Encyclopedia*, edited by Jacques P. Malan, 4:197–98.Cape Town: Oxford University Press, 1986.

Manca, Joseph. "Eoan Group." In *South African Music Encyclopedia*, edited by Jacques P. Malan, 2:26–29. Cape Town: Oxford University Press, 1982.

Manual, George. *Kampvegters* [Campaigners]. Cape Town: Nasau Beperk, n.d.

Martin, Denis-Constant. *Coon Carnival: New Year in Cape Town, Past and Present*. Cape Town: David Philip, 1999.

———. *Sounding the Cape: Music, Identity and Politics in South Africa*. Cape Town: African Minds, 2013.

Moll, J. C. *Akademie 75*. Goodwood: NasionaleBoekdrukkery, 1984.
Muller, Carol Ann. *Focus: Music of South Africa*. New York: Routledge, 2008.
———. *South African Music, a Century of Traditions in Transformation*. Santa Barbara, CA, Denver, CO, and Oxford: ABC-Clio, 2004.
Muller, Carol-Ann, and Sathima Bea Benjamin. *Musical Echoes, South African Women Thinking in Jazz*. Durham, NC, and London: Duke University Press, 2011.
Patterson, Sheila. *Colour and Culture in South Africa*. London: Routledge and Paul, 1953.
Rassool, Ciraj, and Leslie Witz. "The 1952 Jan Van Riebeeck Tercentenary Festival: Constructing and Contesting Public National History in South Africa." *Journal of African History* 34, no. 3 (1993): 447–68.
Roos, Hilde. "Briewe aan 'n diva: Die verswyging van gay-identiteit in Gordon Jephtas se briewe aan May Abrahamse" [Letters to a diva: The concealment of gay identity in the letters of Gordon Jephtas to May Abrahamse]. *Litnet Akademies* 13, no. 1 (March 2016): 31–55.
———. "Eoan—Our Story: Treading New Methodological Paths in Music Historiography." *Historia* 60, no. 2 (2015): 185–200.
———. "Indigenization and History: How Opera in South Africa Became South African Opera." *Acta Academica*, supp. 1 (2012): 132–33.
———. "Opera Production in the Western Cape: Strategies Towards Indigenization." PhD diss., University of Stellenbosch, 2010.
———. "Probing the Boundaries of Opera as Notated Practice in South Africa: The Case of Eoan." *Muziki* 11, no. 2 (November 2013): 79–88.
———. "Remembering to Forget the Eoan Group—the Legacy of an Opera Company from the Apartheid Era." *South African Theatre Journal* 27, no. 1 (March 2014): 1–18.
Stodel, Jack. *The Audience Is Waiting*. Cape Town: Howard Timmins, 1962.
Talbot, Désirée. *For the Love of Singing: 50 Years of Opera at UCT*. Cape Town: Oxford University Press, 1978.
Taruskin, Richard. *The Oxford History of Western Music*. Vol 3. Oxford: Oxford University Press, 2010.
Theron, Erika, and J. B. du Toit. *Kortbegrip van die Theron-verslag* [Brief understanding of the Theron report]. Cape Town: Tafelberg 1977.
Ulster, Dan R. *The Teaching of Music in Primary Schools*. Cape Town: Maskew Miller 1965.
Van der Ross, Richard. "A Political and Social History of the Cape Coloured People, 1880–1970." PhD diss., University of Cape Town, 1973.
———. *The Rise and Decline of Apartheid*. Cape Town: Tafelberg. 1986.
Verdi, Giuseppe. *Rigoletto*. London: Boosey & Co, n.d.
———. *Rigoletto*. Performed by the Eoan Group and the Cape Town Municipal Orchestra, conducted by Joseph Manca. With Lionel Fourie, Joseph Gabriels, Sophia Andrews, Ruth Goodwin, et al. Recorded during a live performance in the Cape Town City Hall in March 1960, released commercially by GSE Claremont Records, 2000. CD.

Waren, Stanley A. "Theatre in South Africa." *Educational Theatre Journal* 20, no. 3 (October 1968): 411.

Weaver, William, and Simonetta Puccini. *The Puccini Companion*. New York: W. W. Norton & Company, 1994.

Witz, Leslie. "From Langa Market Hall and Rhodes' Estate to the Grand Parade and the Foreshore: Contesting van Riebeeck's Cape Town." *Kronos Southern African Histories* 25 (1988/1989): 189–206.

# INDEX

1952 Jan van Riebeeck Tercentenary Celebrations, 42, 90, 180, 221n39, 228n28
1960 Tour, 75–77
1965 Tour, 109–112
1966 Republic Festival, 5, 113, 201
1971 Republic Festival, 144–145, 150, 206

Abrahamse, May, 2, 5, 38, 43, 64, 66, 67, 76, 82, 86, 88, 89, 93, 101, 108, 115, 116, 122, 143, 154, 161, 163, 171, 245n93, 251n46, 256n167–168; biography, 52–53, 149–150, 172–175, 181; performance list, 189–199, 203, 208–210
Adams, Marie, 37, 222n17, 226n95
Adhikari, Mohamed, 9–12, 43, 60, 74
African People's Organization (APO), 33
Alexander Theatre, 77
Alhambra Theatre, 63, 73, 102, 109, 124–127, 137, 148, 155
Allan, Veronica, 173
Andrews, Sophia, xi, 76, 82, 86, 89, 105, 106, 108, 122, 125, 126, 130, 132, 147, 149, 150–151, 237n94; biography, 65–66, 78–80, performance list, 193–200, 202–208
April, Elizabeth, 31, 37; performance list, 188
Arendse, Benjamin, xi, 65, 76, 86, 105, 108, 122, 125, 126, 150; performance list, 190, 193–201, 203–207
Arendse, Gerald, xi, 64, 76, 92; performance list, 193, 194–197, 206

Arendse, Susan, 105, 108, 122, 130; performance list, 196, 199, 200–202, 204

*Babiere di Siviglia, Il* (Rossini), 58, 62, 107, 127, 130, 160, 220n20, 231n25
Bailey, Judith, 169; performance list, 206, 209
Ballet, 83, 97, 104, 120, 136, 147, 152, 160, 163, 168–170, 176, 237n113, 252n70; early history, 11, 15, 17, 19, 22–23, 26, 29, 30–32, 37, 58, 64, 66, 71–72; *The Square* 59, 70, 85, 89–93, 96, 117
Bamford, Brian, 145, 164–166
Battswood College, 43, 87, 102, 229n133
*Behind the Yellow Door* (Stohr), 59, 96, 141
Bernard van Leer Foundation, 122, 135, 245n97
Bishop Sydney Lavis, 19, 40, 222n10
Bizet, George: *Carmen*, 14, 104, 109, 111, 112, 220n20, 231n25, 242n36
Black consciousness, 92, 104, 170, 171, 177, 182
Bloom, Harry, 70, 93
Bloomberg, David, 87–88, 99, 123–126, 135, 172, 227n109, 241n4, 246n103, 248n149
*Bohème, La* (Puccini), 58, 62, 72, 73, 76, 79, 85, 86, 104, 108, 196, 198, 201, 220n20
Budgets, 59, 98, 133, 136, 145, 148, 151, 154

Cape Performing Arts Board (CAPAB), 6, 11, 12, 96, 108–109, 147, 159, 166, 178, 181, 183, 239n141, 243n43, 252n70, 256n167

Cape Town City Hall, 27, 28, 40, 55, 63–64, 66, 72, 74, 91, 113, 122, 127, 130, 132, 137, 155–158, 166, 168
Cape Town Municipal Orchestra, 1, 23, 24, 29, 31, 38, 39, 43, 44, 47, 64, 90, 91, 102, 109, 241n12, 246n103
*Carmen* (Bizet), 14, 104, 109, 111, 112, 220n20, 231n25, 242n36
*Carmen Jones* (Hammerstein II), 123, 138
Caruso, Enrico, 142
*Cavalleria Rusticana* (Mascagni), 37, 58, 64–65, 66, 72, 73, 148, 220n20
Chisholm, Erik, 31, 39, 56, 62–64, 65, 95, 107, 108, 234n36
Coates, Albert, 29, 31, 39
College of Music at the University of Cape Town, 24, 31, 62, 78, 81, 83, 101, 181
Coloured Identity, 8–12
Coloured People's Congress (CPC), 71, 72, 104
Coloured Preference Policy, 103
Community music, 26, 133–134
Coronationville, 110
Council for Culture and Recreation, 120, 132, 159

Damons, Maud (stage name Maxine Day), 92–93
Davids, Virginia (maiden name Virginia Damons), 6, 121, 150, 181, 251n49; performance list, 206–208
Delta House, 83, 137
Department of Coloured Affairs (DCA), 3, 12, 47–49, 95, 99, 113, 114, 118, 132–133, 144, 148, 154–156, 159, 162, 167, 170, 173, 176–177
Deutsche Oper am Rhein, 142
Devereux, Regina, 167
Di Stefano, Giuseppe, 141
District Six, 11, 12, 15, 18, 19, 24, 33, 40, 43, 54, 68, 69, 71, 78, 83, 89, 92, 113–114, 117, 127, 137, 162, 238n116
Documentation Centre for Music (DOMUS), xi, 13, 14, 183, 261
Donizetti, Gaetano: *L'Elisir d'Amore*, 104, 107–108, 122–123, 200, 203
Du Plessis, Winifried, 108, 122, 124; performance list, 200–201, 203

Dunn, Edward, 141
Durban City Hall, 75, 76

Eight Opera Season, 128
Eleventh Opera Season, 162–164
English National Opera, 142
Eoan Group Archive, xi, 7, 19, 33, 35, 49, 50, 54, 55, 73, 75, 78, 80, 96, 103, 105, 109, 111, 116, 135, 136, 152, 170, 183, 185, 187, 220n16, 232n3, 232n8, 261; sources, 11–16, 87–88, 90–92, 113–114, 126–127
Eoan Group Choir, 16, 24–28, 31, 89, 102, 168, 188, 190–191, 199, 209
Eoan Group Cultural Centre, 135–137, 151, 154, 159, 183. *See also* Joseph Stone Auditorium
Eoan Group Trust, 87, 98–99, 113, 119, 123, 129, 134–136, 155, 158, 216, 241n4–5, 247n125
Equal remuneration, 119, 151–152
Erika Theron Commission, 158–159

Feather Market Hall, 75
February, Vernon, 7
Fiasconaro, Gregorio, 39, 57, 62–66, 72, 78, 80, 81, 82, 88–89, 108, 237n111; performance list, 193–199
First Arts Festival, 50–55
*Fledermaus, Die* (Strauss II), 85, 89, 93, 94, 96, 123, 220n20
Fourie, Lionel, 1, 2, 54, 74, 76, 79, 89, 97, 108, 150–151, 219n14, 234n40, 234n46; biography, 66–68; performance list, 192, 194–197, 199
Fourth Opera and Ballet Season, 71–74
Fox, Revel, 136, 248n153
Fraser-Simson, Harold: *The Maid of the Mountains*, 44, 123, 189
Frimi, Rudolph and Herbert Stothart: *Rose Marie*, 64, 123, 124, 194
Funding, 11, 23–24, 27, 33, 47, 56, 60, 63, 74, 84, 88, 93, 95–96, 118–120, 151, 154–155, 165, 167, 176, 181, 184, 231n30, 235n70, 244,67

Gabriels, Joseph, 32, 72, 75, 76, 81, 86, 88, 89, 93, 94, 105–106, 108, 109–110, 146, 240n163, 249n4; biography, 68–70,

78–79, 140–144; performance list, 194, 196–201
Gems of the Opera, 134, 154, 161
Gilbert, W. S. and Arthur Sullivan: *The Mikado*, 47, 54, 63, 94, 123, 192
Gilbert and Sullivan Society, 63, 178
Glasser, Stanley, 59, 70, 85, 89–93, 234n46; *Paljas*, 70, 92–93; *The Square*, 59, 70, 85, 89–93, 96, 117
Golden Dixies Show, 69, 96, 141
Goodwin, Ruth, 1, 53, 66, 76, 78, 79, 88, 97, 108; performance list, 190, 192, 194, 196–7
Gow, Vera, 72, 78, 86, 88, 105, 106, 108, 112, 122, 125, 126, 128, 130, 131, 132, 151, 167; performance list, 197–207, 210
Green and Sea Point Civic Centre, 156–157, 160, 161, 163, 167
Group Areas Act, 6, 41, 83, 103, 114, 156
*Gypsy Princess, The* (Kalman), 44, 123, 190

Hammerstein II, Oscar: *Carmen Jones*, 123, 138
Hartman, Sidwell, 181, 210, 254n132, 257n198
*Hong Kong* (Jessop), 44, 123
Howes, Dulcie, 31, 32, 90

International Festival of Youth Orchestras and Performing Arts, 162, 166–169
Irish, Deon, 183
Isaac Ochberg Hall, 40–41, 83, 117, 137, 228, 238n116, 248n146

Jaffer, Dick, 163, 167, 168, 172
Jansen, Alethea, 22, 37, 55–56, 61, 222n8, 228n126, 231n26
Jansen, Yvonne, 108, 130; performance list, 200–202
Jazz, 26–27, 29, 69, 70, 90, 91–93, 133, 134, 141, 169, 234n46
Jephtas, Gordon, 88, 102, 108, 112, 115–116, 130, 140, 143, 149, 150, 168, 219n14, 237n106, 245n93, 251n46, 255n163, 256n164, 257n198; biography, 81–83, 120–122, 152–153, 172–178
Jessop, Charles: *Hong Kong*, 44, 123
Johannesburg Civic Theatre, 102, 110

Johnson, Martin, 124, 126, 131, 161, performance list, 198–207, 209
Jones, Billie, 22, 37, 38, 53, 189, 194, 227n103
Jones, Ivor, 96
Joseph Stone Auditorium, xi, 5, 12, 40, 83, 122, 135, 136, 139, 145, 158–159, 162, 172, 183, 222n19, 245n97, 248n155

Kaganof, Aryan, xii, 184
Kalman, Emmerich, works of: *Maritza*, 64, 123, 193; *The Gypsy Princess*, 44, 123, 190
Kern, Jerome and Oscar Hammerstein: *Showboat*, 102, 123, 124, 125
Kester-Gabriels, Mabel, 69, 96, 141, 240n163, 249n4
*King Kong* (Matshikiza), 70, 92–93, 240n156
Kramer, Hans, 122, 132

La Guma, Alex, 3, 14, 71, 72
*L'Elisir d'Amore* (Donizetti), 104, 107–108, 122–123, 200, 203
Leoncavallo, Ruggero: *I Pagliacci*, 140, 142–143, 148–149, 154, 220n20, 231n25
Little Theatre, 56, 57, 59, 63, 64, 96, 233n23
London Opera Centre, 120, 167, 168
Luxurama, 124, 125, 139

Mackrill, Andrew, 28, 32, 38, 43, 47–49, 64; performance list, 187, 189, 230n8, 230n9,
*Madama Butterfly* (Puccini), 37, 58, 85, 86, 122, 142, 197, 203, 220n20, 242n26
Magnoni, Olga, 53, 148, 172
*Magyar Melody* (Posford), 44, 123, 191, 229n138
*Maid of the Mountains, The* (Fraser-Simson), 44, 123, 189
Manca, Joseph, 2–4, 10, 32, 37–39, 42, 65, 75, 78–81, 86–87, 89, 92, 95, 104, 107, 109, 111–112, 116, 127, 132, 138, 145, 148, 151, 158, 161–162, 223n41, 230n9, 236n77, 236n83, 242n36, 245n93, 251n58, 252n70, 254n136, 256n164; archive, 7, 14, 55, 73, 105, 114, 170, 232n8; biography, 23–25, 44–50, 224n43, 227n109; performance list, 187–210; politics, 46, 49, 58–61,

Manca *(Continued)*
  83–84, 100–102, 171, 220n16; succession, 120–121, 152, 170–17
Mandela, Nelson, 103, 242n21
*Maritza* (Kalman), 64, 123, 193
Mascagni, Pietro: *Cavalleria Rusticana*, 37, 58, 64–65, 66, 72, 73, 148, 220n20
Matshikiza, Todd: *King Kong*, 70, 92–93, 240n156
Metropolitan Opera House, 30, 69, 140–143, 146, 178
*Mikado, The* (Gilbert and Sullivan), 47, 54, 63, 94, 123, 192
Mohr, Robert, 96, 199
Momberg, James, 108, 122, 130; performance list, 198–205
Mosaval, Johaar, 32, 89, 91

Naudé, Beyers, 147
Nico Malan Theatre Complex, 136; 159, 168, 170, 174–175, 176, 210, 232n6, 254n133, 256n167; color bar, 164–166, inauguration, 145–147
Ninth Opera Season, 148–150, 206
Non-European Unity Movement (NEUM), 71, 103

*Oklahoma!* (Rodgers and Hammerstein), 123–124, 138, 202
Opera for All, 129, 134

*Pagliacci, I* (Leoncavallo), 140, 142–143, 148–149, 154, 220n20, 231n25
*Paljas* (Stanley Glasser), 70, 92–93
Parker, Abeeda, 86–88, 97, 253n111; performance list, 198, 199
Performing Arts Councils, 11, 59, 96, 98, 99, 120, 132, 133, 165, 181
Pheiffer, Roy 149
Pistorius, Juliana, 183, 258n1
Politics, 5, 15, 27, 33, 42, 46, 49, 58–61, 84, 100–102, 171, 179
Poole, David, 11, 32, 64, 66, 89, 90–91, 147, 234n36, 239n144, 252n70
Port Elizabeth Opera House, 110
Posford, George: *Magyar Melody*, 44, 123, 191, 229n138

Posford, George: *Zip Goes a Million*, 47, 54, 123, 192
Puccini, Giacomo, works of: *La Bohème*, 58, 62, 72, 73, 76, 79, 85, 86, 104, 108, 196, 198, 201, 220n20; *Madama Butterfly*, 37, 58, 85, 86, 122, 142, 197, 203, 220n20, 242n26

Rajap, Shafiek, xi, 247n125, 258n202
Remuneration, 72, 88–89, 119, 151–152, 159, 218
Renzi, Emma, 57, 141
*Requiem* (Verdi), 85, 89, 189
*Rigoletto* (Verdi), 55, 58, 66, 68, 72, 73, 76, 79, 127, 130, 141, 145, 148, 150, 194, 196, 206, 207, 220n20
*Rio Rita* (Tierney), 64, 123, 195
Rodgers, Richard and Oscar Hammerstein II, works of: *Oklahoma!*, 123–124, 138, 202; *South Pacific*, 123, 125–127, 138, 139, 204, 248n146
*Rose Marie* (Frimi and Stothart), 64, 123, 124, 194
Rossini, Gioacchino: *Il Babiere di Siviglia*, 58, 62, 107, 127, 130, 160, 220n20, 231n25
Rota, Alessandro, 1, 39, 54, 73, 104, 105, 112, 129, 130, 148, 161, 167, 180, 220n14; performance list, 191, 200–210

Samaai, Gerald, 7, 107, 108, 111, 118, 119, 130, 131, 150, 161, 163, 167, 251n58; performance list, 200, 203, 205–210
Second Arts Festival, 59, 83–89, 93, 98, 197–199
Second Opera and Ballet Season, 58, 64–66, 193–194
Seventh Opera Season, 122–123, 203–204
*Showboat* (Kern and Hammerstein), 102, 123, 124, 125
Silver, Alfred: *A Slave in Araby*, 37–38, 149, 189, 227n103
Silvestri, Antoinette, 132, 174, 175
Sixth Opera Season, 104–109, 199–201
*Slave in Araby, A* (Silver), 37–38, 149, 189, 227n103
Small, Adam, 146, 177
South African Academy for Arts and Science, 161

South African Coloured People's Organization (SACPO), 3, 71
South African Council on Sport (SACOS), 6, 220n21
*South Pacific* (Rodgers and Hammerstein), 123, 125–127, 138, 139, 204, 248n146
Southern-Holt, Helen, 30, 35, 37, 40, 46, 61, 133, 211, 222n10, 222n11, 222n17, 222n19, 223n27, 225n62, 228n126, 231n26; biography, 18–24, 55–56
Southern-Holt, Maisy, 20, 22, 30, 222n18, 226n62
Spes Bona Orchestra, 43, 102, 229n133
*Square, The* (Glasser), 59, 70, 85, 89–93, 96, 117
Stellenbosch, 5, 33, 35, 137, 168, 187, 199, 208, 256n167
Stellenbosch University, xi, 13, 14, 31, 68, 158, 183, 261
Stoffels, Roy, 179
Stohr, Flora: *Behind the Yellow Door*, 59, 96, 141
Stone, Joseph, 12, 135, 248n149
Strauss II, Johann: *Die Fledermaus*, 85, 89, 93, 94, 96, 123, 220n20
Succession, 121–122, 152–154
Swales, Philip, 121, 150; performance list, 206–207
Sydow, Carmen, 106, 162, 172, 245n89
Sydow, Didi, 66, 83, 97, 140, 152, 245n89
Sydow, Ismail, 61, 99–101, 109, 110, 113, 115, 117–120, 129, 133, 135–136, 151–153, 156, 164, 166–168, 170, 174, 219n14, 223n41, 237n106, 245n89, 245n91; biography, 162, 172; politics, 14, 100

Te Wata, Inia, 102–103
Teacher's League of South Africa, 118
Tenth Opera Season, 161–162, 209
Theys, Ronald, 130, 149, 150, 161, 163, 167, 181; performance list, 203–210
Third Opera and Ballet Season, 66–70
Tidboald, David, 102, 104, 109
Tierney, Harry: *Rio Rita*, 64, 123, 195
Timms, Keith, 6, 163, 181; performance list, 209–210
Tobin, Cecil, 108, 118, 130, 198–200, 202–207

*Traviata, La* (Verdi), 1–6, 45, 50–54, 58, 65, 66, 73, 85, 86, 104, 105, 108, 111, 113, 122, 127, 129, 130, 148, 151, 163–164, 219n14, 220n20; performance list, 182–183, 191–210
*Trovatore, Il* (Verdi), 37, 55, 104, 105, 107, 108, 111, 130, 132, 142, 220n20, 231n25
Trussell, Robert, 68, 86, 88, 89, 108, 130; performance list, 192, 194–201

Ulster, Dan, 24, 28, 43, 54, 64, 82, 101, 192, 223n41, 231n22
Ulster, John, xi, 24, 28, 189, 223n41
Ulster, Tillie, xi, 20, 22, 28, 37, 63, 66, 101, 222n8, 222n11, 222n17, 231n26; performance list, 194, 197
University of Cape Town, 59, 95, 127, 145, 223n18, 233n23; Ballet Company, 32; Ballet School, 11, 72, 90; Opera Company, 54, 56, 59, 62–3 65, 108; Opera School, 50, 68, 80
University of Witwatersrand Great Hall, 77

Van Graan, Patricia, xi, 93, 107, 108, 122, 124, 130, 131, 140, 149; performance list, 194–196, 198–206, 208
Verdi, Giuseppe, works of: *Il Trovatore*, 37, 55, 104, 105, 107, 108, 111, 130, 132, 142, 220n20, 231n25; *La Traviata*, 1–6, 45, 50–54, 58, 65, 66, 73, 85, 86, 104, 105, 108, 111, 113, 122, 127, 129, 130, 148, 151, 163–164, 182–183, 191–210, 219n14, 220n20; *Requiem*, 85, 89, 189; *Rigoletto*, 55, 58, 66, 68, 72, 73, 76, 79, 127, 130, 141, 145, 148, 150, 194, 196, 206, 207, 220n20
Verwoerd, Hendrik, 71, 119, 246n103
Voges, Peter, 93, 101, 177, 178

Waren, Florence, 123, 124
Waren, Stanley, 123, 124, 137, 202, 206
Weich, Charlie, 1, 66
Williams, Owen, 124, 125

*Zip Goes a Million* (Posford), 47, 54, 123, 192

www.ingramcontent.com/pod-product-compliance
Lightning Source LLC
Chambersburg PA
CBHW030529230426
43665CB00010B/820